W9-BSC-503

Bloom's Literary Themes

❧

Alienation
The American Dream
Death and Dying
The Grotesque
The Hero's Journey
Human Sexuality
The Labyrinth
Rebirth and Renewal

THE AMERICAN DREAM

THE
AMERICAN DREAM

Edited and with an introduction by
Harold Bloom
Sterling Professor of the Humanities
Yale University

Volume Editor
Blake Hobby

BLOOM'S
LITERARY CRITICISM
An imprint of Infobase Publishing

12/11   LAD   TC

4/14   SAME
        9/12

Bloom's Literary Themes: The American Dream

Bloom's Literary Criticism
An imprint of Infobase Publishing
132 West 31st Street
New York NY 10001

Library of Congress Cataloging-in-Publication Data
The American dream / edited and with an introduction by Harold Bloom ; volume editor, Blake Hobby.
    p. cm. — (Bloom's literary themes)
    Includes bibliographical references and index.
    ISBN 978-0-7910-9801-1 (hc : alk. paper) 1. American literature—History and criticism. 2. American Dream in literature. I. Bloom, Harold. II. Hobby, Blake.
    PS169.A49A44 2009
    810.9'35873—dc22   2008042987

Bloom's Literary Criticism books are available at special discounts when purchased in bulk quantities for businesses, associations, institutions, or sales promotions. Please call our Special Sales Department in New York at (212) 967-8800 or (800) 322-8755.

You can find Bloom's Literary Criticism on the World Wide Web at
http://www.chelseahouse.com

Text Design by Kerry Casey
Cover design by Takeshi Takahashi

Printed in the United States of America

IBT EJB 10 9 8 7 6 5 4 3 2

This book is printed on acid-free paper.

Contents

Contents

Series Introduction by Harold Bloom: Themes and Metaphors

1. Topos and Trope

What we now call a theme or topic or subject initially was named a *topos*, ancient Greek for "place." Literary *topoi* are commonplaces, but also arguments or assertions. A topos can be regarded as literal when opposed to a trope or turning which is figurative and which can be a metaphor or some related departure from the literal: ironies, synecdoches (part for whole), metonymies (representations by contiguity) or hyperboles (overstatements). Themes and metaphors engender one another in all significant literary compositions.

As a theoretician of the relation between the matter and the rhetoric of high literature, I tend to define metaphor as a figure of desire rather than a figure of knowledge. We welcome literary metaphor because it enables fictions to persuade us of beautiful untrue things, as Oscar Wilde phrased it. Literary *topoi* can be regarded as places where we store information, in order to amplify the themes that interest us.

This series of volumes, *Bloom's Literary Themes*, offers students and general readers helpful essays on such perpetually crucial topics as the Hero's Journey, the Labyrinth, the Sublime, Death and Dying, the Taboo, the Trickster and many more. These subjects are chosen for their prevalence yet also for their centrality. They express the whole concern of human existence now in the twenty-first century of the Common Era. Some of the topics would have seemed odd at another time, another land: the American Dream, Enslavement and Emancipation, Civil Disobedience.

I suspect though that our current preoccupations would have existed always and everywhere, under other names. Tropes change across the centuries: the irony of one age is rarely the irony of another. But the themes of great literature, though immensely varied, undergo transmemberment and show up barely disguised in different contexts. The power of imaginative literature relies upon three constants: aesthetic splendor, cognitive power, wisdom. These are not bound by societal constraints or resentments, and ultimately are universals, and so not culture-bound. Shakespeare, except for the world's scriptures, is the one universal author, whether he is read and played in Bulgaria or Indonesia or wherever. His supremacy at creating human beings breaks through even the barrier of language and puts everyone on his stage. This means that the matter of his work has migrated every-where, reinforcing the common places we all inhabit in his themes.

2. CONTEST AS BOTH THEME AND TROPE

Great writing or the Sublime rarely emanates directly from themes since all authors are mediated by forerunners and by contemporary rivals. Nietzsche enhanced our awareness of the agonistic foundations of ancient Greek literature and culture, from Hesiod's contest with Homer on to the Hellenistic critic Longinus in his treatise *On the Sublime*. Even Shakespeare had to begin by overcoming Christopher Marlowe, only a few months his senior. William Faulkner stemmed from the Polish-English novelist Joseph Conrad and our best living author of prose fiction, Philip Roth, is inconceivable without his descent from the major Jewish literary phenomenon of the twentieth century, Franz Kafka of Prague, who wrote the most lucid German since Goethe.

The contest with past achievement is the hidden theme of all major canonical literature in Western tradition. Literary influence is both an overwhelming metaphor for literature itself, and a common topic for all criticism, whether or not the critic knows her immersion in the incessant flood.

Every theme in this series touches upon a contest with anteri-ority, whether with the presence of death, the hero's quest, the over-coming of taboos, or all of the other concerns, volume by volume. From Monteverdi through Bach to Stravinsky, or from the Italian Renaissance through the agon of Matisse and Picasso, the history of all the arts demonstrates the same patterns as literature's thematic struggle with itself. Our country's great original art, jazz, is illumi-nated by what the great creators called "cutting contests," from Louis

Armstrong and Duke Ellington on to the emergence of Charlie Parker's Bop or revisionist jazz.

A literary theme, however authentic, would come to nothing without rhetorical eloquence or mastery of metaphor. But to experience the study of the common places of invention is an apt training in the apprehension of aesthetic value in poetry and in prose.

Volume Introduction by Harold Bloom

I might have thought the American Dream had ended, but the election of Barack Obama makes a difference. He invoked our national dream in his victory speech, an important citation though edged by the ill omens of financial and economic disaster both at home and abroad (I write on 20 November, 2008).

Like so many potent social myths, the American Dream is devoid of clear meanings, whether in journalistic accounts or in academic analyses. The major American writers who have engaged the dream—Emerson, Whitman, Thoreau, Mark Twain, Henry James, Willa Cather, Robert Frost, Wallace Stevens, Ernest Hemingway, Scott Fitzgerald, Hart Crane—have been aware of this haziness and of attendant ironies. And yet they have affirmed, however ambivalently, that it must be possible to have a nation in which all of us are free to develop our singularities into health, prosperity, and some measure of happiness in self-development and personal achievement. Call this Emerson's Party of Hope, whose current prophet and leader is the still untested President-Elect Obama.

Let us call the Other Side the American Nightmare, from Poe, Hawthorne, and Melville through T.S. Eliot and Faulkner onto our varied contemporaries such as Cormac McCarthy, Thomas Pynchon and Philip Roth. Between Faulkner and these came Nathanael West, Flannery O'Connor, and Ralph Ellison. Dreamers of nightmare realities and irrealities, these superb writers are not altogether in Emerson's opposing camp, the Party of Memory because, except for Poe, Eliot and O'Connor, they shared the American freedom from dogma.

But they dwelled on our addiction to violence, endemic from *Moby-Dick*'s Captain Ahab through *Blood Meridian*'s Judge Holden, and on our constant involuntary parodying of hopes for a more humane life.

What are we to believe about our nature and destiny in the sea of history that has engulfed so many other nations? We make terrible blunders, of which the Iraqi War and our current financial panic are merely the most recent, and only rarely can they be mitigated. Our American Dream always is likelier to bring forth another Jay Gatsby than a reborn Huck Finn. Our innocence is difficult to distinguish from ignorance, a problematical theme throughout the novels and stories of Henry James, our strongest novelist even as Walt Whitman remains our more-than-major poet. What Whitman discerned (in Emerson's wake) was the American Adam, unfallen and dazzling as the sun. Is that national myth sustained by the extraordinary rise of Barack Obama?

Eight years from now we may be able to answer that question. A country without a monarch and a hereditary nobility must find its heroes in the American Presidency, an absurd ground for such a search ever since the murder of Abraham Lincoln in 1865, almost a century and a half ago. Emerson's Party of Hope trusts for a reversal, in the name of the American Dream.

THE ADVENTURES OF HUCKLEBERRY FINN (MARK TWAIN)

~ ❧ ~

"Huckleberry Finn and the Problem of Freedom"
by Sanford Pinsker,
in *Virginia Quarterly Review* (2001)

INTRODUCTION

As *The Adventures of Huckleberry Finn* ends, Huckleberry
Finn sets out for the uncharted new Territory. As Twain does
not specify what this new land will be like, we can only speculate about this place to which Huck yearns to go, and about
his reasons for leaving "sivilization." Arguing that Huck's decision to separate from American society is an indictment of
the American dream of freedom, Sanford Pinsker shows how
Twain's novel transcends our traditional understanding of the
American Dream. For Pinsker, Huck's decision to light out for
the Territory indicates a dark understanding of our desire for a
free society. While Pinsker acknowledges that Jim's "gradual
movement toward freedom" marks a sub-text in the novel,
Pinsker claims that Huck ultimately realizes that he can never
be a part of American society and can never be free, "even
should he make it to the Territory and manage to survive."
Thus, Pinsker concludes that, despite the novel's many comic

Pinsker, Sanford. "*Huckleberry Finn* and the Problem of Freedom." *Virginia
Quarterly Review* Vol. 77, No. 4 (Fall 2001): 642–49.

episodes, Twain remains skeptical about the possibility of ever attaining freedom in a flawed society built upon the impossible dream of "freedom and justice for all."

ᏆᏆᏆ

"... he ain't no slave; he's as free as any cretur that walks this earth."

—Tom Sawyer spilling the beans about Jim.

"We're free ...We're free ..."

—Linda Loman at Willy's graveside.

Freedom is America's abiding subject, as well as its deepest problem. I realize full well that I am hardly the first person to ruminate about the yawning gap between our country's large promises and, its less-than-perfect practice, much less the first to comment on the ways in which 19th-century America struggled with the "peculiar institution" known as slavery. But I am convinced that the way these large topics find a local habitation in the pages of *Adventures of Huckleberry Finn* is yet another instance in which George Orwell's prophetic words ring true: 'It is the first duty of intelligent men to restate the obvious." What Twain means to test out in Huck's idiosyncratic telling of how he and Jim made their way down the river is nothing less than what freedom in America means, and does not mean.

Critics of Twain's novel generally shy away from what makes it simultaneously disturbing and important. So, let me offer the following proposition in the spirit of plain Orwellian speech: *Adventures of Huckleberry Finn* is a novel that does not blink about all that militates to keep genuine freedom under wraps and in control. Just as the book is as wide as the Mississippi on which many of its most memorable moments are set, it is also wide enough to take on the full range of American culture—from those elements out to elevate to those which run the gamut from the lower-browed to the downright coarse.

At this point, a thumbnail sketch of how the novel has been read, and misread, may be helpful. *Adventures of Huckleberry Finn* began its long, complicated history as America's most controversial novel shortly after its publication in 1885, when the well-meaning members of the Concord (Mass.) Public Library committee decided to exclude the book from its shelves on the grounds that the story was, in their words, "trashy and vicious." The trouble with Mr. Clemens, they went on to say, was that he had "no reliable sense of propriety." They were, of course, right about this, even if their rightness rather resembles that of a busted watch that tells correct time twice a day. What they worried about, between the words of their carefully crafted objections, is that Twain's novel would corrupt the young—of Concord and, presumably points west and south. The charge is a very old one and has been leveled against those, from Socrates onward, who were regarded as corrupters of the young.

In Twain's case, what he did that so upset the moral arbiters of Concord is boldly announced in the novel's second sentence: "That book [*The Adventures of Tom Sawyer*], Huck tells us by way of introduction] was made by Mr. Mark Twain, and he told the truth, mainly." The operative word is *truth*, although we get a pretty good idea about who Huck is and what he stands for by way of his qualifying "mainly." I shall have more to say about the "mainly" later, but for the moment, let me concentrate on what it means to tell the truth and thus begin our journey down a long, complicated path. One should be aware, for example, that truth-telling, properly understood, is not always what Huck had in mind or what many of Twain's readers imagined when they went about separating lies from the truth. *Truth*, in short, is one of those words—slippery, troublesome, but nonetheless, of great importance. This is even truer, as it were, at a time when many thinkers positioned on theory's cutting edge confidently insist that "truth" be surrounded by sneer quotes and interrogated until all that remains are the easy certainties of nihilism. Twain would have found this brand of postmodernism very strange indeed, although I hasten to add that the "pursuit of truth" in his novel leads to darker conclusions than theory has yet dreamt of.

One way to explain the difference between versions of truth-telling is to sharply distinguish between small-t truths of the sort that conform to observable "facts" and the large-T Truths that philosophers worry about and writers explore in fiction and poetry. In this latter sense, to tell the truth about the world requires more than a careful attention to realistic detail, however much this was certainly part of Twain's aesthetic agenda. Rather, it is a matter of burning away the social conditioning that puts layers of fat around the soul and that covers the eyes with motes.

In the late 1940's Lionel Trilling, perhaps the most influential critic of his time, famously declared that Huck and Tom Sawyer may tell the lies of children but they do not, in Trilling's words, "tell the ultimate lie of adults: they do not lie to themselves." These characters, who (rightly) believe that "the world is in a conspiracy to lie to [them]," are thus swaddled, Trilling argues, in "moral sensitivity."

In general T. S. Eliot is right about the way that Huck, Twain's satiric persona, works, but there are moments when Huck is not quite all that Eliot claims on his behalf. Take, for example, the moment in which Colonel Sherburn beats back a potential lynch mob by standing up to bullies and taking their cowardly measure. Huck describes the last, tail-between-their-legs moments this way: "The crowd washed back sudden, and then broke all apart and went tearing off every which way, . . . I could a staid, if I'd a wanted to, but I didn't want to." Here, despite Eliot's large pronouncement, is a moment where Huck, in his own term, heaves off a "stretcher." In plainer language, he clearly lies to himself; moreover, we see his feeble rationalization as the sham it surely is.

Why, one wonders, would Twain so embarrass his otherwise savvy protagonist? My hunch is that he means to remind us that Huck is a very young, young boy, despite his sound heart and outbursts of good sense. He is, in short, given to backsliding of the human sort. This often overlooked point deserves emphasis if only because so many readers, including quite intelligent ones, fall into fits of disappointment whenever Huck—or by extension, Twain—lets them down. This usually occurs when Tom Sawyer enters the scene and bullies poor Huck with his insider knowledge of romance novels, but it can also happen when such readers tire of satire, even of dark, uncompromising satire, and prefer that the novel head off to other, more morally soothing directions.

Eliot makes much the same point about Huck's honesty when he talks about his "vision." He sees the real world, Eliot argues, but "he does not judge it—he allows it to judge itself." Enter Leo Marx's "Mr. Eliot, Mr. Trilling, and Huckleberry Finn," a 1953 essay that attacks both critics as "tender-minded" because they substitute structural arguments (Eliot's paean to the mythic river) or easy platitudes (Trilling's magisterial assertions about Huck's honesty) for the more sober recognition that Twain's novel ends in shambles and failure.

At this point, let me drag in Huck's comment about Mr. Twain telling the truth, *mainly.* Huck is not especially bothered by this—certainly he is not as lathered up about it as Mr. Marx will be—because, as he puts it, "I never seen anybody but lied, one time or another, without it was Aunt Polly, or the widow, or maybe Mary," Everybody else is given to heaving in "stretchers"; as far as Huck is concerned, they come with the territory. What the novel dramatizes, however, is how dangerous, and indeed, how deadly, certain "stretchers" can become—especially if they are generated by the small-r romantic wish to make quotidian life more glamorous than it in fact is. That romanticism of the sort behind the blood-curdling oaths taken by would-be members of Tom Sawyer's gang is one thing; when it generates the ongoing feud of the Shepherdsons and the Grangerfords, however, this is another matter altogether.

In much the same way that Twain, in *Life on the Mississippi*, argues that the novels of Sir Walter Scott were singularly responsible for the Civil War, *Adventures of Huckleberry Finn* presents one episode after another in which romance trumps his ignorant protagonist. For early generations of believers, Satan was the force to reckon with. He was cunning, shape-shifting, and always threatening to steal away with one's soul. Calvinists took his power seriously; no measures were too stern when it came to resisting the many forms his temptations took, whether it be packaged in a whiskey bottle or a pack of playing cards. Twain may have rather enjoyed kicking Christians in the slats when they refused to act as proper Christians or when their hypocrisy poked out like a sore thumb, but he did not see Satan lurking around every corner. Rather, it was the endless versions of small-r romanticism that got Twain's dander up. They lied—not as simple "stretchers," but as *lies.* And the biggest lie of all is that *anyone*, black or white, could be genuinely free.

This is why the current obsession with Twain's failure to address the implications of slavery comes to half a loaf. Yes, slavery was the most visible manifestation of man's inhumanity to man—not just the shackles and the beatings, but also in the systematic way in which an entire people was reduced to chattel property. Jim's line about being a rich man if he owned himself cracks the heart, and I would add, goes a long way to counter those arguments in which Jim is reduced to minstrel clown. Granted, the tone drips out of Twain's pen, just as it does when Tom dramatically proclaims that Jim is as "free as any cretur that walks the earth." Attentive readers cannot help but ask themselves, given all that the book has demonstrated, *"How free is this?"*—for not only the newly freed Jim, but also for Huck, for Tom, for everyone on the Phelps plantation and for everybody back home.

Granted, no American writer can match Twain when it comes to giving vivid expression to the great abiding dream of being free:

> Soon as it was night, out we shoved; when we got her out to about the middle, we let her alone, and let her float wherever the current wanted her to; then we lit the pipes, and dangled our legs in the water and talked about all kinds of things—we was always naked, day and night, whenever the mosquitoes would let us. . . . Sometimes we'd have that whole river all to ourselves for the longest time . . . It's lovely to live on a raft. We had the sky, up there, all speckled with stars, and we used to lay on our backs and look up at them, and discuss about whether they was made, or only just happened.

The dream, alas, cannot last, however much it remains lodged in the head of every reader with an ear for the music that language at its most supple can make. As my grandfather used to say about the America he both loved and quarreled with, "You could live if they'll let you." No remark better sums up the history of the Jews, or, with a snip here a tuck there, the necessary fate of Huck and Jim. Huck's instinctive goodness turns out to be no match for Tom's book-learning and charisma. Indeed, how could it? After all, it is Tom, not Huck, who knows how a proper "evasion" should be conducted, and how to give Jim the theatrical homecoming his protracted suffering deserves. Huck goes along with the former because, well, that is Huck's modus operandi, but he balks at the latter because he's had a bellyful of Tom foolishness. Granted, Twain knew full well that lighting out for the Territory would put Huck in harm's way, and that the lawlessness of the West was an exaggerated mirror of the more "sivilized" lawlessness of the East. Pursue it as Huck will, freedom remains an elusive promise, one that F. Scott Fitzgerald would later characterize as the boats that forever recede into the past no matter how hard one paddles.

Seen one way, Huck is a survivor, with an eye on a warm meal and a trundle bed; seen from another angle, he is the satiric lens through which we see the world's endless capacity for cruelty. That is why Huck's deadpan descriptions of, say, the Duke and the King are so effective. They know—or think they know—all that con men need to work a crowd—namely, that you can't cheat an honest man and, better yet, that there's a sucker born every minute. The same thing applies to Huck's account of the drunks who populate the shore towns and who take an enormous pleasure in setting dogs on fire. Freedom, for these folks, consists of inflicting as much cruelty as they can. Pap is squarely in their camp. He would vote for slavery if it were on all the ballots—that is, if he could stagger to the local polling place. He is, of course, not alone in this sentiment. Indeed, which voter in the world of Twain's novel felt otherwise?

Small wonder, then, that Leo Marx was so infuriated when he took Trilling and Eliot to task in the early 1950's or that Jane Smiley, a novelist of some reputation, recently argued that Harriet Beecher Stowe's *Uncle Tom's Cabin* is in every way superior to *Adventures of Huckleberry Finn*. Marx is a critic worth taking seriously. Smiley, unfortunately, is not. She sides with propaganda rather than with art, preferring a work that confirms her politically correct certainties rather than one which questions her unquestioned beliefs. For her, it is not enough that Huck *feels* a certain way toward Jim, he needs to act—and it is precisely on the level of action (or more precisely still, *non* action) that Twain's novel so badly fails in Smiley's opinion:

> To invest *The Adventures of Huckleberry Finn* with "greatness" is to underwrite a very simplistic and evasive theory of what racism is and to promulgate it, philosophically, in schools and the media as well as in academic journals. Surely the discomfort of many readers, black and white, and the censorship battles that have dogged *Huck Finn* in the last twenty years are understandable in this context. No matter how often the critics "place in context" Huck's use of the word "nigger," they

can never fully excuse or fully hide the deeper racism of the novel—the way Twain and Huck use Jim because they really don't care enough about his desire for freedom to let that desire change their plans.

Smiley much prefers *Uncle Tom's Cabin* because it is full of people acting against slavery, because it is, unashamedly, an Abolitionist manifesto. But after the Civil War resolved the matter at the end of the rifle barrel, after oceans of blood had been spilled, Stowe's novel no longer packed the same immediacy it once did. True enough, *Uncle Tom's Cabin* retains an importance as an historical novel, but not, I think, as a living (which is to say, disturbing) piece of literature.

As Americans, we bow to no one in our official regard for freedom, but we are also a country whose Pledge of Allegiance insists that, here, there will be "liberty and justice for all." School children mouth the words without every quite realizing that they are a contradiction, that if there is unbridled liberty there cannot be endless liberty. The contradiction also lies at the very heart *of Huckleberry Finn*. Twain wrote well before Sigmund Freud's *Civilization and Its Discontents* explained the small-print costs, in repression, deferred gratification, and neurosis, that inevitably come with the clear benefits of civilization. Huck does not want to return to a world that will insist that what he calls "sivilization" be spelled with a *c*—and moreover that such people are expected to wear shoes and have clean fingernails.

Huck prefers freer space and a separate peace. In this sense, his dream of freedom is the antithesis of Linda Loman's painful recognition that the American Dream of a paid-off house does not, alas, make one "free and clear." Arthur Miller's play is an indictment of a life lived in noisy, manic-depressive desperation. Willy, alas, was a man who never knew who he was, a man who bought into a world where Success lies just around the corner and where "being well liked" will eventually carry the day. But powerful as Miller's play clearly is, it does not limn freedom as darkly as Twain's novel does. For the problem of freedom in *Huckleberry Finn* so co-exists with its humor that readers forget just how broad the brush that Twain uses is. Jim's slavery and gradual movement toward freedom is at best only a small part of what the novel is about. Rather, it is Huck's understanding that, unlike Tom, he can never fit into society, added to our growing realization that he will never be free—even should he make it to the Territory and manage to survive—that makes Twain's novel so problematic. In short, *Adventures of Huckleberry Finn* is a deeply subversive book, not because it is peppered with the N-word or even because some see racism in what is the most anti-racist book ever written in America, but because it tells the Truth—not "mainly," but right down to the core.

THE AMERICAN DREAM
(EDWARD ALBEE)

"Albee's *The American Dream* and the Existential Vacuum"
by Nicholas Canaday, Jr.,
in *South Central Bulletin* (1966)

INTRODUCTION

In his highly influential essay on Albee's play, Nicholas Canady identifies *The American Dream* as an example of the Theater of the Absurd, describing the play as a comic response to the "meaninglessness of American life." For Canady, The Young Man appearing near the end of the play "is the symbol of the American Dream, beautiful in appearance but without real substance," and the other characters represent ways of responding to the void of modern life. Canady sees Daddy as a fatalist, Mommy as a fanatic, "who seeks to manipulate and dominate people in order to get her own 'satisfaction,'" Mrs. Barker as a "representative of organizations" consistently seeking to align herself with others, and Grandma as a realist who accepts the meaninglessness of life by responding creatively. Thus, Canady argues that Grandma offers the only positive response to the American Dream in the play, suggesting "that whatever meaning is possible is achieved

Canaday, Nicholas Jr. "Albee's *The American Dream* and the Existential Vacuum." *South Central Bulletin* Vol. 26, No. 4 (Winter 1966): 28–34.

through an attitude of courageous realism that can enable
man to conduct himself with dignity, through the simple enjoyment of whatever experience can be enjoyed, and through the
creative act of the artist."

༄༅

The many varieties of probings in and around the center of life in our
time—whether sociological, philosophical, religious, or literary—are
so well known by now that terms like "anguish" and "estrangement"
and "nothingness" have become, if not household words, at least basic
to the jargon of the academy.[1] Edward Albee's *The American Dream* is
what might be called a textbook case of the response of the American
drama to this existential vacuum, and at the same time this play of
1961 is perhaps our best example of what has come to be known as the
"theatre of the absurd."[2] Thus *The American Dream* is appearing with
increasing frequency in the drama anthologies and the American literature survey texts. By means of caricature and the comic irrelevancy
of its language the play mirrors the meaninglessness of American life.
The Young Man, who appears on stage near the end of the play, is the
symbol of the American Dream, beautiful in appearance but without
real substance. He embodies Albee's view of the present extension
of this familiar myth. The general critical view that "Edward Albee's
plays are ferocious attacks on lethargy and complacency in American society" and "a savage denial that everything is just dandy"[3] is
supported by Albee's own remarks in his introduction to the Coward-
McCann Contemporary Drama Edition of the play.[4] Thus the void at
the center of modern life is the basic assumption upon which this play
rests; the action is primarily concerned with typical responses to this
existential situation. It is the purpose of this essay to categorize these
responses and then to offer the suggestion that in this play there are
certain positive values that have thus far been overlooked by critics. It
seems to me that such values are implied in the absurd world of *The
American Dream*, even though the center has gone out of life, all forms
are smashed, and—to coin a cliché—God is dead.

The first type of response is represented in the play by Daddy. His
attitude is fatalistic. In his opening speech, as he and Mommy are
vaguely awaiting the arrival of "them"—whether Mrs. Barker, the Van

Man, or just for something to happen—he answers Mommy's remark that "they" are late: "That's the way things are today, and there's nothing you can do about it." From the very beginning Daddy's tone is resigned, particularly in contrast to the whining, griping qualities in the complaints of Mommy. Even when Daddy goes on to list the needed repairs to icebox, doorbell, and toilet, it is clear that he really does not expect to get anything done about them. "That's the way things are today," he says, "You just can't get satisfaction."

Both ineffectualness and resignation have so reinforced each other in Daddy's character that "Oh dear; oh dear" becomes his typical reaction to whatever happens. The past is meaningless to him; he cannot even recall the name of the son they had adopted some years before. After Mrs. Barker has been present for some time on stage and then leaves, Daddy cannot recall her name; and when Mommy sends him off to break Grandma's television set, he cannot even find her room. His resignation seems to be due to the meaninglessness of his life and to his subjection to the dominating presence of Mommy. His response to this domination, like everything else he does, is characterized by a typical lack of resolution: "I do wish I weren't surrounded by women; I'd like some men around here." His only defense against Mommy is to withdraw into his own empty world, pretending to listen to her and responding just enough to keep her satisfied, which of course is all that she requires. There is nothing in life he wants anymore: "I just want to get it over with."

Mommy represents a second characteristic response to the void of modern life. She is a fanatic, who seeks to manipulate and dominate people in order to get her own "satisfaction." Heedless of the opinions or feelings of others, she is capable of casual cruelty (as when she tells Daddy she has the right to live off him because she married him and is entitled to his money when he dies) or nauseating flattery (as when she praises Daddy's firm masculinity in an attempt to make him get rid of Grandma)—capable of any means to attain her own ends. When she tells of her shopping expedition to purchase a hat, she makes it clear that her method of dealing with people is to create such an unpleasant scene that she finally has her way. By throwing hats around and screaming as loudly as she can she finally manages to get "satisfaction." The rest of the play demonstrates how she practices this method.

Mommy's treatment of everyone is imperious and demanding. Her attacks on Daddy show a ruthless disregard for his personality, and her relationship with Grandma is one long terrible scene of cruel bullying insult. She rages at Grandma, alternately telling her that she has nothing to say or that she is a liar. She threatens to hide Grandma's teeth, break her television, and send her away. This last embarrasses Daddy, who would rather not think about it. But Grandma refuses to be bullied by the woman that Grandma herself had warned Daddy not to marry because she was "a tramp and a trollop and a trull to boot." Grandma regards her as not having improved any with age. Mommy responds angrily that Grandma is *her* mother, not Daddy's, but Mommy fails to break up whatever relationship there is between Grandma and Daddy.

At the end of the play Mommy is quite pleased to have the Young Man waiting on her as a servant might. She sends him to fetch sauterne to celebrate their new family relationship, and he certainly will provide no resistance to her aggressiveness. She orders everyone to take a glass and drink to "satisfaction," which they all do as the play ends.

Mrs. Barker represents a third response to the existential vacuum. Her thoughts and actions are based not upon any principle or principles she holds within herself, for she has none. Instead she is a sensitive weather vane constantly seeking to align herself with the opinions of others and especially sensitive to the ideas (insofar as she knows what they are) of the various groups with which she is associated. Mrs. Barker represents a collectivistic response to absurdity, although not in the political sense. She is rather a kind of caricature of the other-directed person. From the beginning of the play Mrs. Barker is identified as a representative of organizations. She participates in Responsible Citizens Activities, Good Works, the Ladies Auxiliary Air Raid Committee, the Woman's Club, and of course the Bye-Bye Adoption Service, which explains her presence on stage. She announces when she first appears that she is a "professional woman"—that is to say an organization woman—and then reveals that she has been listening outside the door before coming in. This bit of eavesdropping allows her to blend into the conversation as soon as she enters, because she knows who is in the room and the tone of their remarks. In this way she avoids offending anyone. As it happens, Daddy has had a change of heart about sending Grandma away just before Mrs. Barker enters, and since she may be the person coming to get Grandma, he wishes aloud that Mrs. Barker might now just go away. Mrs. Barker's answer is characteristic: "Oh no; we're much too efficient for that." She represents an efficient organization and carefully chooses to have no view on the matter for herself.

Mrs. Barker is a caricature of amiability, ignoring the inconsistencies that arise when she agrees with everyone in turn. She talks enthusiastically about this "jolly family," as she calls it, finds their stories "engrossing" or "gripping," and exclaims several times about the "good idea" or the "nice idea" that someone had. In the end she remarks how glad she is that they are all pleased with the solution to their problem, a solution which has actually been engineered by Grandma. On three separate occasions in the dialogue Mrs. Barker takes contradictory positions on both sides of an argument. In effect, her method is to agree with the last speaker. When she and Mommy are talking about Woman Love in the country, the chief exponent of the movement seems to be Mrs. Barker's dear brother with his dear little wife, and Mrs. Barker agrees that the national tendency to hate women is deplorable. Just after that Daddy makes his complaint about being surrounded by women and wanting the companionship of men, and Mrs. Barker enthusiastically agrees with him. Later the question arises whether Mommy is being polite enough to Mrs. Barker. She allows Mommy to persuade her of her good will, but as soon as Mommy leaves the room she agrees with Grandma that Mommy is mistreating her as a guest in the house. Finally, when confronted with the Young Man, who may be about to take Grandma away. Mrs. Barker says indignantly: "How dare you cart this poor old woman away!" But when he answers that he is paid to do it, Mrs. Barker says: "Well, you're quite right, of course, and I shouldn't meddle." Such confrontations show Mrs. Barker's shallowness and within her an element of fear that makes her so quick to please.

When she is asked a direct question, even about a simple matter, Mrs. Barker becomes pathetic. After Grandma has arranged for Mrs. Barker to introduce the Young Man into the family, Grandma asks Mrs. Barker if this has helped her accomplish her mission. It has helped, of course, because she has had no idea of what to do or even why she is there. When she accepts the credit for the "happy" ending from Mommy, she does it in the name of "professional women," so in a sense she does not claim to have solved the problem herself. About the usefulness of Grandma's assistance, however, she says: "I can't tell, yet. I'll have to . . . what is the word I want? . . . I'll have to relate it . . . that's it . . . I'll have to relate it to certain things that I *know*, and . . . draw . . . conclusions." What Mrs. Barker knows, when she knows anything at all, is the opinion of others, the rules of the various organizations, the collective mind of any group, however small, with which she comes in contact. Without such knowledge she is completely unable to respond even on a trivial subject. It is no wonder that at one point in the play she remarks pathetically: "But . . . I feel so lost . . . not knowing why I'm here." Is it possible that her name characterizes her? Could she be a barker for a cheap show, an amiable front woman who represents those inside the seductive but shaky tent of consensus?

It is to Grandma—the most appealing character in Albee's play— that we must look for a positive response to the existential vacuum. Although there seems to be no solution in the cosmic sense to the absurdity of our world, there is at least a way to make this world bearable. Among the commentators on the play there is general critical agreement that Grandma stands apart from the other characters. One critic writes: "The characters are dehumanized types, played in a mannered, marionette style—except Grandma, who is honest and therefore a real person."[5] Another critic relates her to the American Dream motif: "Grandma is an anachronism: she represents the solid pioneer stock out of which the American Dream might have come had it not been corrupted instead."[6] Having said these things, however, few critics see in Grandma or in the play generally any positive values applicable to the present. According to one writer, Albee "imparts no sense of a cure, the knowledge of paths toward enlargement, not the diminution of life."[7] The observation has also been made that Albee "attempts to satirize a situation which he sees as both painful and irremediable," and thus his work is "largely a negation of the possibility of meaningful human action."[8] Such lack of hope for the future is also reflected in this comment: "Sadly, however, we cannot say that Albee's outlook produces any . . . hope. As he perceives the future, he can see only annihilation, performed by a devouring world."[9] One critic demurs by observing that Albee's "harshly satirical stance presupposes positive sense and meaning."[10] This critic does not spell out precisely what the meaning is, but perhaps there are positive values implicit in this play, and, if so, we must turn to an analysis of the character of Grandma to find them.[11]

The first positive value that Grandma represents is one of attitude. She is realistic; she has a sense of her own freedom and especially of her own dignity. Amid all the whining and sighing her most characteristic speech is cheerful: "How do you like them apples?" Her attitude is tinged with cynicism in her present situation, but this is a necessary antidote to the more than slight nausea we feel about the relationship between Mommy and Daddy. Even in her first comic entrance Grandma maintains her dignity. To Mommy's question about the boxes she is carrying Grandma replies: "That's nobody's damn business." One of her early speeches concerns the sense of dignity that is so important: ". . . that's all that's important . . . a sense of dignity. You got to have a sense of dignity, even if you don't care, 'cause if you don't have that, civilization's doomed." We see dignity in Grandma when she responds to Mommy's threats. "You don't frighten me," she says, "I'm too old to be frightened."

There is value also in Grandma's realistic attitude. She says that she is a "muddleheaded old woman," but the fact is that she sees more clearly than anyone else in the play. Through her the audience learns why Mommy married Daddy and much about their present relationship. Through Grandma we learn about Daddy's disillusionment with Mommy and with marriage, and of course the whole story of their adoption of a son years before is told by Grandma to Mrs. Barker. In three separate speeches Grandma gives a realistic picture of old age, yet manages at the same time to retain her own dignity. She knows about the threat of the Van Man who may take her away—whether he is the keeper of an old folks' home or Death itself—and when Mommy begins to talk about his arrival, Grandma says contemptuously, "I'm way ahead of you." The fact is that she is far ahead of all the other characters in the play.

Still another value is in Grandma's enjoyment of living. She apparently has lived a full and pleasant life, although we are given few details. But the good is enjoying the experience of life, which she has done. The things she has collected in her boxes, "a few images, a little garbled by now," do provide comedy, but the old letters, the blind Pekinese, the television set—even the Sunday teeth—all of which she thinks of sadly, indicate that she did enjoy life in the past. This cannot be said of any of the others. Some of Grandma's old spirit is revealed as she greets with appreciation the Young Man. She is the only one who knows the essential vacuity of the Young Man, but she can still enjoy his handsome, muscular appearance with an honest pleasure unlike that of the simperingly coy Mommy. "My, my, aren't you something!" Grandma says to the Young Man. And later she adds with a characteristic view of herself: "You know, if I were about a hundred and fifty years younger I could go for you."

Most important, however, Grandma is the only one in the play who shows a creative response to life. It is not merely that she makes plans, sees them carried out, and thus significantly exercises a freedom that the others do not. The baking contest represents Grandma's plan by which she intends to escape her dependence on Mommy and Daddy, and its $25,000 prize enables her to do just that at the end of the play. This in itself is significant enough compared to the aimless activities of Mommy, Daddy, and Mrs. Barker. But Grandma also is a kind of creative artist in her own way. Mommy tells how Grandma used to wrap the lunch boxes that Mommy took to school as a little girl, wrap them so nicely, as she puts it, that it would break her heart to open them. Grandma did this in spite of the poverty of the family. There is much comic nonsense in this story as Mommy tells it, but it also points to a creativity only partly suppressed. Certainly Grandma's use of language and her comments about language reveal another creative response to life. In general the comic irrelevance of the language mirrors the meaninglessness of life and demonstrates especially that language as gesture has replaced language as communication. For Grandma, however, language does serve to communicate, and her comments on style are both amusing and significant. Mommy tries to imitate her, but Grandma scornfully points out Mommy's failure to achieve harmony of rhythm and content.

Finally, another kind of creativity is shown in the way Grandma provides the resolution of the play by suggesting to Mrs. Barker what to do about the Young Man and by prompting the Young Man about taking a place in the family. Having arranged all this, Grandma steps outside of the set, addresses herself to the audience, and as a kind of stage manager observes the "happy" ending she has created. It is happy because, as she says, "everybody's got what he thinks he wants." She is satisfied: "Well, I guess that just about wraps it up. I mean, for better or worse, this is a comedy, and I don't think we'd better go any further." Life may have a void at its center, but perhaps how you wrap it up—one recalls the lunch boxes—has in itself a value.

Thus Albee's *The American Dream* makes the assumption that the dream is hollow and shows the causes and symptoms of a sick society. Through comic caricature it reveals three desperate responses to the existential vacuum, and then it goes on to do one thing more. In the character of Grandma the play suggests that whatever meaning is possible is achieved through an attitude of courageous realism that can enable man to conduct himself with dignity, through the simple enjoyment of whatever experience can be enjoyed, and through the creative act of the artist.

NOTES

1. The phrase "existential vacuum" is found in the writings of Viktor E. Frankl, professor of neurology and psychiatry at the University of Vienna. I am also indebted to Professor Frankl for his discussion of the categories of response to this vacuum, upon which discussion I have drawn in analyzing *The American Dream.* See especially *The Doctor and the Soul,* trans. Richard and Clara Winston (New York: Alfred A. Knopf, 1957).

2. Martin Esslin, *The Theatre of the Absurd* (Garden City, N.Y.: Doubleday & Company [Anchor Book], 1961), judges the play to be a "promising and brilliant first example of an American contribution to the Theatre of the Absurd" (p. 227).

3. Henry Goodman, "The New Dramatists: 4. Edward Albee," *Drama Survey,* II (1962), 72.

4. *The American Dream* (New York: Coward-McCann, Inc., 1961), p. 8. All further quotations from the play are taken from this edition.

5. Allan Lewis, "The Fun and Games of Edward Albee, *Educational Theatre Journal,* XVI (1964), 32.

6. George E. Wellwarth, "Hope Deferred—The New American Drama," *Literary Review,* VII (1963), 13.

7. Lewis, p. 39.

8. Wendell V. Harris, "Morality, Absurdity, and Albee," *Southwest Review*, XLIX (1964); 254, 255.

9. Jordan Y. Miller, "Myth and the American Dream: O'Neill to Albee," *Modern Drama*, VII (1964), 198.

10. Goodman, p. 79.

11. For a critical view different from the consensus indicated above, see Kenneth Hamilton, "Mr. Albee's Dream," *Queen's Quarterly*, LXX (1963), 393–399. Hamilton maintains that Albee "has a dream of his own, one no less hollow than that which he attacks and perhaps even more at odds with reality" (393). In this dream, "the Huckleberry Finn dream," Hamilton holds that "the lost innocence of the Young Man is regarded as infinitely precious and its destruction as the supreme crime" (395). This interpretation views the Young Man as the "key figure" (395) in the play. My own view accords him a central symbolic significance, but sees Grandma as the key figure from whom positive values emerge. Hamilton believes that both Grandma and the Young Man "remain dominated by the pleasure-principle" (399), while I would argue that Grandma has never been so dominated.

THE AUTOBIOGRAPHY OF BENJAMIN FRANKLIN
(BENJAMIN FRANKLIN)

~~~

"Franklin's *Autobiography*
and the American Dream"
by J.A. Leo Lemay,
in *The Renaissance Man
in the Eighteenth Century* (1978)

INTRODUCTION

J.A. Leo Lemay sees Franklin's *Autobiography* as the "definitive formulation of the American Dream." Enumerating the
work's literary qualities and socio-political concerns, Lemay
finds the book's "primary function" is "to demonstrate that
man does have choice in the New World, that man can create
himself." This ability to create and recreate the self lies at the
center of Franklin's idea of the American Dream.

~~~

The genres that Franklin wrote are the proverb, essay, editorial, *jeu
d'esprit*, hoax, *bagatelle*, satire, letter, pamphlet, speech, almanac,
periodical, and, of course, autobiography.[1] Critics generally concede

---

Lemay, J.A. Leo. "Franklin's Autobiography and the American Dream." *The
Renaissance Man in the Eighteenth Century*. William Andrews Clark Memorial
Library, Los Angeles: 1978.

that he wrote the greatest bagatelles in any language, and I am of
the heretical opinion that, in the age of letters as literary art, he was
incomparably the greatest letter writer.[2] He wrote so much, so well,
that I could not list, in my remaining minutes, the titles of his more
artful writings. So I will instead limit myself to some remarks about
one aspect of his best-known work.

Franklin's *Autobiography* is the first great book in American
literature, and, in some ways, it remains the most important single
book. One cannot claim for it the structural perfection of, say, Henry
James's *Ambassadors* or Nathaniel Hawthorne's *Scarlet Letter*, nor
does it possess the grandiloquent language of Melville, Whitman, or
Faulkner. But Franklin's *Autobiography* contains those "short quick
probings at the very axis of reality,"[3] which, in Melville's opinion, were
a touchstone of literary greatness. The youthful Franklin lapsed from
his vegetarian diet after observing that big fish ate smaller fish (and
after seeing and smelling the fresh fish sizzling hot in the pan), and
so he ate the fish; and the old man who was writing the *Autobiography*
ironically commented on the young man's justification: "So convenient a thing it is to be a *reasonable creature*, since it enables one to
find or make a Reason for every thing one has a mind to do" (p. 88).
Franklin's profound skepticism concerning reason, his implied positions on eighteenth-century theological and psychological debates on
voluntarism, and his pessimism concerning the vanity and selfishness
of mankind are important themes of the *Autobiography* (and of that
quotation), present for those who read it carefully.

But few people read the *Autobiography* for its satire on the
nature of man, or for its important contributions to the key questions of ethical and moral philosophy which racked eighteenth-
century thought, or for its ridicule of various religions and religious
doctrines. It is not because of these themes that the book has been
an important influence upon such disparate current Americans as the
Chinese-born Nobel Prize winner in physics in 1957, Chen Ning
Yang, and the Georgia-born Democratic nominee for president in
1976, Jimmy Carter.[4] No, these themes add a depth to its greatness,
a richness and complexity to its thought, a texture and subtlety to
its language and content that is generally unseen and unappreci-
ated, although friends of Franklin with whom he corresponded
about aspects of the book, like Joseph Priestley and Henry Home,

Lord Kames, or those who read it in manuscript at his request, like Richard Price and La Rochefoucauld, would have appreciated its subtleties.[5] But everyone knows, or thinks he knows, one major theme and subject of the *Autobiography*. Everyone can say why the book has been enormously popular and why it is among the classics of American literature.

It is because Franklin gave us the definitive formulation of the American Dream. What is the American Dream? The simplest possible answer, as well as the most common general impression, is expressed by the standard cliché, the rise from rags to riches. This theme was certainly not new to Franklin's *Autobiography* or even to American literature, though Franklin is often commonly supposed to be the progenitor of the Horatio Alger success story of nineteenth-century American popular literature.[6] Actually such stories are later versions of popular Renaissance and seventeenth-century ballads and chapbooks such as *The Honour of a London Prentice* and *Sir Richard Whittington's Advancement*. Such ballads usually portray the rise of the hero by a sudden stroke of good fortune, or by knightly feats of heroic courage.[7] Franklin's version of the rise is similar to the motif as presented in miniature in the numerous promotion tracts of America, such as John Hammond's *Leah and Rachal*, which stress the possible rise of the common man by industry and frugality.[8] On this basic level of the American Dream motif, the *Autobiography* combines the kinds of popular appeal present in the old ballads with the view of life in America as possibility, which is the constant message of the promotion tracts and which echoes the archetypal ideas of the West, both as the terrestrial paradise and as the culmination of the progress of civilization.[9]

But the *Autobiography*, as every reader knows, is not primarily about Franklin's economic rise. At best, this is a minor subject. When he refers to it, he generally does so for a number of immediate reasons, nearly all of which are as important as the fact of his wealth. For example, Franklin tells that Deborah Franklin purchased "a China Bowl with a Spoon of Silver" for him "without my Knowledge." He relates this anecdote partly for the sake of its ironic quality ("she thought *her* Husband deserv'd a Silver Spoon and China Bowl as well as any of his Neighbours" [p. 145]), partly for its testimony of the rewards of Industry and Frugality (it follows a passage praising

Deborah as a helpmate), and, of course, partly as a testimony of the beginning of their wealth. Although Franklin writes of his early poverty a number of times, he rarely mentions his later wealth. It might be said that in twice telling of his retirement from private business, Franklin indirectly boasts of his financial success. But the sentence structure on both occasions demonstrates that the major subject is public business, not private wealth.[10] The rags to riches definition of the American Dream is a minor aspect of the American Dream theme in Franklin's *Autobiography*. Those readers who are unhappy with the *Autobiography* because it is primarily a practical lesson in how to become rich, themselves emphasize the demeaning message that they decry.

A second and more important aspect of the American Dream theme in the *Autobiography* is the rise from impotence to importance, from dependence to independence, from helplessness to power. Franklin carefully parallelled this motif with the rags to riches motif in the opening of the *Autobiography*: "Having emerg'd from the Poverty and Obscurity in which I was born and bred, to a State of Affluence and some Degree of Reputation in the World . . ." (p. 43). The *Autobiography* relates in great detail the story of Franklin's rise from "Obscurity" to "some Degree of Reputation in the World."

This aspect of the American Dream motif gives the book much of its allegorical meaning and its archetypal power. Readers frequently observe that the story of Franklin's rise has its counterpart in the rise of the United States. Franklin was conscious of this. In the later eighteenth century he was the most famous man in the Western world. Even John Adams, in an attack on Franklin written thirty years after his death, conceded: "His reputation was more universal than that of Leibnitz or Newton, Frederick or Voltaire, and his character more beloved and esteemed than any or all of them."[11] And Franklin was famous as an *American*.[12] He frequently wrote about America, was familiar with all the eighteenth-century ideas about America, and knew that his *Autobiography* would be read, at least by some Englishmen and Europeans, as a book about America. As Benjamin Vaughan pointed out in a letter urging Franklin to go on with the *Autobiography*: "All that has happened to you is also connected with the detail of the manners and situation of a *rising* people" (p. 135). And critical articles, such as that by James M. Cox, show that the book has frequently been read as an allegory of the rise to power and to independence of the United States.[13]

A more fundamental reason for the book's power and popularity lies in the archetypal appeal of the individual's rise from helplessness to power, from dependence to independence. In that normal development that every human being experiences from nebulousness to identity, from infancy to maturity, we all recapitulate the experience of the American Dream.[14] That is why the American Dream has been and is so important to so many people, as well as to American literature. That explains the appeal of the myth of the log-cabin birth of our American presidents and the popularity of the role of the self-made man. The American Dream, on this archetypal level, embodies a universal experience. *But* what is the identity, the strength, the power, or the independence that we adults enjoy? There's the rub. To an infant, the adult's power seems unlimited. To a child or adolescent, it seems a goal that cannot be too quickly achieved. But the achieved status is no great shakes, as every suicide bears ample witness. And we all recognize the lamentable truth of what Poor Richard said: "9 Men in 10 are suicides."[15] Who could not feel disenchanted with life? It is not only every person who ever reads a newspaper or has many dealings with the public; it is every person who goes through infancy and childhood anticipating that glorious state of adult freedom and independence, and who achieves it—as, of course, we all have. How many qualifications there are, how little real independence, how constraining nearly all occupations, how confining the roles we must act, and how unpleasant all the innumerable forces that are so glumly summed up under the forbidding heading of *the realities of life*. Who could not feel disenchanted with the American Dream?

That brings us to a third aspect of the American Dream as it appears in Franklin's *Autobiography*. The American Dream is a philosophy of individualism: it holds that the world can be affected and changed by individuals. The American Dream is a dream of possibility—not just of wealth or of prestige or of power but of the manifold possibilities that human existence can hold for the incredible variety of people of the most assorted talents and drives. Generalized, the American Dream is the hope for a better world, a new world, free of the ills of the old, existing world. And for the individual, it is the hope for a new beginning for any of the numerous things that this incredible variety of human beings may want to do.[16] Although these desires can be as varied as the different people who exist, they have one thing in common. Before anyone can achieve any measure of competence, much less extraordinary success, in any field, it is necessary to believe in the possibility of accomplishment. Franklin graphically expressed his attitude in a woodcut (America's first political cartoon) which portrays a Conestoga wagon stuck in the mud, with the wagoner beside it praying to Hercules. Under it, Franklin printed the opening of Cato's well-known speech in Sallust. In effect, Hercules tells the wagoner to get up, whip up the horses, put his shoulder to the wheel, and push.[17]

Before we apply to the American Dream the common sense of today, we should appreciate its eighteenth-century significance. The fictive world of Franklin's *Autobiography* portrays the first completely modern world that I know in Western literature: nonfeudal, nonaristocratic, and nonreligious. One has only to compare it with the fictive world of Jonathan Edwards's autobiography to realize that Franklin's world, like Edwards's, was indeed a world of his imagination, although that imaginative world, as portrayed in the *Autobiography*, suspiciously corresponded to an ideal democratic world as imagined by European philosophers and men of letters. Franklin's *persona*—that runaway apprentice whose appetite for work and study is nearly boundless, that trusting youth flattered and gulled by Governor Keith, that impecunious young adult who spent his money supporting his friend Ralph and his friend's mistress—that youth is the first citizen in literature who lives in a democratic, secular, mobile society.[18] The *persona* has the opportunity of choosing (or, to put it negatively, faces the problem of choosing) what he is going to do in life and what he is going to *be* in life. Will he be a tallow chandler and soap maker like his father and his older brother John? A cutler like his cousin Samuel? Or a printer like his older brother James? Or will he satisfy his craving for adventure and run off to sea like his older brother Josiah?[19] These choices—presented in poignant terms early in the *Autobiography* and presented against the background of his father's not being able to afford to keep even Benjamin, "the Tithe of his Sons" (p. 52), in school so that he could become a minister—these choices actually function as a series of paradigms for the underlying philosophical questions of the role of man in society. But their primary function in the *Autobiography* is to demonstrate that man does have choice in the New World, that man can create himself. This is the primary message of Franklin's American Dream, just as it had been the fundamental message of the American Dream in the promotion tracts of the seventeenth and eighteenth centuries and in the writings of the European intellectuals.

Most sentences in Franklin's *Autobiography* are unrevised, but that sentence at the opening of the *Autobiography* in which he presented the American Dream motif caused him trouble, and he carefully reworked it. The finished sentence coordinates two participial phrases: one concerns Franklin's rise both from rags to riches and from obscurity to fame; the other tells us that Franklin generally had a happy life; but the main clause says that Franklin will inform us *how* he was able to accomplish these. "Having emerg'd from the Poverty and Obscurity in which I was born and bred, to a State of Affluence and some Degree of Reputation in the World, and having gone so far thro' Life with a considerable Share of Felicity, the conducing Means I made use of, which, with the Blessing of God, so well succeeded, my Posterity may like to know, as they may find some of them suitable to their own Situations, and therefore fit to be imitated" (p. 43). Franklin sees *the means* that a person can use in order to create himself, to shape his life into whatever form that he may choose, as the primary subject of his book—insofar as it is a book about the American Dream.

Some readers (notably D. H. Lawrence) have mistaken Franklin's means as his ends.[20] That famous chart of the day, and that infamous list of virtues to be acquired, are not the ends that Franklin aims at; they are merely the means of discipline that will allow the ends to be achieved.[21] Franklin's own ultimate values are there in the book as well, for it is a book about values even more than it is a book about the means to achievement, but that is another, and larger, subject, and I have time only to sketch out some of the implications of this one.

With consummate literary artistry, Franklin embodied his portrait of the American Dream not only in that youth seeking to find a calling, a trade, but also in that scene which long ago became the dominant visual scene in all American literature, Franklin's entry into Philadelphia.[22] Franklin prepares the reader for the scene by saying: "I have been the more particular in this Description of my journey, and shall be so of my first Entry into that City, that you may in your

Mind compare such unlikely Beginnings with the Figure I have since
made there" (p. 75). We all recall Franklin's entrance into Philadelphia: dirty, tired, hungry, broke, his "Pockets . . . stuff'd out with
Shirts and Stockings," buying his three great puffy rolls of bread. That
image echoes throughout the *Autobiography* and resounds throughout
American literature. Near the end of the *Autobiography*, it is contrasted
with the Franklin who, in 1756, was escorted on a journey out of town
by the officers of his regiment: "They drew their Swords, and rode
with them naked all the way" (pp. 238–239). Franklin writes that
the display was foolish and embarrassing and that it ultimately did
him considerable political disservice. And Franklin ironically points
out the absurdities of such ceremonies: "The first Time I review'd
my Regiment, they accompanied me to my House, and would salute
me with some Rounds fired before my Door, which shook down
and broke several Glasses of my Electrical Apparatus. And my new
Honour prov'd not much less brittle; for all our Commissions were
soon after broke by a Repeal of the Law in England" (p. 238). My
point in citing this passage is partly to show that the American Dream
motif provides one of the elements that unify the book, but mainly to
show how Franklin himself undercuts the value of the public honors
paid to him, even as he tells us of those honors. Such complexities
are found in every aspect of Franklin's presentation of the American
Dream, even while Franklin nonetheless demonstrates that he is, in
Matthew Arnold's words, "a man who was the very incarnation of
sanity and clear sense."[23] Amidst all of Franklin's complexities and his
radical skepticism, no one ever doubts his uncommon possession in
the highest degree of common sense.[24]

This third aspect of the American Dream, which holds that the
world can be affected by individuals, goes much beyond the common
sense enshrined in Franklin's wagoner cartoon and in such sayings as
"God helps those who help themselves."[25] For there is something most
uncommon implied in the American Dream. It posits the achievement
of extraordinary goals, a distinction in some endeavor, whether football or physics, politics or scholarship, a distinction not to be achieved
by ordinary application or by ordinary ability. And common sense,
though hardly so common as the phrase would have it, is still nothing
extraordinary. This third motif of the American Dream believes in
the possibility of extraordinary achievement. When Franklin tells of

his early grand scheme to promulgate the Art of Virtue (which, in his own mind, amounted to a new and better religion), he succinctly expresses a philosophy of belief in the individual, a philosophy that allows for the extraordinary accomplishments of mankind: "And I was not discourag'd by the seeming Magnitude of the Undertaking, as I have always thought that one Man of tolerable Abilities may work great Changes, and accomplish great Affairs among Mankind, if he first forms a good Plan, and, cutting off all Amusements or other Employments that would divert his Attention, makes the Execution of that same Plan his sole Study and Business" (p. 163).

A fourth aspect of the American Dream is, like the third, an underlying implication of the first two themes. Philosophically, it subsumes the earlier three motifs I have mentioned. The fourth theme takes a position on the age-old dialectic of free will versus determinism; or, to put this opposition in its degenerate present guise, between those people who think that what they do (whether voting in an election, teaching in a classroom, or answering questions from behind the reference desk) might make a difference and those who think it does not. Obviously Franklin is to be placed with those who believe in the possible efficacy of action. But Franklin is nothing if not a complex man and a complex thinker. Several long passages in his writings—as well as his only philosophical treatise—argue just the opposite.[26] Even in that consummate and full statement of the American Dream, the *Autobiography*, he has discordant notes.

At one point, he says that his early mistakes had "something of *Necessity* in them." That is, the world is not governed solely by free will: experience, knowledge, and background—or the lack of them— may determine, indeed predestine, the actions of an individual. Franklin speaks of his conviction as a youth that "*Truth, Sincerity and Integrity* in Dealings between Man and Man, were of the utmost Importance to the Felicity of Life" (p. 114). He goes on: "And this Persuasion, with the kind hand of Providence, or some guardian Angel, or accidental favourable Circumstances and Situations, or all together, preserved me . . . without any *wilful* gross Immorality or Injustice that might have been expected from my Want of Religion. I say wilful, because the Instances I have mentioned, had something of *Necessity* in them, from my Youth, Inexperience, and the Knavery of others" (p. 115).

In addition to the species of necessity which arises from inexperience and from trusting in humanity, Franklin also mentions the Marxian version of predestinarianism, economics. Because Franklin's father could not afford to keep him in school, he took the boy home at ten to teach him his own trade, and so Franklin writes: "there was all Appearance that I was destin'd to . . . be a Tallow Chandler" (p. 57). As I have suggested, Franklin's painful series of constricting choices concerning what he was going to be in life is played out against a backdrop of free will versus determinism, and necessity nearly carries the outcome. As Poor Richard said, "There have been as great Souls unknown to fame as any of the most famous."[27] But the necessitarian notes are deliberately minor. Franklin's classic statement of the American Dream rests firmly upon the belief in man's free will, but Franklin is not blind to the realities of economics, education, innocence, or evil. To regard his version of the American Dream as in any way simple is to misread the man—and the book.

A fifth and final aspect of the American Dream is, like the last two, a concomitant of the first two, as well as a precondition of their existence. It is a philosophy of hope, even of optimism. Belief in individualism and in free will, like the prospect of a rise from rags to riches or from impotence to importance, demands that the individual have hope. And so the *Autobiography* is deliberately optimistic about mankind and about the future. Nor is Franklin content with the implication. He gives a practical example of the result of an opposite point of view in his character sketch of the croaker, Samuel Mickle. It opens: "There are Croakers in every Country always boding its Ruin." Franklin tells of Samuel Mickle's prediction of bankruptcy for Franklin and for Philadelphia. Franklin testifies that Mickle's speech "left me half-melancholy. Had I known him before I engag'd in this Business, probably I never should have done it." And he concludes the sketch by telling that Mickle refused "for many Years to buy a House . . . because all was going to Destruction, and at last I had the Pleasure of seeing him give five times as much for one as he might have bought it for when he first began his Croaking" (p. 116).[28]

What makes this sketch particularly interesting to me is that Franklin falsifies the conclusion for the sake of the moral. No one knows anything about the personality of Samuel Mickle, who may well have been a pessimist. We do know that he was a real estate operator who owned numerous properties.[29] Franklin certainly knew it, although for the sake of showing the impractical results of a philosophy of pessimism, he falsifies the facts.

And we all know that, though the facts may be false, Franklin is right. It is better to be optimistic than pessimistic, better to be hopeful than hopeless. But we may not be able to be. Franklin knew too that men are at the mercy of their personalities, their world views, as well as of their ability, background, finances, health, and age. To his Loyalist son, Franklin wrote after the Revolution: "Our Opinions are not in our own Power; they are form'd and govern'd much by Circumstances, that are often as inexplicable as they are irresistible."[30]

When Franklin's old friend Hugh Roberts wrote him of the deaths of two of their former fellow members of the junto, Franklin wrote back: "Parsons, even in his Prosperity, always fretting! Potts, in the midst of his Poverty, ever laughing! It seems, then, that Happiness in this Life rather depends on Internals than Externals; and that, besides the natural Effects of Wisdom and Virtue, Vice and Folly, there is such a Thing as being of a happy or an unhappy Constitution."[31]

Franklin himself seems to have been blessed with a happy constitution, but it is better never to be too certain of Franklin. He was capable of enormous self-discipline and had the common sense to know that it is better to be happy than miserable. Poor Richard advised hosts: "If you wou'd have Guests merry with your cheer,/ Be so your self, or so at least appear."[32] Since a dominant theme of the *Autobiography* is the American Dream, and since this theme holds that it is desirable and beneficial to have hope, even optimism, Franklin's *Autobiography* is an optimistic work. But that is too partial a view of life to satisfy Franklin. He tells us in the *Autobiography* that at age twenty-one, when he began to recover from a severe illness, he regretted that he had not died: "I suffered a good deal, gave up the Point in my own mind, and was rather disappointed when I found my Self recovering; regretting in some degree that I must now some time or other have all that disagreable Work to do over again" (p. 107). This pessimism surprises no Franklinist, for his writings contain numerous similar passages. I'll cite just one more. In his only straightforward philosophical treatise, he defined life as suffering and death as the absence of pain: "We are first mov'd by *Pain*, and the whole succeeding Course of our Lives is but one continu'd Series of Action with a View to be freed from it."[33]

In the *Autobiography* Franklin balances optimism against the realities of life, and this tension in the *persona* is presented by an authorial voice that calls attention to the wishful, self-deceiving nature of the *persona*, and of man, who sees only what his vanity allows him to see. And Franklin had other good reasons to make the foolish vanity of man a major subject of the *Autobiography*, for the vanity of the autobiographer, as Franklin well knew, was the greatest literary pitfall of the genre. But the ways that Franklin dealt with this is another major theme of the book, and I have already outstayed my time.

I hope, though, to have shown that even dealing with its most obvious theme, the American Dream, the *Autobiography* possesses unity and complexity. Franklin deliberately creates a certain kind of fictive world, embodies that world in some unforgettable scenes, creates and sustains one character who is among the most memorable in American literature, and writes vivid truths that strike us with a shock of recognition. For these, among other reasons, I believe that the *Autobiography* is a major literary achievement, more complex, and in many ways, more artful, than a beautifully constructed novel like *The Rise of Silas Lapham*, which, of course, is much indebted to Franklin's *Autobiography*. Even so, Franklin would, I believe, have a much greater reputation as a literary artist if he had not written his masterpiece. We ordinary mortals want to turn against him, for what excuse does it leave us? Howells, in *The Rise of Silas Lapham*, gives that usual businessman's apology for financial failure: I was not a cheat; I was honest; therefore I failed. Its comforting implication is that all men who make fortunes are dishonest. Franklin maintains that cheats fail and honest men rise. We can say (what is partially true) that Franklin's book is written for young people, but that offers us little solace. And I can maintain that it portrays a fictive world of Franklin's imagination, and that offers us a little solace. But the Franklin portrayed in the *Autobiography* allows us older people little comfort for our comparative failure. That's part of the reason why we want to disbelieve him. The laws of physics, the moral wisdom of the ancients, and our own visions of reality say that everything rises but to fall.[34] The Franklin of the *Autobiography*, however, displays himself behind that sturdy peasant's face and that old man's heavy figure, nimbly, magically dancing to his own complex music, while permanently suspended in the heights above us.

NOTES

1. Both Richard E. Amacher, *Benjamin Franklin* (New York: Twayne, 1962), and Bruce Ingham Granger, *Benjamin Franklin: An American Man of Letters* (Ithaca: Cornell University Press, 1964) are organized by genre.
2. Many of my reasons for this heresy are detailed in my "Benjamin Franklin," pp. 217–26.
3. Herman Melville, "Hawthorne and His Mosses," in Walter Blair, Theodore Hornberger, and Randall Stewart, eds., *The Literature of the United States: An Anthology and a History*, 2 vols. (Chicago: Scott, Foresman & Co., 1953), 1:1005.
4. See Jeremy Bernstein, *Encyclopedia Britannica*, 15th ed., s.v. "Yang, Chen Ning"; and Hugh Sidey's article on Carter's reading, "The Presidency," *Time*, 6 September 1976, p. 15.
5. Franklin to Priestley on moral algebra, 19 September 1772, in Smyth, 5:437–38; Franklin to Kames, 3 May 1760, in *P*, 9:104–5; *Autobiography*, p. 27; Franklin to La Rochefoucauld, in Smyth, 9:665.
6. Wecter, p. 61.
7. For *The Honour of a London Prentice*, see Donald Wing, *Short-Title Catalogue of Books Printed . . . 1641–1700*, H 2592, and *The National Union Catalog: Pre-1956 Imprints*, 253:502, NH 0500961; John Ashton, *Chap-Books of the Eighteenth Century* (1882; reprint ed., New York: B. Blom, 1966), pp. 227–29; William Chappell and Joseph Woodfall Ebsworth, eds., *The Roxburghe Ballads*, 9 vols. (Hertford: Ballad Society, 1871–99), 7:587–91; and Claude M. Simpson, *The British Broadside Ballad and Its Music* (New Brunswick: Rutgers University Press, 1966), p. 13. For *Sir Richard Whittington's Advancement*, see *London's Glory and Whittington's Renown*, Wing, L 2930, and the British Museum, *General Catalogue of Printed Books . . . to 1955*, vol. 256, cols. 1086–89; and William Chappell, *The Ballad Literature and Popular Music of the Olden Time*, 2 vols. (1859; reprint ed., New York: Dover, 1965), 2:515–17.

8. See the discussion of *Leah and Rachal* in Lemay, *Men of Letters*, pp. 38–42.
9. Charles Sumner, "Prophetic Voices About America: A Monograph," *Atlantic Monthly* 20 (September 1867): 275–306, gathers together a number of authors from the ancients to the mid-nineteenth century who use one or both of these motifs. On the West as terrestrial paradise, see William H. Tillinghast, "The Geographical Knowledge of the Ancients Considered in Relation to the Discovery of America," in Justin Winsor, ed., *Narrative and Critical History of America*, 8 vols. (Boston: Houghton Mifflin & Co., 1884–89), 1:1–58; and Loren Baritz, "The Idea of the West," *American Historical Review* 66 (1960–61): 618–40. On the *translatio* idea (the theory of the westward movement of civilization), see Rexmond C. Cochrane, "Bishop Berkeley and the Progress of Arts and Learning: Notes on a Literary Convention," *Huntington Library Quarterly* 17 (1953–54): 229–49; Aubrey L. Williams, *Pope's Dunciad: A Study of Its Meaning* (London: Methuen & Co., 1955), pp. 42–48; Lewis P. Simpson, ed., *The Federalist Literary Mind* (Baton Rouge: Louisiana State University Press, 1962), pp. 31–41; Lemay, *Men of Letters*, pp. xi, 131–32, 191, 257, 296, 299, 303, 307, 311; William D. Andrews, "William Smith and the Rising Glory of America," *Early American Literature* 8 (1973): 33–43; and Kenneth Silverman, *A Cultural History of the American Revolution* (New York: Thomas Y. Crowell, 1976), pp. 9–11, and see the index. Although he gives no indication of being aware of the intellectual and historical backgrounds of these motifs, Paul W. Conner, in *Poor Richard's Politicks: Benjamin Franklin and His New American Order* (New York: Oxford University Press, 1965), gathers together many of Franklin's allusions to these typical promotion tract topics in his subchapter "Muses in a Cook's Shop," pp. 96–107.
10. *Autobiography*, pp. 195–96.
11. Adams, *Works*, 1:660.
12. See, for example, the popular 1777 French medallion of Franklin, which bears the inscription "B Franklin Americain," in Charles Coleman Sellers, *Benjamin Franklin in Portraiture* (New Haven: Yale University Press, 1962), pp. 344–46 and pl. 10.

13. James M. Cox, "Autobiography and America," *Virginia Quarterly Review* 47 (1971): 256–62.

14. As far as I know, I first suggested this line of thought; see my "Benjamin Franklin," pp. 240–41.

15. *Poor Richard*, October 1749, in *P*, 3:346.

16. See my remarks toward a definition of the American Dream in *Men of Letters*, pp. 6–7, 41–42, 59.

17. *P*, 3:xiv and 190. The quotation is from Sallust, *The War with Catiline*, chap. 52, sec. 29. The Loeb Library translation is "Not by vows nor womanish entreaties is the help of the gods secured" (John C. Rolfe, trans., *Sallust*, rev. ed. [Cambridge: Harvard University Press, 1931], p. 107).

18. For some remarks on the democratic and modern background of Franklin's *Autobiography*, see Paul Ilie, "Franklin and Villarroel: Social Consciousness in Two Autobiographies," *Eighteenth-Century Studies* 7 (1973–74): 321–42.

19. *Autobiography*, pp. 53, 57–59; *P*, 1:lii, lvi–lix.

20. D. H. Lawrence, "Benjamin Franklin," in his *Studies in Classic American Literature* (New York: T. Seltzer, 1923), pp. 13–31.

21. See especially Herbert W. Schneider, "The Significance of Benjamin Franklin's Moral Philosophy," Columbia University, Department of Philosophy, *Studies in the History of Ideas* 2 (1925): 293–312.

22. I echo my earlier claim in "Franklin and the *Autobiography*: An Essay on Recent Scholarship," *Eighteenth-Century Studies* 1 (1967–68): 200–201.

23. Matthew Arnold, *Culture and Anarchy*, in *The Complete Prose Works of Matthew Arnold*, ed. R. H. Super (Ann Arbor: University of Michigan Press, 1960–), 5:110.

24. On the general topic of common sense in the *Autobiography*, see the discerning essay by John Griffith, "Franklin's Sanity and the Man behind the Masks," in Lemay, ed., *The Oldest Revolutionary: Essays on Benjamin Franklin* (Philadelphia: University of Pennsylvania Press, 1976), pp. 123–38.

25. Franklin's form was "God helps them that help themselves," in *Poor Richard*, June 1736 (*P*, 2:140), and in "The Way to Wealth" (*P*, 7:341).

26. For Franklin's *Dissertation on Liberty and Necessity, Pleasure and Pain*, see *P*, 1:55–71.

27. *P*, 1:355.

28. Compare Benjamin Franklin's account of his brother's starting a newspaper (*Autobiography*, p. 67), which implicitly makes the same point.

29. See the biographical sketch in the *Autobiography*, p. 291.

30. Smyth, 9:252.

31. *P*, 8:159–60.

32. *P*, 1:358.

33. *P*, 1:64.

34. Sallust, *The War with Jugurtha*, chap. 2, sec. 3, in Rolfe, trans., *Sallust*, p. 135.

"Children's Rhymes"
(Langston Hughes)

~❧~

"The American Dream and the Legacy of Revolution in the Poetry of Langston Hughes"
by Lloyd W. Brown,
in *Studies in Black Literature* (1976)

Introduction

Lloyd Brown argues that Langston Hughes' poetry deals with an all-encompassing notion of the American Dream. Rather than focus merely on the "contradiction between the American promise of 'liberty and justice,'" and "the political and socio-economic disadvantages of the Black American" in Hughes' poetry, Brown opens with an analysis of "Children's Rhymes," arguing that "if Blacks have been excluded outright from the American Dream, White Americans have also denied themselves the substance of those libertarian ideals that have been enshrined in the sacred rhetoric, and history, of the American Revolution." In turning to the American Revolution as subject during the country's Bicentennial year (1976), Brown traces notions of the American Dream in several of Hughes' poems. Finding that Hughes ultimately distances himself from the skepticism of his early "dream" poems,

---

Brown, Lloyd W. "The American Dream and the Legacy of Revolution in the Poetry of Langston Hughes." *Studies in Black Literature* (Spring 1976): 16–18.

Brown concludes by demonstrating how Hughes' late poems invest themselves in the very dream his early poems decried. In drawing upon the ideas of Amiri Baraka (LeRoi Jones) at the essay's close, Brown creates a powerful contrast, offering two radically different visions of the American Dream.

∽×∽

In his poem, "Children's Rhymes," Langston Hughes offers a brief but rewarding glimpse of Black children at play on city streets, complete with jingles that have been improvised out of the Black experience to replace more innocent ditties:

> What's written down
> for white folks
> ain't for us a-tall:
> "Liberty and Justice—
> Huh—For All."[1]

The contrast which Hughes offers here is familiar enough: it is the well known contradiction between the American promise of "liberty and justice," on the one hand, and on the other hand, the political and socioeconomic disadvantages of the Black American. But, looked at more closely, Hughes' poem is interlaced with additional ironies. The assertion that "liberty and justice . . . for all" is a concept "written down for white folks" is suggestively ambiguous. It not only points to the historical exclusion of Blacks from White America's "written down" ideas, but the very emphasis on a "written down" tradition raises questions about the substance of these ideals in the lives of "white folks" themselves. In other words, the ironic ambiguity of Hughes' poem implies that if Blacks have been excluded outright from the American Dream, White Americans have also denied themselves the substance of those libertarian ideals that have been enshrined in the sacred rhetoric, and history, of the American Revolution. Liberty and justice, he seems to suggest, have been "written down" for, but not actualized by, White Americans.

Of course, the ironic insights that I am attributing here to Langston Hughes are rooted in a well-known historical judgment on Black–White relations in America: that is, no group, including Whites, can be significantly free as long as any one group is denied the full rights of the society as a whole. But the implications of Hughes' poetic logic both include and go beyond that historical truism. To return to the provocative nuances of that phrase, "written down for white folks," Hughes is also invoking a *time* reference—a reference to that period, the America Revolution, in which certain notions of liberty, justice and equality were cited, justified, and of course, written down, in various guises, in the Declaration of Independence and later in the Constitution of the United States. So that in effect the doubts which Hughes' irony casts on the substance of liberty and justice in American history also extend to the American Revolution itself: the essential limitations, or insubstantiality, of revolutionary rhetoric about freedom raise questions about the substance of the Revolution. In other words, how revolutionary *was* the American Revolution? The identity of the speakers in Langston Hughes' poem is crucial here. The image of children at play and the traditionally innocent connotations of children's rhymes seem deliberately to invoke an image of innocence upon which Americans have always insisted in their cultural history—an innocence defined by allegations that the American War of Independence was not simply a rebellion but a revolution, that as a revolution it radically transformed the sociopolitical structure of the erstwhile colonies, that this sense of a newly created order in the New World is intrinsic to the American Dream of new beginnings in the human condition and new possibilities for individual fulfillment. But, to repeat, Hughes associates these revolutionary notions with only an **image** of childhood innocence. It is manifest that the children of his poem are not innocent in a behavioral sense (they are noisy, rambunctious window-breakers), and as their knowing sneers about nonexistent liberty and justice imply, they are not innocent in the sense of ignorance or inexperience.

Altogether, their own lack of innocence and their archetypal roles as deprived outsiders have the effect of stripping away their society's complacent mask of innocence: the American Revolution is not an indisputable historical fact, but part of America's myth of innocence. Moreover, to return, finally, to that tell-tale phrase, "written down for white folks," Hughes implies a contrast between his children's truthful rhymes, on the one hand, and on the other hand, the false innocence of the Founding Fathers' "Revolution" and the mythic structures through which generations of historians and writers have perpetuated the dubious notion, in the light of certain perspectives on the events, and results, of 1775–1776. When one considers the fact of Black enslavement, the disenfranchisement of large groups, and the disadvantages of women, to name but a few areas, there seems little basis, apart from the usual dreams of American mythology, to believe that the American rebellion involved a fundamental re-structuring of the social order. Thus even Bernard Bailyn's preoccupation with an ideologically inspired American Revolution concedes that the Revolution "was not the overthrow or even the alteration of the existing social order."[2] Similarly, Raymond Aron who pays the usual homage to the myth of the social melting pot finds it prudent to restrain himself on one point, for he does not go so far as to suggest that the "transformations" of American society have constituted any fundamental (i.e. revolutionary) re-structuring of political and social institutions. Indeed, Aron's main point is to emphasize the essentially continuous and evolutionary, rather than revolutionary, nature of American history.[3] As for some of those political and social institutions, their structures and functions have been less "revolutionary" in relation to the eighteenth century than some of our myth-makers and historians have allowed. So that the American constitution has *always* had more in common with British constitutional practice of the eighteenth century than one would suspect of a "revolutionary" process: the road between the eighteenth-century corruptions of Britain's Prime Minister, Robert Walpole, and the Watergate traditions of our own time is a very short one indeed. Conversely, the distance between revolution and the popular use of the word "revolutionary" is much greater than may of us would like to think. Indeed the word revolutionary is an excellent semantic example of the culture's obsession with the *appearance* of revolution—or, to be more specific, an obsession with revolution as an image, or appearance, of newness rather than as fact. The preoccupation with an *image* rather than with the reality of revolution fits in with the American Dream of innovative transformations and novel beginnings. And it operates on our perception of a wide variety of things in our cultural history—from the War of Independence to the television commercial that hawks the latest "revolutions" in laundry detergents and bathroom cleaners.

I do not offer these observations by way of registering a complaint. Whether or not there should have been a *real* revolution, of whatever kind, in the course of American history is not my main objective here. My primary interest is to point out those "written down" historical assumptions and those cultural norms which have created a mythos of revolution in the American Dream of "progress" as "change," and which, in turn, have a significant bearing on attitudes towards revolution in the Black American's literature. In essence the majority culture's dream of a progressive society based on individual fulfillment and social harmony, that majority dream has created its own inevitable legacy—that is, the Black American Dream of realizing those dreams and ideals that have been written down for white folks. Moreover, and this is a crucial corollary, that mythos of revolution which has always been integral to the majority dream has been ironically transformed in the Black American Dream: for while the majority culture mythologizes revolution as an historical fact that guarantees present and future "progress," the Black American experience has nurtured inclinations toward revolution which have been stimulated by the Black American's exclusion from that majority dream, complete with its myth of a revolutionary past. In short, the majority culture's mythos of revolution has been ironically transformed into the Black American's legacy of revolutionary possibilities. So that writers like Langston Hughes are exploring the nature of these revolutionary inclinations in order to determine whether they are fundamental revolutions against the majority dream and culture as a whole, or whether they are actually rebellious attempts to break down barriers to their realization of the majority dream.

On the whole Langston Hughes' poetry inclines towards the latter direction. Hence, to take a work like "Children's Rhymes," he ironically invokes the myth of the American Revolution, with its attendant dream of equality and socioeconomic fulfillment, and then pits these against the Black American condition of deprivation and rebellious impatience. For there is nothing inherently revolutionary in the poem's emphasis or assumptions. The acid reminders of a tradition of revolutionary rhetoric are really taunts directed at the majority culture rather than some species of exhortation aimed at Black Americans. Here, too, the child-identity of the poem's protagonists is revealing. Their truant sidewalk games and their destruction of neighborhood property are presented as rebellious acts of frustration (i.e. protest) rather than as the result of some calculated revolutionary posture. The child-identity minimizes the possibilities of such a posture, at the same time that it emphasizes the Black American as child-heir to the American dream-legacy of freedom, equality, and individual fulfillment. But, in turn, these connotations of an inheritance confer an additional dimension on Hughes' rebel-heir archetypes. As I have already suggested, this rebellion is not only a protest against exclusion from the political and socioeconomic promises of the American Dream; it is also directed at the "revolutionary" antecedents of the Dream itself, in that the expose of the failure of the American Dream in Black America is, simultaneously, an implicit challenge to America to make its tradition of revolution or sociopolitical reality rather than a semantic imposture. Altogether, Hughes' poem explores the essentially *rebellious disposition* of the disinherited Black American while at the same time implying the very real possibilities for revolution in the *situation* of Black Americans: their situation as the dispossessed heirs to a mythic revolution encourages an intensely partial interest in the threat of a genuine American Revolution.

This is the kind of threat, or promise, that remains implicit in the well-known Langston Hughes poem, "Harlem":

> What happens to a dream deferred?
> Does it dry up
> like a raisin in the sun?
> Or fester like a sore—
> And then run?
> Does it stink like rotten meat?
> Or crust and sugar over—
> like a syrupy sweet?
> Maybe it just sags
> like a heavy load.
> *Or does it explode?*

The frustrations of the disinherited Black American, the reflections which that disinheritance casts on the substantiality of the American Revolution—all these are concentrated in the rebellious query of protest, "What happens to a dream deferred?" But as he does in so many of his "dream" poems, Hughes hints at the revolutionist possibilities that are inherent in the very fact that the Black American has an interest in the mere notion of an American Revolution. Thus the prophetic query ("Or does it explode?") with which the poem ends reflects that legacy of revolution which, ironically, has fallen to Black Americans, precisely because the rhetoric and dreams of that other revolution have failed them.

But here again it must be emphasized that Hughes does not explore this legacy of revolution in any exhortatory sense. That is, he obviously identifies with the Black rebel-heirs to the American Dream—indeed their rebellion is the very essence of his own poetic protest—but he does this without necessarily espousing any concept of a radically transforming revolution. And here we are brought face to face with a basic ambiguity in some of Hughes' "dream" poems: on the one hand, his satiric expose of the deferred dream in Black America is invariably couched in terms which taunt White America about the essentially non-revolutionist nature of *its* Revolution; but, on the other hand, his identification with the Black American's rebellion does not go beyond protest to any revolutionary ideology of his own. Indeed, one may speculate that it is easier for Hughes to demand that White America make good on the promises of its Revolution precisely because a satisfactory fulfillment of these promises, from Hughes' point of view, would not necessitate that fundamental restructuring of the social order, which even an historian like Bernard Bailyn associates with revolution. The point is not that Hughes is being hypocritical, or even muddle-headed; rather that his interest in sociopolitical reform is sharply defined by his basic loyalty to the unfulfilled promises of the American Revolution. So that in the final analysis his overall protest is not that the deferred dream is non-revolutionist but, quite simply, that it has been deferred. And in the light of all this, it is logical that the war-time poem, "Freedom's Plow" reaffirms the people's faith in the eventual fulfillment of the American Dream, with its "revolutionary" promises of freedom and democracy—at the same time that the poet defies both the external Nazi threat and the (pro-Communist) revolutionary stirrings at home:

America is a dream.
The poet says it was promises.

The people say it is promises—
that will come true. . . .
Who is America? You, me!
We are America!
To the enemy who would conquer from without,
We say, NO!
To the enemy who would divide
and conquer us from within,
We say, NO!
  FREEDOM!
       BROTHERHOOD!
       DEMOCRACY!

Interestingly enough, Hughes affirms this faith in the American Dream by identifying with a popular mass view ("The people say it *is* promises") which is sharply distinguished from the scepticism of the Black poet ("The poet says it was promises"). By identifying himself with the popular faith Hughes has, in effect, abjured the deep-seated scepticism which his earlier "dream" poems share with the Black rebel-heirs to the American Revolution. On the basis of "Freedom's Plow" it would appear that his always undeniable loyalty to the American Dream has become less ambiguous, and even more detached from a sense of revolutionist possibilities. At the same time, the distinction which he offers between the quasi-revolutionary scepticism of the poet-intellectual and the firm faith of the masses, has significant implications for pro-revolutionary themes in Black American literature, especially since the sixties. For, in general, what one finds in these themes is an emphasis on the Black artist-intellectual as the revolutionary archetype whose mission is the bringing of a revolutionist consciousness to the supposedly receptive Black masses. This view of the artist as revolutionary teacher/preacher underlies Imamu Baraka's (LeRoi Jones') definition of "revolutionary theatre": "The change. . . . The Revolutionary Theatre must take dreams and give them a reality. . . . Americans will hate the Revolutionary Theatre because it will be out to destroy them and whatever they believe is real. . . . The force we want is of twenty million spooks storming America with furious cries and unstoppable weapons. We want actual explosions and actual brutality.[4]

Jones leaves us with no illusions about the nature of his revolutionary "dreams", they are not the yearnings of the rebel-heir who is impatient to realize the American Dream (i.e., what ever White Americans "believe is real"), instead, they are another kind of dream—the dream of the Black artist/intellectual for a revolutionary process that will reject the traditional American order by changing the cultural revolution envisaged by his poem, "Black Art":

> Let Black people understand
> that they are the lovers and the sons
> of lovers and warriors and sons
> of warriors Are poems & poets &
> all the loveliness here in the world
> We want a black poem. And a
> Black World.[5]

The poetic insights of Hughes' "Freedom's Plow" insist on a frank, if unflattering, admission of the gulf between the artist/intellectual and the masses, a gulf which Hughes as poet deliberately crosses in order to share a popular faith in the American Dream. On the other hand, the current trend in Black revolutionary literature assumes a rather easy identification of the artist with some mass revolutionary taste, a taste, one should add, that is often postulated but never really demonstrated as fact. Hughes' admission may very well irk the revolutionary enthusiasts among us; but in the absence of any obvious enthusiasm for radical revolution (as distinct from rebellious impatience) among those masses, one is left with the suspicion that Hughes is perhaps more realistic about the actual relationships between the Black American masses and the American Dream, and that, conversely, Jones' prophetic vision of Black people as Black poets, Black poem as Black world is another dream legacy—that is, another revolution as dream.

NOTES

1. References to Langston Hughes' poems are based on *Selected Poems of Langston Hughes* (New York: Alfred A. Knopf. 1971).

2. Bernard Bailyn, *The Ideological Origins of the American Revolution* (Cambridge, Mass: Harvard University Press, 1967). p. 19.
3. Raymond Aron, *The Opium of the Intellectual* (New York: Norton. 1962).
4. LeRoi Jones, *Home: Social Essays* (New York: William Morrow. 1966), pp. 210, 211, 214.
5. LeRoi Jones, *Black Magic: Collected Poetry 1961–1967* (Indianapolis: Bobbs-Merrill, 1969), p. 117.

DEATH OF A SALESMAN
(ARTHUR MILLER)

"Arthur Miller's *Death of a Salesman*"
by Merritt Moseley,
University of North Carolina at Asheville

Death of a Salesman is centrally concerned with dreams and dreaming. What are the dreams of its protagonist, Willy Loman? What is their worth? This question occupies the surviving characters at the play's conclusion. Son Biff, the most lucid among the Loman men and thus the most despairing, cries to his father, as things are falling apart: "Will you let me go, for Christ's sake? Will you take that phony dream and burn it before something happens?" (133).

Willy, typically, misses the point, reading Biff's outcry not as a call to become wiser but as a confession of love. And in the Requiem, standing at Willy's grave, younger son Happy insists:

> All right, boy. I'm gonna show you and everybody else that Willy Loman did not die in vain. He had a good dream. It's the only dream you can have—to come out number-one man. He fought it out here, and this is where I'm gonna win it for him. (138-39)

Willy is dreaming, in a literal sense, throughout much of the play. Explaining to his wife Linda why he has returned early, and empty-handed, from his selling trip, he acknowledges that his mind wanders too much for driving:

I was driving along, you understand? And I was fine. I was even observing the scenery. You can imagine, me looking at scenery, on the road every week of my life. But it's so beautiful up there, Linda, the trees are so thick, and the sun is warm. I opened the windshield and just let the warm air bathe over me. And all of a sudden I'm goin' off the road! I'm tellin' ya, I absolutely forgot I was driving. If I'd've gone the other way over the white line I might've killed somebody. So I went on again—and five minutes later I'm dreamin' again, and I nearly—*He presses two fingers against his eyes.* I have such thoughts, I have such strange thoughts. (14)

This is an important passage in setting up the way the tragedy will unfold. It is the audience's first indication that Willy is unable to continue his job as a traveling salesman, which he has followed for many years. Linda suggests in response that he ask the company to let him work in town; Willy, still proud at this point ("I'm vital in New England"), declines. Later, when he makes just this request, he is spurned on the basis of pure business calculations.

Willy is drawn to death. We learn later that he has attached a little hose to the gas line in his basement and is flirting with the idea of suicide. At the end of the play he carries through with it, apparently by crashing his car. Though he tells Linda that by crossing the center line he might have killed "somebody," rather than himself, it is himself that he eventually kills. Perhaps it is his suicide fantasies that Willy refers to in his "strange thoughts."

One reason that Willy can no longer be a functioning salesman—aside from age, exhaustion, and the death or retirement of his old friends in the territory—is his increasing inability to remain psychologically in the here and now. Throughout the play he slips his moorings, comes unstuck in time, and is living through a past event while, in some cases, still interacting with those who are in his present. A small glimpse of this phenomenon is visible in the passage above, when he tells Linda that he opened the windshield to enjoy the warm air. Later, when she refers to opening the windshield, Willy corrects her—"the windshields don't open on the new cars"—and realizes that he was "thinking of the Chevvy" that he had in 1928. But it is more than thinking of it: "I coulda sworn I was driving that Chevvy today." (19).

Everyone thinks of the past, but Willy involuntarily *relives* it. Whether we consider these events daydreams or reveries, they are a crucial part of the play. Increasingly they erupt at moments of crisis, and they are most often related to Willy's troubled relations with his male relatives, particularly his older brother Ben and his older son Biff.

If we read the reveries as Willy reliving the past, then we must grant them the status of authentic events that have happened. Miller has sometimes suggested that this is what they are: "There are no flashbacks in this play but only a mobile concurrency of past and present . . ." (Miller, "Introduction" 26). So are the past moments supposed to be entirely believable? When Willy "relives" a scene starring Biff, in which Linda tells Biff "the cellar is full of boys. They don't know what to do with themselves" (34), and Biff decides to have his adoring followers sweep out the furnace room, there is reason to believe that Willy's mind has edited and revised his past. And why not? Everybody revises the past, and Willy, especially, is a dishonest man in his ordinary interactions. Even in his own reveries, we see him lying to his wife and sons. In real time, he edits and revises reality. He claims "I was sellin' thousands and thousands, but I had to come home"; then, "I did five hundred gross in Providence and seven hundred gross in Boston"; then, when Linda eagerly begins to compute his commission, "Well, I—I did—about a hundred and eighty gross in Providence. Well, no—it came to—roughly two hundred gross on the whole trip" (35). When Biff insists, near the end of the play, "We never told the truth for ten minutes in this house!" (131) the audience is prepared, for it has seen Willy's routine dishonesty, which has helped to make his sons dishonest as well. (Biff is as given to fantasizing and dishonest braggadocio as Willy, until the end, and Happy has the same traits, on a mundane level, mostly about his sexual conquests.)

There has been a great deal of discussion about the question of tragedy in *Death of a Salesman*, most of it focusing on the unadmirable protagonist, Willy Loman. It is not necessary to worry about whether Willy is a tragic hero in the Aristotelian sense (he is not), or whether the pity and fear aroused through the play's action are properly purged or clarified. It is enough to realize that Willy Loman is delivered to catastrophe by aspects of his character that move him inexorably in that direction.

The scene at Willy's burial, which Miller called "Requiem," provides
a chorus of comments on his death. Linda is simply baffled. Neighbor
Charlie, who has been a sympathetic friend to Willy through his dete-
rioration—and, it seems, a model of how to succeed in business and
in child-rearing where Willy failed—delivers a mawkish testimony
to the salesman's risky profession. Happy, a superficial thinker at all
times, reaffirms Willy's dream to be number one in the terms quoted
earlier. Only Biff seems to judge adequately:

> Biff: He had the wrong dreams. All, all, wrong.
> Happy, *almost ready to fight Biff*: Don't say that!
> Biff: He never knew who he was. (138)

What were Willy's dreams? And were they, in some real sense,
"wrong"? Or was he wrong in his way of going about realizing them?

Willy does indeed dream of business success, though "the
meaning of that need extends beyond the accumulation of wealth,
security, goods, and status" (Jacobson 247). Willy would like to have
his refrigerator paid for and be freed from nagging financial worries,
but except for wistful reflections on his brother Ben, he never
seems to aspire to great wealth. He wants to "succeed" in business
by being recognized as a success and being admired, like legendary
salesman Dave Singleman. He likes the idea of many people coming
to his funeral (in the end there are five in attendance). His business
dreams are based on the idea of being "well liked." In part he insists
on this because of his own self-doubts. He frets to Linda, "They
seem to laugh at me . . . I don't know the reason for it, but they just
pass me by. I'm not noticed. . . . I joke too much . . . I'm fat. I'm
very—foolish to look at, Linda . . . I'm not dressing to advantage,
maybe" (37).

He stifles his doubts, though, submerging them in his dream that
business success comes from personality. In reverie, he tells the boys:

> You and Hap and I, and I'll show you all the towns. America
> is full of beautiful towns and fine, upstanding people. And they
> know me, boys, they know me up and down New England. The
> finest people. And when I bring you fellas up, there'll be open
> sesame for all of us, 'cause one thing, boys: I have friends. I can

park my car in any street in New England, and the cops protect
it like their own." (31)

Willy's dreams of success based on being liked are linked to his obsession with his brother Ben, a mysterious business tycoon (who in some
interpretations of the play is a product of Willy's anxious imagination) and his son Biff. Ben and Biff are both older brothers; each has
an under-prized younger brother, Willy himself—and Happy, who
struggles unsuccessfully to get his share of his father's attention.

   Biff is popular (that cellar full of admirers), handsome, and
athletic. The high point of his life was playing a football game at
Ebbets Field. Since that time he has been a loser and a petty criminal
(he was actually a petty criminal before, as Willy laughingly encouraged him to steal footballs from school and lumber from construction
sites). Willy cannot understand it: "In the greatest country in the
world a young man with such—personal attractiveness, gets lost. And
such a hard worker. There's one thing about Biff—he's not lazy" (16).
At other times Willy accuses Biff of being a lazy bum who fails in life
only to spite his father.

   Willy's accusations against Biff are incoherent. The larger problem
for him is that *his dreams* are incoherent. He wishes to be a successful
salesman (Happy's "number-one man") on the basis of being liked by
everyone. He believes that salesmanship is based on "sterling traits of
character" and "a pleasing personality" (Murphy 9). But Willy does
not have the requisite sterling traits of character; people simply do not
like him as much as he thinks is necessary for success. In any case,
business success does not actually come from being a nice man whom
others respect. The models of business success provided in the play
all argue against Willy's personality theory. One is Charley, Willy's
neighbor and apparently only friend. Charley has no time for Willy's
theories of business, but he provides for his family and is in a position to offer Willy a do-nothing job to keep him bringing home a
salary. Howard, Willy's present-day boss and the son of the man who
originally hired Willy, is a heedless man with no time for personal
relations, who spurns Willy's appeal to family friendship. Howard
not only denies Willy the easier position that Willy believes he's due,
(based on their long personal relationship) but fires him from his
selling job. Ben—a ruthless, hard man—is the richest figure in the

play. As he tells Biff and Happy, "when I was seventeen I walked into the jungle, and when I was twenty-one I walked out. [*He laughs.*] And by God I was rich" (48). Willy's semi-legendary older brother, who appears to him in reveries, Ben is the very opposite of the idea of business success based on being nice. Ben demonstrates his "personality" by tripping his nephew Biff, threatening his eye with an umbrella point and advising "Never fight fair with a stranger, boy. You'll never get out of the jungle that way" (49).

It is true that Willy and Ben's father seems to have had business success, in a rather hard-to-imagine career as an itinerant flute salesman and inventor, taking his family across the country in a covered wagon. He abandoned his family before Willy could ever learn his secret, and the days of that kind of life are past by the time Willy has settled in Brooklyn. But he longs for them anyway, and his pride in his ability to use tools, as well as his pathetic plans to grow a garden (he is putting seeds in the stony, sunless ground the night before he dies), are part of his nostalgic dream of an entirely different way of life.

No one Willy knows, except for the old salesman, Dave Singleman, (whose career Willy seems to have misunderstood) has "succeeded" by the force of personality, a nice suit, a good line of jokes, and being well-liked. Willy's capacity for believing in this possibility leads critics to invoke "the American dream." In an influential early review of Miller's play, Harold Clurman staked out this critical position:

> *Death of a Salesman* is a challenge to the American dream. Lest this be misunderstood, I hasten to add that there are two versions of the American dream. The historical American dream is the promise of a land of freedom with opportunity and equality for all. This dream needs no challenge, only fulfillment. But since the Civil War, and particularly since 1900, the American dream has become distorted to the dream of business success. A distinction must be made even in this. The original premise of our dream of success—popularly represented in the original boy parables of Horatio Alger—was that enterprise, courage and hard work were the keys to success. Since the end of the First World War this too has changed. Instead of

the ideals of hard work and courage, we have salesmanship. Salesmanship implies a certain element of fraud: the ability to put over or sell a commodity regardless of its intrinsic usefulness. The goal of salesmanship is to make a deal, to earn a profit—the accumulation of profit being an unquestioned end in itself. (212-13)

Before there were any Horatio Alger stories there was Benjamin Franklin, maybe the best embodiment of the classic stereotype of "the American dream": a self-made man, starting in Philadelphia with nothing and making his way by sheer hard work and ingenuity, Franklin was a rich retiree by age 40. His well-known aphorisms, published periodically in "Poor Richard's Almanac," were collected in a volume with the telling title *The Way to Wealth*.

The more one tries to understand and name "the American dream," though, the more slippery it becomes. Likewise, we wonder if Willy is at fault for believing at all in the American dream, called by Susan Harris Smith "possibly a driving delusion that many Americans actively participate in and promote" (32) or for his faulty way of trying to actualize it, when it is reachable only by radically different approaches, such as Ben's ruthlessness.

But Willy's incoherent longing extends beyond his confusion about the route to success. Joseph A. Hynes has provided a compelling analysis:

> When we solicit more precise information about the "dream" we find it composed, by Willy and Biff, of several elements: Ben's hard-fisted independent acquisition of vast wealth; the geographical and economic freedom enjoyed by Willy's father, an improbable flute-hawking salesman of the plains, who "made more in a week than a man like [Willy] could make in a lifetime"; the fixed idea that Dave Singleman's ability to sell his product by telephone somehow revealed the pregnant power and value of being "well-liked"; the longing for sufficient peace of mind to enjoy his considerable manual skill and to raise chickens in the open air; the defensive insistence that he is popular and financially successful; and, to

come full circle, the theory that Biff's high school popularity and athletic prowess will (must) inevitably make him as "successful" as Willy. (287)

We should add one more dream, though it is never precisely articulated: that of family life. Willy's father abandoned his family (Willy never mentions his mother, though she must have brought him up after his father left when he was not yet four; his lack of interest in her is echoed in his frequent condescension or cruelty toward his long-suffering wife). When Ben offers Willy the chance to go to Alaska with him—and become wealthy—he cannot go because he has a family. In his almost certainly "improved" reveries, Biff and Happy idolize him. In turn he idolizes Biff—caring for him, certainly, in a way his own father had never cared for him. Willy's problem is that the incoherence and inconsistency of his various dreams complicate his relationship with Biff, whom he looks to as the one who can live those dreams. Biff should succeed because people like him. He should impose his will on the world by sheer magnetic masculinity—being well-built and athletic. But when Biff lives an outdoor life in the West (a modern, reduced version of old Mr. Loman's romantic life) he fails Willy because he isn't making a name for himself or a lot of money.

It is true that Biff has rejected Willy because of his discovery that Willy is a "fake"—that is, an unfaithful husband—but in a broader sense Biff has seen through the illusions. Biff is an aging high school football star, too lazy to make his way up and casually criminal. Happy is a bum. Willy is a minimally successful salesman, now no longer able to sell. *Willy's* dream, never relinquished, fuels his end—he kills himself for the insurance money so Biff can make a great business success. The climax of the play comes not because Willy has been victimized by fate, or capitalism, or some implacable abstraction. It comes not because he has seen through the illusion of his manifold dreams, and the sobering truth makes life no longer livable. It comes because of the irreconcilable conflict between those dreams and reality, a reality that Biff—and the audience—perceive at that bleak funeral. Biff tries to shine the light of reality on Willy when he tells him "Pop! I'm a dime a dozen, and so are you! . . . I am not a leader of men, Willy, and neither are you. You were never anything but a hard-working drummer who landed in the ash can like all the rest of them! I'm one dollar an hour, Willy!" (132)

Is there something heroic about refusing to abandon one's dreams? And does it matter if those dreams are false, or "wrong"? Willy Loman goes to his grave holding some version of the American Dream—some romantic insistence that every man can be extraordinary.

Works Cited

Clurman, Harold, "[The Success Dream on the American Stage]," from *Lies Like Truth*. New York: Macmillan, 1958; rpt. in *Death of a Salesman: Text and Criticism*, Ed. Gerald Weales. New York: Viking, 1967: 212–216.

Hynes, Joseph A. "Attention Must Be Paid . . . ," from *College English* 23 (April 1962): 574-78; rpt. in *Death of a Salesman: Text and Criticism*, Ed. Gerald Weales. New York: Viking, 1967: 280–89.

Jacobson, Irving. "Family Dreams in Death of a Salesman," *American Literature* 47 (May, 1975): 247–58.

Miller, Arthur. *Death of a Salesman: Certain Private Conversations in Two Acts and A Requiem*. New York: Viking, 1949.

———. "Introduction" to *Collected Plays*. New York: Viking, 1957: 3–55.

———. "Tragedy and the Common Man," *The Theater Essays of Arthur Miller*, Ed. Robert A. Martin. New York: Viking, 1978: 3-7.

Murphy, Brenda, "'Personality Wins the Day': 'Death of a Salesman' and Popular Sales Advice Literature," *South Atlantic Review* 64 (Winter, 1999): 1–10.

Smith, Susan Harris, "Contextualizing *Death of a Salesman* as an American Play," in *Approaches to Teaching Miller's Death of a Salesman*, Ed. Matthew C. Roudané. New York: Modern Language Association, 1995: 27–32.

"The Gift Outright"
(Robert Frost)

"The Dream of Possession: Frost's Paradoxical Gift"
by Jeffrey Gray,
Seton Hall University

How am I theirs,
If they cannot hold me,
But I hold them?

—Emerson, "Earth Song" from "Hamatreya"

Although Robert Frost's poem "The Gift Outright" was written in 1936, its fame today rests mainly on Frost's recitation of it at President John F. Kennedy's inauguration, televised worldwide in 1961. Kennedy had originally wanted a poem written especially for the occasion, but Stewart Udall, Kennedy's Secretary of the Interior, reminded the president that "Not once in his career had [Frost] written a verse for an occasion" (Udall 12). Kennedy then suggested "The Gift Outright," which Frost himself thought an excellent choice, indeed his "most national poem." Curiously, though this agreement had been reached, Frost wrote a poem for the occasion anyway. Still more curiously, that poem, called "Dedication," was not read for the occasion. At the ceremony, Frost *began* to read it, then cast it aside, gazed out at the audience, and recited by heart "The Gift Outright."

Frost was 86 at the time of the inauguration. The usual reasons given for his change of mind were his frailty, his relative unfamiliarity with the new work, and the fact that he was apparently blinded by the noon light and wind, though the new vice president held his top hat out in front of the poet to keep the wind off the paper and the glare from his eyes. But Frost's instinct in discarding "Dedication" may have had less to do with the weather than with the poem itself. A long, unabashedly nationalistic ode, written in Augustan rhymed couplets (with occasional three rhymed lines in a row), "Dedication" tells the story of the rise of American democracy. It claims that "God nodded his approval" of the victory of the British over the French, the Spanish, and the Dutch. It also praises the role of the Declaration of Independence in encouraging other peoples ("our wards") to revolt, and America's role in "teach[ing] them how Democracy is meant."

In spite of some wry asides, Frost on the whole subscribed to these sentiments, arguing in the poem that "Our venture in revolution and outlawry / Has justified itself in freedom's story / Right down to now in glory upon glory." He then turns to praise the new president and presages "The glory of a next Augustan age," indeed "A golden age of poetry and power / Of which this noonday's the beginning hour."

This was the poem Frost did *not* read. Before turning to the poem he *did* read, we might note the dramatic effect of this apparent breaking of protocol: the faltering of the aged poet indicating his frailty but also his sincerity, the impromptu "botched" reading; and the sudden shift to something older, seeming to come, as Bob Perelman suggests, straight from the body, since reciting is often heard as more authentic than reading (111). Thus, the effect was more powerful than it would have been had Frost simply stood up and read a poem. It seems likely not only that Frost was more comfortable with reciting this earlier poem but also that, on the spot, he realized it was the right poem to read—a shorter, unrhymed poem, with an historical reach almost as great as "Dedication" but, more importantly, a poem that examines the American Dream in ways that the simplistic "Dedication" could not. "The Gift Outright" is certainly not obscure, but both its mysteries and its music have ensured it an immortality that "Dedication," with its confident nationalism, would never have achieved.

"The Gift Outright" is a 16-line blank verse poem that Frost first published in the *Virginia Quarterly Review* in spring of 1942; it appeared later the same year in the poet's eighth book, *A Witness Tree*. Like the poem "Dedication," it alludes to American history, especially in relation to England and, even more than "Dedication," it explores the American Dream in terms of the promise of ownership of land. The poem presents two particular problems for contemporary readers. First, the matter of the first-person plural pronoun and whom it represents—the "we" to whom the continent is promised; and second, the vocabulary of possession—the multiple forms of the words *possess*, *give*, and *gift*—and the larger issue of owning and belonging that these words indicate.

The earliest promises of America were based on the idea of fresh opportunity—to escape from the oppression of history to a virgin land where one could make oneself anew. By the time the term "American Dream" was actually coined (by James Truslow Adams in 1931), it had come to mean prosperity and possession of land. After World War II, the American Dream became more specifically identified as the citizen's possession of a free-standing home. Thus the postwar move to the suburbs is central to the definition we retain today of this term, even where it is used cynically. By the time of the Kennedy inauguration, that later meaning of the dream had been fulfilled by white middle-class Americans.

Readers of "The Gift Outright" have often dwelt on the word "possess," which sometimes seems to connote sexual possession and mastery, especially given the masculine perspective throughout, the rhetoric of weakness and strength, and the use of the word "she," however conventional, to refer to the continent. It is difficult, in ordinary usage, to find a positive nuance to the word "possess." Frost himself said the poem was about the Revolutionary War. But the line, "the deed of gift was many deeds of war," in parentheses and not grammatically connected to the rest of the poem, raises specters other than those of war. As Albert von Frank notes, "the deed of gift" seems to be lifted from *Dr. Faustus*, where it appears three times in connection with that bargain that entails the signing of "a deed of gift with thine own blood," "a deed of gift of body and soul." (Frost knew the play well; indeed, he composed a short version of it for his students at Pinkerton Academy [Von Frank 23].) This aspect of a Faustian bargain, Western expansion at the cost of the American soul, makes "possession" seem far from auspicious. Indeed, it hints not at the

Whitmanian, spiritual side of the American dream but rather at the dark, materialistic side of that dream.

In spite of the poem's musicality and playful punning, the vaguery of "possessed" is just one example of several dark nuances that run through the "The Gift Outright." The hypnotic lines "Possessing what we still were unpossessed by, / Possessed by what we now no more possessed," introduce the concept of possession not as fulfillment but as puzzle and paradox. History, in the speaker's view, leads us toward possession. Lack of possession is construed as a failure to fulfill the promise of the new continent. In this view, one *should* be possessed by territory. But "we" colonials—unpossessing and dispossessed—were still floating free of the land, our dream unfulfilled, without the satisfaction that would come once we surrendered ourselves "outright"—that is, unconditionally—to it. Instead, these lines argue, we were still possessed—psychologically, culturally, and legally—by England. Obligation lay there, but true connection lay there also: roots, family, the personal and historical past. Though that reality possessed us, we could no longer lay claim to it: we no longer possessed it.

These musical, repetitive, and balanced lines suggest the idea of economic reciprocity, exchange, and commensuration, just as the balanced couplets, witty closures, and verbal economy of eighteenth-century English verse reflect the birth of industry and capitalism. The Frost poem plays with these ideas of reciprocity, as if in search of a formula through which to express the modern American condition of belonging neither here nor there. The first line—"The land was ours before we were the land's"—offers the first example. The second and third lines constitute another. The third example is the sentence beginning "She was ours . . ." and ending "but we were England's . . .," which also contains the two lines at the poem's heart, quoted above ("Possessing what . . ." etc.). Other lines in the poem perform similar balances and oppositions: the next sentence after those just cited begins "Something we were withholding . . ." and proceeds to "it was ourselves / We were withholding. . . ." The last long sentence absorbs the last five lines. It begins with the giving of ourselves, "Such as we were . . ." and ends with the payment of the land, "such as she was, such as she would become." Within that long sentence floats the parenthetical, disconnected sentence that balances "The deed of gift" against "many deeds of war," in the most explicit economic exchange of all.

In the world of exchange set up in Frost's poem, the idea of a "gift outright" is something of a conundrum. To give something "outright" means to give it without expectation of a return. Yet Marcel Mauss's essay *The Gift*—as well as Jacques Derrida's lectures on Mauss (in *Donner le Temps*, or *Given Time*)—argues persuasively that such a gift is an impossibility. Economy is characterized by exchange, and Frost, as we have seen, is talking precisely about exchange. A gift without return, therefore, is an interruption in economy, a contradiction. The paradox may be stated as follows: If the gift *appears* as gift, it constitutes itself as part of an economy and therefore cannot *be* a gift. Early ethnographers—Malinowski, Boas, and others—believed, idealistically, that some primitive peoples had a pre-capitalist economy based on gifts that did not require returns—that is, gifts "outright." However, as Mauss suggests, those gifts might well have had expectations attached to them—not visible to the ethnographers—as gifts do in every other culture. Derrida and Mauss, in other words, in their reading of Malinowski *et al*, argue that the gift is a figure for the impossible, since gifts inevitably reinscribe themselves within a cycle of exchange and return, even if only in the subjective form of gratitude or enhanced self-esteem for the giver. In other words, in giving, the giver expects something *back*.

This then—the question of possession and gift—is one of the two chief problems of "The Gift Outright." The second, perhaps most egregious problem, concerns the pronoun "we." Writing of the choice of this poem for the Kennedy inauguration, and particularly of the three lines beginning "The land was ours," Derek Walcott comments:

> This was the calm reassurance of American destiny that provoked Tonto's response to the Lone Ranger [the joke whose punch line is "What do you mean *we*, white man?"]. No slavery, no colonization of Native Americans, a process of dispossession and then possession but nothing about the dispossession of others that this destiny demanded. The choice of poem was not visionary so much as defensive. A Navajo

> hymn might have been more appropriate: the "ours" and the
> "we" of Frost were not as ample and multihued as Whitman's
> tapestry, but something as tight and regional as a Grandma
> Moses painting, a Currier and Ives print, strictly New England
> in black and white. (93-94)

Indeed, says Walcott, the poem ends up sounding "more like an
elegy than a benediction" (94). In a similar vein, Jerome McGann
writes that the name "Massachusetts" "reminds us that this supremely
Anglo-American poem cannot escape or erase a history that stands
beyond its white myth of Manifest destiny"; Massachusetts reveals
Virginia to be a "lying, European word" (qtd. in Perelman 111-112).

As such comments suggest, "The Gift Outright" was a poem
written for 1940s America, not for late twentieth-century America.
The *e pluribus Unum* melting-pot version of the American Dream
suggested by "salvation in surrender" has for some time in the United
States been replaced, for better or worse, by a view that prizes identity
in ethnic *difference*. The myth on which Frost draws, of course, had
been shaped in the 1890s, as the frontier vision of influential American historian Frederick Jackson Turner. More than a century later,
that vision is in disrepute, since it underwrote suffering on a massive
scale. Thus, the American "we" that Walcott examines is one with
which fewer Americans today are likely to sympathize.

But perhaps we should pause and credit Frost's well-known cynicism as well as his instinct for paradox and ambiguity. While the
poem certainly can be read as nationalist, it is not only ambiguous—its
music and word play enhancing that ambiguity—but surprisingly
dark. Although the image of the weathered, shaggy-haired Vermont
poet traipsing through the leaves continues to enable readings of
Frost's poems as embodiments of country wisdom, modern commentary focuses more on the darkness and sorrow of most of Frost's
poetry. A popular self-help book titled *The Road Less Traveled*, for
example, interprets Frost's "The Road Not Taken" as a poem about
the victories of individualism, when in fact that poem has regret and
loss written into every line. The title alone reveals the theme of regret,
yet the poem's famous last line—"and that has made all the difference"—which locates the speaker in the future, at the end of his life's
road, has suggested triumph to thousands of readers.

In the same manner, "The Gift Outright," with its upbeat title—what could be better than a gift? How better to give than "outright"?—suggests the forging of the American soul in the New England wilderness and its subsequent self-invention as the population moved westward. Yet, underneath the vocabulary of nationalism, the poem's more troubling currents are unmistakable, especially in the concluding lines. Hamida Bosmajian points out that the poem's direction is not just toward the frontier but also toward a sunset, and that "its expanse compares well with the expanse of a wasteland, but unlike Eliot's poem of that name, the American land lacks even the fragments of a civilization" (102).

In this context of sunsets and endings, the last three lines of the poem are those with perhaps the most disturbing nuances for Americans living in a later time: the land is described as "vaguely realizing westward," a phrase that suggests anything but Manifest Destiny. Does the phrase apply then to the land? The grammatical position of "the land," after all, makes it both the object of what "we" gave, and the noun that "vaguely realizing westward" seems to modify. If so, how might the land, existing in geological time, devoid of human plans, be said to realize itself? It has no inherent potential to be fulfilled; any such vision has to reside in the mind of the pioneer or empire builder who is doing the "realizing," in both senses of the word. For a recent revision of these closing lines, we might turn not to a critical essay but to a contemporary poem, one that suggests how "The Gift Outright" is still very much part of the American cultural canon, though chiefly in the sense of something to work *against*.

In "Legacy," a poem about his French grandparents' move to the American desert, the poet Frank Bidart writes that the West his ancestors "made" was "never unstoried, / never / artless" and follows this with an italicized indictment that summons both William Carlos Williams and Robert Frost: *Excrement of the sky our rage inherits / there was no gift / outright we were never the land's* (21). "Excrement of the sky" comes from Section XVIII of William Carlos Williams' "Spring and All," in which the New Jersey poet laments that a rural and suburban working-class of the 1940s is "without peasant traditions to give them / character," and, perhaps thinking of the Puritan poet Edward Taylor, speaks of the earth as "an excrement of some sky," under which we are "degraded prisoners / destined / to hunger until we eat filth" (Williams 132). This debased existence is set against a dream of fields of goldenrod and, implicitly, a dream of poetry. The section ends with one of the best-known poetic images of a lost America: No one / to witness / and adjust, no one to drive the car (133). As for the "gift / outright," it appears here as a demurral to Frost's vision of a wedding of human and land, of the economic exchange by which human and land would belong to each other. Bidart's point is not to debunk Frost, but to assert the later poet's anxiety at his own failure to find anything approaching meaning in his American childhood, family, and subsequent homes. The disconnection that Frost's poem *apparently* sees as fated to become a connection has not been realized. The disconnection is still a disconnection: not only was the land never ours, but equally, in Bidart's poem, "we were never the land's."

Bidart juxtaposes these two American views: Frost's view, in which the American westward prospect is still hopeful and the American dream of possession of a virgin land still realizable; and Williams's, in which the Puritans brought with them the seeds of their own moral destruction, and conquered the new continent with massacres and dispossession.

But, surprisingly, not only the lines of the two critiques but also the two vocabularies of Frost and Williams converge. In Frost's closing lines— ". . . the land vaguely realizing westward, / But still unstoried, artless, unenhanced, / Such as she was, such as she would become"—one sees the process of an unfocused consciousness groping toward something it could never grasp. Frost's "unstoried, artless" land is Williams's land "without peasant traditions" and without "character." And this condition, Frost's poem concedes, is not merely the state of the continent before the Europeans' history might make it (according to the poem's logic) "storied" and "enhanced," it is the land "such as she was," but also "such as she would become." The phrase "Such as we were," suggests also the condition of rootlessness and culturelessness; of newcomers adrift on a continent, derivative from and secondary to a land they were still possessed by. They were capable neither of witnessing nor adjusting to the new place and the new condition, since those had not yet, and perhaps never did, come together for them. "The Gift Outright" crystallizes not an historical moment but rather four centuries of the "in-betweenness" of Americans. It suggests not so much a destiny as a long-standing and uncomfortable situation, one in which the reciprocal exchange contemplated in the poem is thwarted, and in which the American Dream remains just that: a dream.

WORKS CITED

Bidart, Frank. *Star Dust*. New York: Farrar, Straus & Giroux, 2005.

Bosmajian, Hamida. "Robert Frost's 'The Gift Outright': Wish and Reality in History and Poetry." *American Quarterly* 22 (1970): 95–105.

Derrida, Jacques. *Given Time: Counterfeit Money*. Trans. Peggy Kamuf. Chicago: U Chicago P, 1992.

Frye, Northrup. *Anatomy of Criticism*. Princeton: Princeton UP, 1957.

Jarrell, Randall. *Poetry and the Age*. New York: Vintage, 1953.

McGann, Jerome. "Dialogue on Dialogue." *A Poetics of Criticism*. Ed. Juliana Spahr et al. Buffalo: Leave Books, 1994.

Perelman, Bob. *The Marginalization of Poetry: Language, Writing and Literary History*. Princeton: Princeton UP, 1996.

Shapiro, Harvey. "Story of the Poem." *New York Times*, 15 January 1961. SM6.

Udall, Stewart L. "Frost's 'Unique Gift Outright.'" *New York Times*, 26 March 1961. SM12.

Von Frank, Albert J. "Frost's 'The Gift Outright.'" *Explicator* 38.1 (1979): 22–23.

Walcott, Derek. "The Road Taken." *Homage to Robert Frost*. Joseph Brodsky, Seamus Heaney, Derek Walcott. New York: Noonday, 1996.

Williams, William Carlos. "Spring and All." *Imaginations*. Ed. Webster Schott. New York: New Directions, 1970: 88–151.

THE GREAT GATSBY
(F. SCOTT FITZGERALD)

"*The Great Gatsby*: The Tragedy of the American Dream on Long Island's Gold Coast"
by Tanfer Emin Tunc,
Hacettepe University

The first literary reference to the "American Dream" appeared in 1931, in J.T. Adams's novel *Epic of America*. But without using this exact expression, F. Scott Fitzgerald had already published a novel commenting on the myth of American ascendancy in 1925—*The Great Gatsby*. With the Gold Coast mansions of Long Island, New York as its setting, this literary classic captures the aspirations that represented the opulent, excessive, and exuberant 1920s. As Fitzgerald illustrates through this microcosm of American society, despite the optimism of the era, the dreams of status-seeking Long Islanders soon become nightmares. Using Jay Gatsby to exemplify the rise and fall of the American Dream, Fitzgerald's novel traces the arc of a life as it begins in wonder, reaches for the stars, confronts society's spiritual emptiness and gratuitous materialism, and ends in tragic death.

Throughout *The Great Gatsby*, narrator Nick Carraway searches for a world that is "in uniform, and at a sort of moral attention forever" (2). Disillusioned by the death and destruction of World War I, Nick decides to relocate from the Midwest to New York during the summer of 1922 to seek his fortune as a Wall Street bonds trader. On the advice of his affluent cousin Daisy Buchanan, he rents "a house

in one of the strangest communities in North America": Long Island.
Nick expects to find personal fulfillment

> ... on that slender riotous island which extends itself due east
> of New York ... twenty miles from the city ... [where] a pair
> of enormous eggs, identical in contour and separated only by
> a courtesy bay, jut out into the most domesticated body of salt
> water in the Western Hemisphere, the great wet barnyard of
> Long Island Sound. (3)

But all he finds is the "foul dust" of moral decay. At the center of
Nick's empirical observations lies Jay Gatsby. Like the Long Island he
inhabits, Gatsby lives in a world of deception that replaces the "moral
attention" Nick is so desperately seeking. Gatsby refashions himself
by changing his name from the ethnic-sounding James Gatz to Jay
Gatsby, claiming he is Oxford-educated, speaking in a staged British
accent, and addressing everyone as "old sport." Fitzgerald reinforces
this image of moral vacuity by portraying Long Island as a "valley of
ashes" or "wasteland"—a metaphorical device he most likely borrowed
from T. S. Eliot's 1922 poem of the same name (Wunderlich 122):

> This valley of ashes [halfway between West Egg and New
> York City] is where ashes grow like wheat into ridges and
> hills and grotesque gardens ... where ashes take the forms
> of houses and chimneys and rising smoke and finally, with a
> transcendent effort, of [ash grey] men who move dimly and
> already crumbling through the powdery air ... But above the
> grey land and the spasms of bleak dust which drift endlessly
> over it are ... the eyes of Doctor T. J. Eckleburg. The eyes of
> Doctor T. J. Eckleburg are blue and gigantic—their retinas are
> one yard high. They look out of no face but, instead, from a pair
> of enormous yellow spectacles which pass over a nonexistent
> nose ... But his eyes, dimmed a little by many paintless days
> under sun and rain, brood on over the solemn dumping ground.
> (Fitzgerald 15)

The hues of the terrain—grey, cloudy, faded—reflect the polluted
environment and offer a bleak depiction of humanity. Dr. Eckleburg's

piercing, unblinking, blue billboard eyes glare over this new generation of Americans. Like an omnipresent God, Dr. Eckleburg monitors Long Island and its inhabitants, his golden spectacles glittering over the wasteland of despair.

Fitzgerald contrasts the valley of ashes with the "Eggs," the two peninsulas described by Nick that jut out of Long Island's north shore. Gatsby's West Egg (present-day Great Neck) is the domicile of nouveau riche Americans who made their fortunes during the booming years of the United States stock market and lived like Gilded Age robber barons. Gatsby, who acquired his wealth through organized crime (e.g., distributing illegal alcohol, trading in stolen securities, and bribing police officers), is part of this new element of society. As such, he can never participate in the arrogant, inherited "old wealth" of Tom and Daisy Buchanan, who live in East Egg (present-day Manhasset and Port Washington), the playground of upper-class, white Anglo-Saxon Protestant Americans.

Unlike the inhabitants of East Egg (where the sun symbolically rises), Gatsby and the other newly minted, self-made millionaires of the Gold Coast are crude, garish, and flamboyant. Gatsby exposes his questionable background through numerous *faux pas* (e.g., he states that San Francisco is in the Midwest). Nick even characterizes his manners as having "sprung from the swamps of Louisiana or from the lower East Side of New York" (32). Gatsby lives in "a colossal affair by any standard—it was a factual imitation of Hôtel de Ville in Normandy, with a tower on one side, spanking new under a thin beard of raw ivy, and a marble swimming pool and more than forty acres of lawn and garden" (3-4). He bought the mansion from another nouveau riche family that was so tactless they sold the estate with their father's black funeral wreath "still [hanging] on the door" (58).

Gatsby, just like the brand new monstrosity he inhabits, is "flashy": he wears pink suits, gaudy shirts, and drives an extravagant Rolls Royce. Despite all of their obvious wealth, the nouveau riche are imposters—cheap materialistic imitations of the American Dream. They can never possess the Buchanans's old-wealth taste, epitomized by their "cheerful red and white Georgian Colonial mansion, overlooking the bay" (4). On Long Island, aristocratic grace and elegance cannot be purchased, only inherited. Try as they may, the inhabitants of West Egg will never be able to acquire *true* opulence. Daisy

Buchanan's white roadster and "spotless" flowing gowns, "gleaming like silver, safe and proud above the hot struggles of the poor," (100) will always remain a dream to them.

While members of the East Coast aristocracy possess understated sophistication, refinement, and breeding, they do not embody the American Dream with the passion and intensity of self-made individuals. As Nick elaborates, members of the aristocracy are cruel: "They are careless people . . . they smash up things . . . and then retreat back into their money or their vast carelessness . . . and let other people clean up the mess they have made" (120). Tom's racism provides important insight into the sinister and arrogant nature of old wealth. However, his fears about the "dangers" facing white, upper-class America, such as racial corruption, were not the isolated, lunatic rantings of a white supremacist zealot. Turn-of-the-century Long Island was a center of pseudo-scientific experimentation and research. Cold Spring Harbor Laboratories, where eugenicists such as Charles Davenport devised "scientific" solutions to the United States' growing race "problem" of the United States, was a mere 15 miles from Great Neck and Manhasset (Emin 1-3). The Ku Klux Klan, which re-emerged during the post-WWI era in response to the rising tide of second-wave immigrants, also fueled nativism by scaring Americans into thinking that "undesirables" would outbreed the "desirable" population. The KKK was active on Long Island during the Roaring Twenties, inflaming hatred of African-American, Jewish, and foreign-born groups who lived in Nassau and Suffolk Counties (Wunderlich 121). As Tom conveys in a conversation with Nick and Daisy:

> Civilization's going to pieces . . . I've gotten to be a terrible pessimist about things. Have you read "The Rise of the Colored Empires" by this man Goddard? . . . Well, it's a fine book, and everybody ought to read it. The idea is if we don't look out the white race will be—will be utterly submerged. It's all scientific stuff; it's been proven . . . This fellow has worked out the whole thing. It's up to us who are the dominant race to watch out or these other races will have control of things . . . This idea is that we're Nordics. I am, and you are and you are and . . . After an infinitesimal hesitation he included Daisy with a slight nod . . .

> we've produced all the things that go to make civilization—oh,
> science and art and all that. Do you see? (9)

Even though the book to which Tom refers does not exist (Fitzgerald was most likely alluding to Madison Grant's *The Passing of the Great Race* [1916] and/or Lothrop Stoddard's *The Rising Tide of Color Against White World Supremacy* [1920], both of which were bestsellers), Tom's nonsensical fear of miscegenation, which, for a brief moment, even caused him to suspect his wife of being not-quite-white, gains the approval of his audience. Moreover, it further dramatizes his pseudo-scientific explanations of American eugenic theory. As he exclaims to Gatsby:

> I suppose the latest thing is to sit back and let Mr. Nobody from Nowhere make love to your wife. Well, if that's the idea you can count me out.... Nowadays people begin by sneering at family life and family institutions and next they'll throw everything overboard and have intermarriage between black and white. Flushed with his impassioned gibberish he saw himself standing alone on the last barrier of civilization...
> We're all white here, murmured Jordan. (86)

While this quote can clearly lead to speculation about Gatsby's race, the more likely explanation was that during the 1920s, groups that were considered to be "true" whites, such as upper-class Anglo-Saxon Protestant Americans like Tom, derived their whiteness, and also class authority, from all "non-whites" against whom they could be compared and deemed socially dissimilar. As Matthew Frye Jacobson delineates, skin color itself did not simply determine race, but was coupled with a set of social or cultural arbiters, such as mannerisms, employment, and housing. Because they lived and worked comfortably with immigrants and minorities, working-class Americans, including rags-to-riches, self-made men like Gatsby, were also considered "non-white," and culturally unfit for inclusion within the ranks of high society (Jacobson 57-58).

Given the anti-Semitism that was brewing on Long Island in the 1920s, it is not surprising that Fitzgerald focused on "sneaky Jewish" business partners, "hostile Jewesses," and "little kikes." Gatsby's

Jewish underworld connection, Meyer Wolfsheim, even whistled "The Rosary" out of tune, and owned "The Swastika Holding Company." As a minor character, Lucille McKee, explains:

> I almost made a mistake, too ... I almost married a little kike who'd been after me for years. I knew he was below me. Everybody kept saying to me: "Lucille, that man's way below you!" But if I hadn't met Chester, he'd got me for sure. Yes, but listen, said Myrtle Wilson ... at least you didn't marry him ... Well, I married him [i.e., George Wilson], said Myrtle, ambiguously. And that's the difference between your case and mine ... I married him because I thought he was a gentleman ... I thought he knew something about breeding, but he wasn't fit to lick my shoe. (23)

While Lucille McKee's account is a clear example of anti-Semitism, Myrtle Wilson's comment only allows the reader to speculate about her husband's potentially Jewish roots. Nick and Gatsby's road trip into New York City is yet another racist vignette. This time both African- Americans and Jews are targets of discrimination:

> As we crossed Blackwell's Island a limousine passed us, driven by a white chauffeur, in which sat three modish Negroes, two bucks and a girl. I laughed aloud as the yolks of their eyeballs rolled toward us in haughty rivalry. Anything can happen now that we've slid over this bridge ... anything at all ... Even Gatsby could happen [another allusion to Gatsby's racial/class identity] ... [Wolfsheim], a small, flat-nosed Jew raised his large head and regarded me with two fine growths of hair which luxuriated in either nostril. After a moment I discovered his tiny eyes in the half darkness. (45)

Tom's violent attitudes towards those he deems inferior are not only evident in his racism, but also through sexist encounters with his wife Daisy, and his mistress du jour, Myrtle Wilson, an aspiring social climber whom he met while riding the Long Island Railroad into the city. Tom is not afraid to lash out against women (especially his lower-class mistress whose materialism makes him feel powerful) in order to exert authority over them. He cheated on Daisy a week after they were married with the chambermaid from their honeymoon resort, and speaks to all women with a tone of paternal contempt, even calling Myrtle's "mongrel" dog (and presumably its owner) a "bitch" (18). When Myrtle oversteps her boundaries, Tom becomes abusive, and with "a short deft movement [breaks] her nose with his open hand" (25). After he discovers Daisy's relationship with Gatsby, he becomes outraged, and threatens to beat his wife. Afraid of what Tom might do to her, Gatsby keeps vigil outside the Buchanans's home, all night long, to "protect" Daisy, just as a hero would his lady: "I'm just going to wait here and see if he tries to bother her about that unpleasantness this afternoon. She's locked herself into her room and if he tries any brutality she's going to turn the light out and on again . . . I want to wait here till Daisy goes to bed" (97-98).

Despite the racism, sexism, and vice-laden violence of old wealth, the nouveau riche continue to be attached to their lifestyle. As Nick notes, "Americans, while occasionally willing to be serfs, have always been obstinate about being peasantry" (58). Gatsby escapes this "peasantry" through conspicuous consumption, his accumulation of meaningless materialistic trophies, such as his piles of silk shirts, ostentatious car, extravagant mansion, and library full of unread books. To Gatsby, these status symbols *are* the American Dream:

> [Gatsby] opened for us two hulking patent cabinets which held his massed suits and dressing-gowns and ties, and his shirts, piled like bricks in stacks a dozen high . . . He took out a pile of shirts and began throwing them, one by one before us, shirts of sheer linen and thick silk and fine flannel which lost their folds as they fell and covered the table in many-colored disarray. While we admired [them] he brought more and the soft rich heap mounted higher—shirts with stripes and scrolls and plaids in coral and apple-green and lavender and faint orange with monograms of Indian blue. (61)

When Daisy realizes that the shirts represent Gatsby's self-destructive obsession with the American Dream (which he perceives to be the accumulation of wealth), she begins to cry with a passion that foreshadows Gatsby's eventual demise: "'They're such beautiful shirts,' her voice muffled in the thick folds. 'It makes me sad because I've never seen such—such beautiful shirts before'" (61).

Fitzgerald uses Gatsby's elaborately staged weekend parties as another metaphor for the greed, material excess, and unrestrained desire for pleasure that resulted in the corruption and disintegration of the American Dream. The anonymous guests, who are nouveau riche social climbers and freeloaders, attend Gatsby's spectacles with the hope of acquiring aristocratic wealth, power, and status. On the other hand, the parties, where guests dance to jazz music on tables, mingle with Roosevelts, and drink bootleg "champagne . . . in glasses bigger than finger bowls," subsume Gatsby's real identity (31). Illusion, conjecture, intrigue, and gossip sustain this identity: "Well, they say he's a nephew or a cousin of Kaiser Wilhelm's. That's where all his money comes from . . . I'm scared of him. I'd hate to have him get anything on me . . . Somebody told me they thought he killed a man once . . . he was a German spy during the war" (21, 29).

Daisy Buchanan, Jordan Baker, and Myrtle Wilson epitomize yet another bitter manifestation of the American Dream: the fickle, bored, selfish, and materialistic "new woman" of the 1920s. Although Gatsby creates an aura of sublime purity around his "flower" Daisy, she is anything but innocent. When Nick begins to question Daisy about her empty existence, she admits, in a jaded tone of experience, that it is all a "sophisticated" act: "I think everything's terrible anyhow . . . Everybody thinks so—the most advanced people. And I KNOW. I've been everywhere and seen everything and done everything . . . Sophisticated—God, I'm sophisticated!" (12). Gatsby is so entranced by Daisy, however, that he embraces her façade: "it excited him that many men had already loved Daisy—it increased her value in his eyes" (99). Tom's relatively public love affair with Myrtle Wilson has turned Daisy into a caustic cynic who maintains her aristocratic socialite image because it strokes her vanity and camouflages her husband's infidelities. She is indifferent to her daughter Pammy, and plans on raising her to be "a fool—that's the best thing a girl can be in this world, a beautiful little fool," most likely so she will not have to suffer the indignity of struggling with a moral conscience (12).

Daisy, whose voice is "full of money," is Gatsby's "silver idol" of illusion (76, 120). Obsessed with the idea of recreating the past "just as it was," Gatsby is blind to Daisy's selfish, juvenile, and self-destructive personality. He cannot confront the fact that she would never abandon her family to be with him, and refuses to acknowledge Tom and Pammy, for to do so would extinguish the nostalgic flame of their romance. The innocence and hope with which Gatsby stares at the "green light that burns all night at the end of [Daisy's] dock," is, like his own future, metaphorically shrouded in an impenetrable mist (61). In the end, Gatsby becomes Daisy's victim, and a victim of the elusive American Dream.

Jordan Baker, like Daisy, also represents the "new woman" of the 1920s: independent, intelligent, and witty, yet cynical, elusive, and conniving. A well-known amateur golfer, Jordan, like Daisy, suffers from spiritual emptiness; her constant yawning symbolizes her empty life and adolescent ennui. She is constantly manipulating her surroundings in a childish effort to maintain her superficial image:

> She was dressed to play golf and I remember thinking she looked like a good illustration, her chin raised a little, jauntily, her hair the color of an autumn leaf, her face the same brown tint as the fingerless glove on her knee . . . She told me without comment that she was engaged to another man. I doubted that though there were several she could have married at a nod of her head but I pretended to be surprised. (119)

Jordan applies the same strategies to her romantic entanglements as she does to her career. She deceives Nick into thinking that they have a future together and then, when she realizes that he cannot secure her materialistic needs, she capriciously decides to marry someone who can. Unlike Gatsby, Nick is able to see through the charade of innocence feigned by Daisy and Jordan, and is able to save himself from their self-destructive influence.

Like her East Egg counterparts, Myrtle Wilson, who lives "on the other side of town" in the "valley of ashes," is also consumed by materialism, spiritual emptiness, and elusive dreams. As Tom's mistress, Myrtle endures his constant abuse because she is attracted to the old wealth and glamour he represents. Tom indulges her, even acquiring a small apartment in New York City for their romantic trysts. Aspiring to join the ranks of the East Egg aristocracy, she, like Gatsby, tries to transcend her working-class roots by mimicking their nonchalant sophistication and superior manners (she allows four taxi cabs to pass before summoning a stylish lavender one with grey upholstery, and even buys a puppy from a John D. Rockefeller look-alike). However, Myrtle's act is inherently flawed because she does not possess the social skills that would allow her to detect the subtleties of her chosen role. Myrtle naively believes that dressing like a member of the old wealth elite will grant her instant admission into their exclusive world:

> Mrs. Wilson had changed her costume some time before and was now attired in an elaborate afternoon dress of cream colored chiffon, which gave out a continual rustle as she swept about the room. With the influence of the dress her personality had also undergone a change. The intense vitality that had been so remarkable in the garage was converted into impressive hauteur ... "It's just a crazy old thing," Myrtle said. "I just slip it on sometimes when I don't care what I look like." (20)

Clearly, Myrtle is conscious of the way in which clothing serves as a class marker. Like Gatsby, she cannot comprehend that attaining the American Dream is far more complicated than slipping into a disguise of cream-colored chiffon, and is therefore doomed to a life of disillusionment.

Even though for a fleeting moment, Gatsby is able to recapture his past with Daisy, he eventually realizes that his fascination with Daisy is grounded not in genuine love, but in deceptive memories of their romance in Louisville. When Daisy refuses to admit that she never loved Tom, Gatsby's ability to reclaim his lost years and feel he is married to Daisy, if only in spirit, disappears. Cynicism replaces enchantment when he painfully comprehends that it is "saddening to look through new eyes at things upon which you have expended your own powers of adjustment" (69). Gatsby "wanted to recover something, some idea of himself perhaps, that had gone into loving Daisy. His life had been confused and disordered since then, but if he could at once return to a certain starting place and go over it all slowly, he could find out what that thing was" (73). After devoting so many years to this elusive dream, Gatsby cannot go back in time and relive these lost years. His dream comes to a bitter end.

Myrtle's accident, which Fitzgerald describes in graphic detail, is important not only for its conflation of sex and violence, but also for its role in the death of Gatsby's idealism. Daisy accidentally kills Myrtle with Gatsby's Rolls Royce—the quintessential symbol of Jazz Age materialism—and then leaves the scene of the crime for the security and respectability of East Egg:

> When [two passersby tore open Myrtle's] shirtwaist ... they saw that her left breast was swinging loose like a flap and there was no need to listen for the heart beneath. [Her] mouth was wide open and ripped at the corners as though she had choked a little in giving up the tremendous vitality she had stored so long. (92)

The fact that Myrtle's breast was violently ripped open "like a flap" illustrates how she, and her breast, were simply sexualized pawns, objects to be played with by old-wealth men like Tom who had social permission to abuse, and then discard, working-class women when they grew tired of them. Myrtle died with her mouth ripped open, as if gasping for air, because her vision of the American Dream had left her suffocating in the valley of ashes. The only way out became using her body to acquire the materialism that she believed defined happiness.

In the end, Daisy ultimately chooses Tom over Gatsby, and then allows Gatsby to take the blame for killing Myrtle. She rationalizes her selfish behavior, claiming, "it takes two to make an accident" (39). This sequence of lies leads George Wilson to believe, erroneously, that Gatsby is having an affair with his wife, and was behind the wheel of the Rolls Royce that killed her. The shame of the affair compels Wilson to shoot Gatsby and then commit suicide. Instead of attending Gatsby's funeral, Daisy hastily flees Long Island without leaving any forwarding address. She could have intervened and saved Gatsby's life. But for Daisy, self-preservation is far more valuable than personal honor. As Nick comments, Daisy is no more than a "grotesque rose" (108). Gatsby, as Nick knows, is "worth the whole damn bunch put together" (103).

Gatsby's death, like his unrelenting quest for personal fulfillment, is marked by solitude and desecration. Daisy flees with Tom, while Gatsby's perpetually freeloading houseguest, Ewing Klipspringer, moves on to his next target in Greenwich, Connecticut, and a boy even scrawls an obscene word on Gatsby's pure white steps (we are left to imagine what sort of slur this could be). Even his underworld connection, Meyer Wolfsheim (who allegedly fixed the 1919 World Series), refuses to get "mixed up" with the mess, declaring that the only way to survive in this world is to "move on" (110). The only souls worthy enough to accompany Gatsby on his final journey are the three characters who, at the end of the novel, still have their moral integrity intact: Nick, Henry Gatz (Gatsby's father), and Owl-Eyes, a party guest who is in perpetual awe of Gatsby's library of unread books. Gatsby's party is over, and the only tangible proofs of his life are the possessions—the books, the mansions, the cars—he acquired.

Gatsby's indomitable optimism and his insistence that the past can be recreated destroys any hope for a salvageable future. While standing outside the Gatsby mansion, looking across Manhasset Bay, Nick realizes that Gatsby's death, like his life, is the product of an elusive, outlived dream. As the moon shines in the night sky, Nick wonders how "for a transitory enchanted moment, man must have held his breath in the presence of this continent, compelled into an aesthetic contemplation he neither understood nor desired, face to face for the last time in history with something commensurate to his capacity for wonder" (182). Daisy had been Gatsby's "continent," the "new world" that he had once wished to conquer. But Gatsby became a victim of the greed, apathy, and indifference that corrupts dreams, betrays promises, and destroys possibilities.

Nick's final commentary serves as a poetic epilogue on the futility and emptiness of Jay Gatsby's life. His conversation with Gatsby's father at the end of the novel reveals what made Gatsby, and the American Dream that he tried to achieve, "great": individualism, a dedication to self-improvement, an unwavering "capacity for wonder," and a steadfast devotion to a "righteous" set of moral and social values. Gatsby "had a big future before him . . . He was only a young man but he had a lot of brain power . . . If he'd of lived he'd of been a great man . . . He'd of helped build up the country" (112). Gatsby, like the young men who perished during WWI, does not live to realize this impossible dream. Despite all of his efforts, Gatsby is unable to disown his humble past; he manages to obtain the artificial security of wealth, but can never secure the respectability of old money that Daisy represents. In his blind pursuit of wealth, status, and success for his own gain, Gatsby follows a dream that ultimately becomes a nightmare.

WORKS CITED

Emin, Tanfer. "Freaks and Geeks: Coney Island Sideshow Performers and Long Island Eugenicists, 1910—1935." *The Long Island Historical Journal* 14.1/2 (Fall 2001/Spring 2002): 1–14.

Fitzgerald, F. Scott. *The Great Gastby*. New York: Charles Scribner's Sons, 1953.

Jacobson, Matthew Frye. *Whiteness of a Different Color*. Cambridge, Massachusetts: Harvard University Press, 1998.

Wunderlich, Roger. "The Great Gatsby as Long Island History." *The Long Island Historical Journal* 7.1 (Fall 1994): 118–124.

THE HOUSE ON MANGO STREET
(SANDRA CISNEROS)

_____

"In Search of Identity in Cisneros'
The House on Mango Street"
by Maria Elena de Valdes,
in _The Canadian Review_
of American Studies (1992)

INTRODUCTION

In _The House on Mango Street_ Sandra Cisneros reflects
upon her experience growing up in a Chicago Latino
neighborhood. The novel contains many autobiographical
elements, including a fictionalized narrator, Esperanza, who
records not only her dreams but also the dreams of her
people. Writing lies at the center of the text, representing
the ability to re-inscribe ourselves in the terms we desire.
Animated by two dreams—of being a writer and of owning
her own home, two means of attaining freedom—Cisneros'
protagonist comes of age as she writes, not only defining
herself but also envisioning a better world by imagining a
house that will enable her to create and to connect with
those around her. Maria Elena de Valdés draws the disparate chapters of Cisneros' collection together by analyzing

Valdes, Maria Elena de. "In Search of Identity in Cisneros' _The House on Mango
Street_." _The Canadian Review of American Studies_, Vol. 23, No. 1 (Fall 1992):
55–72.

the way writing functions in the text. For Valdés, writing is a means of liberation for Esperanza, who "has taken the strength of trees unto herself and has found the courage to be the house of her dreams, her own self-invention." Finding Esperanza a subversive figure who writes against the grain, Valdés describes how Esperanza's writings resist the cultural norms she knows, "for she lives in a patriarchal Mexican American culture whose stories silence women and determine the roles they can play." Esperanza's dream house becomes both a representation of the American Dream and also a symbol of her personal freedom, the emancipation of women, and the liberation of a culture.

∽◌∽

Sandra Cisneros (1954–), a Chicago-born poet of Mexican parentage, published her first novel in 1984.[1] *The House on Mango Street* is written in the manner of a young girl's memoirs.[2] The forty-four pieces are, however, not the day-to-day record of a preadolescent girl, but rather a loose-knit series of lyrical reflections, her struggle with self-identity and the search for self-respect amidst an alienating and often hostile world. The pieces range from two paragraph narratives, like "Hairs," to the four-page "The Monkey Garden."

There are a number of significant issues to be discussed concerning *The House on Mango Street*[3] but I believe that the most pressing issue is the ideological question of a poetics of identity in the double margin-alization of a Chicana.[4] [. . .] In this study, I shall present the highly lyrical narrative voice in all its richness of a "persona" to which my commentary will seek to respond.

[. . .]

My commentary is aimed at establishing a historically based, critical model of reading for the presentation of self. The narrating presence is a composite of a poetic enunciating voice and a narrative voice, and this presence can best be described as a formal function within the literary structure who, as a speaker, is only knowable as a story-teller in her response to the extratextual, societal, and historical, determinate referents. Notions of self or voice are implicitly controlled by the spectrum of the world of action as known to the reader, and notions of character are explicitly linked to the notions of person in the world. The union of the self and person is the hallmark of the lyrical text. If voice or self is an impulse toward the world, person or character is a social structure of dispositions and traits. In brief, the text in *The House on Mango Street* presents the exterior and the interior of living in the world.

The narrative situation is a familiar one: a sensitive young girl's reflections of her struggle between what she is and what she would like to be. The sense of alienation is compounded because ethnically she is a Mexican, although culturally a Mexican American; she is a young girl surrounded by examples of abused, defeated, worn-out women, but the woman she wants to be must be free. The reflections of one crucial year in her life are narrated in the present from a first person point of view. This was the year of the passage from preadolescence to adolescence when she discovered the meaning of being female and Mexican living in Chicago, but, most of all, this was the year she discovered herself through writing. The girl who did not want to belong to her social reality learns that she belongs to herself, to others, and not to a place.

The frame for the short narratives is simple but highly effective. The family has been wandering from place to place, always dreaming of the promised land of a house of their own. When they finally arrive at the house on Mango Street, which is at last their own house, it is not the promised land of their dreams. The parents overcome their dejection by saying that this is not the end of their moving, that it is only a temporary stop before going on to the promised house. The narrator knows better. The conflict between the promised land and the harsh reality, which she always recognizes in its full force of rejection, violence, fear, and waste, is presented without compromise and without dramatization. This is just the way things are on Mango Street, but the narrator will not give up her dream of the promised house and will pursue it. The lesson she must learn is that the house she seeks is, in reality, her own person. She must overcome her rejection of who she is and find her self-esteem. She must be true to herself and thereby gain control of her identity. The search for self-esteem and her true identity is the subtle, yet powerful, narrative thread that unites the text and achieves the breakthrough of self-understanding in the last pieces.

We can trace this search through some of its many moments. The narrative development begins in the first entry, "The House": "I knew then I had to have a house. A real house. One I could point to. But this isn't it. The house on Mango Street isn't it. For the time being, Mama says. Temporary, says Papa. But I know how those things go" (9). The narrator goes on to establish the family circle where she has warmth and love but is lonely and, most of all, estranged from the world outside. Her name, Esperanza, in English means hope: "At school they say my name funny as if the syllables were made out of tin and hurt the roof of your mouth. But in Spanish my name is made out of a softer something, like silver" (13). Fear and hostility are the alienating forces she tries to understand. Why do people of other colour fear her? And why should she fear others? That's the way it is. "All brown all around, we are safe" (29). Changes are coming over her, she is awakening to sexuality and to an adult world. It is in "Four Skinny Trees," that the identity question is explored: "They are the only ones who understand me. I am the only one who understands them" (71).

"A Smart Cookie" touches one of the most sensitive areas of the text: the mother–daughter relationship. Her mother remains nostalgic not for what was, but for what could have been: "I could've been somebody, you know?" (83) Being somebody is full of unarticulated significance, but in its impact on Esperanza, it means primarily to be herself and not what others wanted her to be. Her mother tells her she had brains, but she was also self-conscious and ashamed not to look as well as other more affluent girls. She quit school because she could not live looking at herself in the mirror of the other girls's presence. She states forthrightly: "Shame is a bad thing, you know. It keeps you down" (83). The syndrome is there; it is a closed circle. You are poor because you are an outsider without education; you try to get an education, but you can't take the contrastive evidence of poverty and "[i]t keeps you down." The constant movement of the narrative takes up one aspect after another of the circumstances of the emerging subject that is Esperanza Cordero.

There is a subtle sequential order to the short sections. The text opens with the description of the house and its significance to the narrator, moves on to a delicate image of the family group, and with the third piece, "Boys and Girls," begins the highly lyrical exposition of the narrator's world, punctuated with entries of introspection in the narrator's struggle with her identity. "My Name," "Chanclas," "Elenita, Cards, Palm Water," "Four Skinny Trees," "Bums in the Attic," "Beautiful and Cruel," "The Monkey Garden," "The Three Sisters," and "A House of My Own," are the most significant pieces because they mark the narrative development of identity. The text ends with the anticipated departure from the house and the literary return to it through writing. Although each piece can be seen as a self-contained prose poem, there is the subtle narrative unity of the enunciating voice's search for herself as she observes and questions her world and its social, economic, and moral conventions.

Esperanza Cordero observes, questions, and slowly finds herself determined through her relationship to the others who inhabit her world. She is drawn to the women and girls as would-be role models; within her family, her mother and her younger sister Magdalena (Nenny) are characterized, but the most searching descriptions are of girls her own age or, as she says, a few years older. Marin from Puerto Rico is featured in "Louie, His Cousin and His Other Cousin" and "Marin," Alicia in "Alicia Who Sees Mice," Rafaela in "Rafaela Who Drinks Coconut and Papaya Juice on Tuesdays," and, most important of all, Sally in "Sally," "What Sally Said," "Red Clowns," and "Linoleum Roses." The older women are treated with a soft-spoken sympathy through imagery: Rosa Vargas in "There Was an Old Woman She Had So Many Children She Didn't Know What to Do," Ruthie in "Edna's Ruthie," the neighbour Mamacita in "No Speak English," and her own mother in "A Smart Cookie."

The enunciating voice never breaks her verisimilar perspective. She speaks about what she sees and what she thinks. Her style is one of subtlety, understatement, and generosity. When she reflects on social hostility or the brutality of wife-beating, it is not with violence or rancour, but with a firm determination to describe and to escape the vicious circle of abused women: Rosa Vargas is the mother "who is tired all the time from buttoning and bottling and babying, and who cries every day for the man who left without even leaving a dollar for bologna or a note explaining how come" (30); Marin who is not allowed out and hopes to get a job downtown so that she "can meet someone in the subway who might marry and take you to live in a big house far away" (27); "Alicia, who inherited her mama's rolling pin and sleepiness" and whose father says that "a woman's place is sleeping so she can wake up early with the tortilla star" (32); "Rafaela, who is still young but getting old from leaning out the window so much, gets locked indoors because her husband is afraid Rafaela will run away since she is too beautiful to look at" (76); "Minerva is only a little bit older than me but already she has two kids and a husband who left . . . she writes poems on little pieces of paper that she folds over and over and holds in her hands a long time" (80). And, there is Sally whose father hits her and "her mama rubs lard on all the places where it hurts. Then at school she'd say she fell. That's where all the blue places come from. That's why her skin is always scarred" (85).

The first person moves effortlessly from observer to lyrical intro-spection about her place in the world. The language is basic, idiomatic English with a touch of colloquial speech and a few Spanish words. The deceptively simple structure of sentences and paragraphs has a concep-tual juxtaposition of action and reaction where the movement itself is the central topic. For example, "Those Who Don't," which consists of three short paragraphs, is about alienation and fear in a hostile society, but it is only fourteen lines in total. It begins with a direct statement about life as she sees it: "Those who don't know any better come into our neighborhood scared. They think we're dangerous. They think we will attack them with shiny knives. They are stupid people who are lost and got here by mistake" (29). The second paragraph, five lines long, begins with the "we" that is the implicit opposite of the "they" of the preceding paragraph. "But we aren't afraid. We know the guy. . . ." With the economy of a well-written sonnet the third five-line para-graph brings the "they" and the "we" into an inverted encounter: "All brown all around, we are safe. But watch us drive into a neighborhood of another color and our knees go shakity-shake and our car windows get rolled up tight and our eyes look straight. Yeah. That is how it goes and goes" (29). The description has been that of a keen observer, the composition is that of a poet.

This structure operates through a conceptual back and forth move-ment of images, like the action of the shuttle in the loom.[5] An image appears which moves the reader forward, following the woof of the first-person through the warp of referential world, but as soon as the image takes shape it is thrust back toward the enunciator. The process is repeated again and again slowly weaving the tapestry of Esperanza's Mango Street. For example, in "Those Who Don't," the initial image is about the others, "Those who don't know any better," but it reaches culmination with the observation that "they think we're dangerous." The counter-move is that "They are stupid people." The new thrust forward is the reassurance of familiarity with the ostensible menacing scene that greeted the outsiders and led them to fear they would be attacked. But, when the shuttle brings back the narrative thread, it presents the inversion. The "we" are the "they" in another neighbour-hood. The movement back and forth will go on, the narrator says, "That is how it goes and goes." The colour of the warp is different in each community, the woof keeps them next to each other, but their ignorance and fear keeps them separate. The tapestry that is being woven by this constant imagistic back and forth movement of the narrator's perceptions and thoughts is not a plotted narrative, but rather a narrative of self-invention by the writer-speaker. The speaker and her language are mutually implicated in a single interdependent process of poetic self-invention.

The poetic text cannot operate if we separate the speaker from her language; they are the inseparable unity of personal identity. There is no utterance before enunciation. There is a fictional persona, Espe-ranza Cordero, who will speak, and there is the implicit continued use of idiomatic American English. But the enunciation that we read is at once the speaker and the spoken which discloses the subject, her subjectivity, and ours. An inescapable part of this subject is what she is expected to be: "Mexicans, don't like their women strong" (12). "I wonder if she [my great-grandmother] made the best with what she got or was she sorry because she couldn't be all the things she wanted to be. Esperanza. I have inherited her name, but I don't want to inherit her place by the window" (12). This close reading of the text with attention to how it operates, suggests a movement and a counter-movement which I have described metaphorically as the movement of a loom weaving the presence of subjectivity. Subjec-tivity is always seen against the background of her community that is Chicago's changing neighbourhoods. This determinate background gives narrative continuation, or narrativity, to the narrator's thoughts. The narrative development of this text can be described as the elabo-ration of the speaker's subjectivity. The symbolic space she creates should not be abstracted from the writing, because the writing itself is the creation of her own space.[6] The structure of this text, therefore,

begins as a frame for self-invention and as the writing progresses so
does the subject. She is, in the most direct sense of the word, making
herself and in a space of her own.

[...]

In order to draw out the subject of this text I will comment
on three of the numerous images which are part of this work. The
imagery in this text functions on three levels, in the manner of prose
poems. Images in this text are effective because they function at the
level of form, of plot, and of symbolic significance. Each of these
images serves, first, to establish the identity of the enunciating voice;
this is primarily a poetic function of creating the lyric presence who
experiences and speaks. But, the images also have a narrative function
as a part of the plot line which is the search for the promised house.
And, finally, each image takes on symbolic proportions because it
participates in the rich intertextuality of literature.

"Four Skinny Trees" presents the most iconic image in the entire
text. The trees are personified in the image of the narrator: "Four
skinny trees with skinny necks and pointy elbows like mine" (71), but
the description is also markedly referential to the specific urban setting
of the text: "Four who grew despite concrete" (71). At the primary
level of the enunciating voice's identity, the image evokes a powerful
statement about belonging and not belonging to the place where they
happen to have grown: "Four who do not belong here but are here"
(71). The narrative is composed of four short paragraphs. The first,
with lyrical rhythm, establishes reciprocity between "I" and "they,"
"four skinny trees." The second completes the personification: "they"
completely supplants "trees." The third paragraph introduces their
function: "they teach"; and the fourth gives the lesson: to reach and
not forget to reach and to "be and be."

At the level of plot, the trees serve as a talisman of survival in a
hostile environment:

> Let one forget his reason for being, they'd all droop like tulips
> in a glass, each with their arms around the other. Keep, keep,
> keep, trees say when I sleep. They teach.
>
> When I am too sad and too skinny to keep keeping, when I
> am a tiny thing against so many bricks, then it is I look at trees.
> When there is nothing left to look at on this street. Four who

grew despite concrete. Four who reach and do not forget to reach. Four whose only reason is to be and be. (71)

Esperanza's survival amidst surroundings that are negative and a rejection of her sensibility is not a denial of where she is and who she is, but rather a continuous fight to survive in spite of Mango Street as Esperanza from Mango Street. It is, however, at the symbolic level that the image of the trees attains its fullest significance. There is a secret to survival that the trees make manifest—an unconquerable will to fight without respite in order to survive in an urban setting:

> Their strength is secret. They send ferocious roots beneath the ground. They grow up and they grow down and grab the earth between their hairy toes and bite the sky with violent teeth and never quit their anger. This is how they keep. (71)

I want to emphasize that the visual aspects of the textual imagery engage the reader in the visual figuration of vertical movement in trees. Is this a form of intertextuality? I think it would be more appropriate to say that this visual imagery is a woman's prose painting.

The highly lyrical presentation of "The Three Sisters" evokes the fairy godmothers of fairy-tale lore, each with a unique image and gift for the heroine. Their gift is the gift of self: "When you leave you must remember to come back for the others. A circle, understand? You will always be Esperanza. You will always be Mango Street. You can't erase what you know. You can't forget who you are" (98). This poem-piece is unlike any of the others in form because it combines the prose-poem quality of the rest of the book with the most extended dialogue sequence. The three sisters speak to Esperanza. The speaking voices are of crucial importance for through their enunciation they become full participants in the story-telling evocation with Esperanza.

At the level of plot the sisters serve as revelation. They are the narrative mediators that enter the story, at the crucial junctures, to assist the heroine in the trial that lies ahead. It is significant that they are from Mexico and appear to be related only to the moon. In pre-Hispanic Mexico, the lunar goddesses, such as Tlazolteotl and Xochiquetzal, were the intermediaries for all women (Westheim 105). They are sisters to each other and, as women, sisters to Esperanza. One has laughter like tin, another has the eyes of a cat, and the third hands like porcelain. This image is, above all, a lyrical disclosure of revelation. Their entrance into the story is almost magical: "They came with the wind that blows in August, thin as a spider web and barely noticed" (96), for they came only to make the gift to Esperanza of her self-hood. At the symbolic level, the three sisters are linked with Clotho, Lachesis, and Atropos, the three fates. Catullus depicts them weaving their fine web of destiny: "These sisters pealed their high prophetic song, / Song which no length of days shall prove untrue" (173).[7] The tradition of the sisters of fate runs deep in Western literature from the most elevated lyric to the popular tale of marriage, birth, and the fate awaiting the hero or heroine. In Cisneros's text, the prophecy of the fates turns to the evocation of self-knowledge.

The last image I shall discuss is based on the number two, the full force of opposition between two houses, the one on Mango Street and the promised house which is now the projection of the narrator. Although this image runs throughout the text, "The House on Mango Street," "Alicia," "A House of My Own" and "Mango Says Goodbye Sometimes," are the principal descriptions. The imagery of the house is in constant flux between a negative and a positive, between the house the narrator has and the one she would like to have: "I knew then I had to have a house. A real house. One I could point to. But this isn't it. The house on Mango Street isn't it" (9). On the level of the narrative voice's sense of belonging and identity, it is clear from the first piece that the house is much more than a place to live. It is a reflection, an extension, a personified world that is indistinguish-able from the occupant. The oppositional pull and push continues throughout and reaches its climax in the last three pieces. In "Alicia and I Talking on Edna's Steps," it is in the form of reported dialogue: "No, this isn't my house I say and shake my head as if shaking could undo the year I've lived here. I don't belong. I don't ever want to come from here . . . I never had a house, not even a photograph . . . only one I dream of" (99). Because the house has become an extension of the person the rejection is vehement. She knows the person she is does not belong to the hostile ugly world she lives in.

"A House of My Own" expands on the promised house of her dreams in subtle, yet evocative, intertextuality to Virginia Woolf's *A Room of One's Own*:[8] "Only a house quiet as snow, a space for myself to go, clean as paper before the poem" (100). The house is now a meta-phor for the subject and, therefore, the personal space of her identity. The last piece resolves the oppositional tension by transforming it into writing, into the metaphor of going away from Mango Street in order to return.

At the level of plot, the opposition of the house on Mango Street and a house of her own provides the narrative thread for the text. It is the movement implicit in the description of hostility and poverty and the belief in a better life that gives the story its inner cohesion and builds the consistency of the narrator's reflections. The fact that this conflict between alienation and the need to belong is common to persons of all cultures and across history gives the text its thematic link to world literature. There is a perfect circularity in the plot insofar as the text ends when the writing begins. The opening lines of the text are the closing. Esperanza has made her tension a tension creative of her subjectivity.

[. . .]

In all patriarchal societies, but especially in this one, there is the imposition of the sign of gender which serves to silence women, to force them to particularize themselves through the indirect means of the way and style in which they serve others. This is the ideological meaning of "a daddy's house." By writing, this young woman has created herself as a total subject and not a gender role or a disem-bodied voice.

The symbolic level of the image of the house is the most basic expression of existence. Everything about the house on Mango Street repels the lyric narrator. This house is not hers and does not reflect her presence. The house of her dreams is first described in negative terms, by what it cannot be: "Not a flat. Not an apartment in back. Not a man's house. Not a daddy's" (100). This is followed by its attri-butes: "A house all my own. With my porch and my pillow, my pretty purple petunias. My books and my stories. My two shoes waiting beside the bed" (100). And it also excludes: "Nobody to shake a stick at. Nobody's garbage to pick up after" (100). The problem is that she belongs to the house on Mango Street and to deny it would be at the expense of herself, of her identity. She belongs to a world that is not hers; it is an opposition that will not be resolved in a synthesis or a compromise. The metaphor of a place of her own draws upon the continuing tensional opposition. She learns not only to survive but to win her freedom, and the text itself with its title and its search for the promised house is the creative tension of poetry. The semantic impertinence of belonging and not belonging creates the metaphorical meaning of identity as one who does not forget to reach and to reach and whose only reason is to "be and be."

[. . .]

Sandra Cisneros's text is a fictional autobiography of Esperanza Cordero. This is a postmodern form of fiction stitching together a series of lyrical pieces, "lazy poems" Cisneros calls them ("Writer's Notebook" 79), into the narrativity of self-invention through writing.

[. . .]

Cisneros begins the end of her text with the affirmation of self-invention that displaces men's stories about women: "I like to tell stories. I am going to tell you a story about a girl who didn't want to belong" (101). By writing, Esperanza has not only gained control of her past, she has created a present in which she can be free and belong at the same time. Her freedom is the fundamental freedom to be herself and she cannot be herself if she is entrapped in patriarchal narrativity. Mango Street will always be part of this woman, but she has taken the strength of trees unto herself and has found the courage to be the house of her dreams, her own self-invention.

NOTES

1. Cisneros was National Endowment for the Arts Fellow in 1982 for Poetry and in 1988 for Narrative, graduated from the Iowa Writers Workshop, taught creative writing at one of Chicago's alternative high schools, and in 1988 held the Roberta Halloway writer-in-residence lectureship at the University of California, Berkeley. She has lectured extensively in North America and during the last three years has dedicated most of her time to writing another book of fiction, *Woman Hollering Creek and Other Stories*, published by Random House in 1991. *The House on Mango Street* was published in 1984 with a publication grant from the National Endowment for the Arts. The book was written from 1977 to 1982 and is now in its fourth printing

which is the second revised edition (1988). In an interview I
had with Cisneros on 30 December 1988 in New Orleans, she
informed me that the first edition of *The House on Mango Street*
had some overcorrections the publishers had made; she was not
able to revise the edition until the fourth printing in 1988. It
was reissued in 1991 by Vintage.

2. Dorrit Cohn has given us an analysis on the kinds of
   narrating voices we find in *The House on Mango Street* in what
   she terms "Diary and Continuity": "There are many reasons
   why the fictional diary is a close relative—and an important
   ancestor—of the autonomous monologue. For one thing, the
   two forms share the fiction of privacy; diarists ostensibly write,
   as monologists speak, only for themselves. Neither has any use
   for over exposition; the fiction of privacy collapses the moment
   either one of them explains his existential circumstances to
   himself in the manner of an autobiographer addressing future
   readers (or an oral narrator a listener)" (208).

3. In one of the first articles written about *The House on Mango
   Street*, Julian Olivares gives a sensitive reading of the text and
   also provides a balanced review of some of the debate provoked
   by this text. The two issues debated are genre and Chicano
   ideology. Olivares cites Cisneros's remarks on the question of
   genre: "I wanted to write a collection which could be read at
   any random point without having any knowledge of what came
   before or after. Or that could be read in a series to tell one big
   story" ("Do You Know Me?" 78). She has done what she set
   out to do. The ideological debate is much more serious. I am
   in agreement with Olivares's assessment. He cites the review
   of *Mango Street* by Juan Rodriguez and comments on his
   ideological critique: "That Esperanza chooses to leave Mango
   St., chooses to move away from the social/cultural base to
   become more 'Anglicized,' more individualistic; that she chooses
   to move from the real to the fantasy plane of the world as the
   only means of accepting and surviving the limited and limiting
   social conditions of her barrio becomes problematic to the
   more serious reader." Olivares disagrees, he writes: "Esperanza
   transcends her condition, finding another house which is the
   space of literature. Yet what she writes about—third-floor flats,

and fear of rats, and drunk husbands sending rocks through
windows, anything as far from the poetic as possible—reinforces
her solidarity with the people, the women, of Mango Street"
(169).

4. My feminist criticism has developed out of my study of
Kristeva's writings. Although I now have moved toward my
own position of literary criticism as social critique, it would be
less than forthright not to acknowledge my debt to Kristeva.
It is primarily Kristeva's concept of language as social being
and her insight into the *sujet en proces* which has given me the
theoretical basis to examine all literary texts in a social critique
that is neither coopted by the patriarchal system of historicist
literary criticism nor by the reductionist tendencies of the
feminist essentialists. I am primarily concerned in my criticism
with the question of identity and gender in the third world of
Latin America and its extension into the United States with the
Chicana writing. In addition to her book *Desire in Language*, I
have made use throughout the present study of the article "The
System and the Speaking Subject."

5. I use the metaphor of the loom, not only because of its
usefulness in describing the movement of the discourse, but also
quite consciously that this is a woman's writing and it privileges
the gradual emergence of a woman's poetic space rather than a
plot. If my study were to concentrate on the topic of women's
discourse, the metaphor of the quilt would have been more
appropriate. But whether loom or quilt there is the unmistakable
design of imagistic narrativity in place of emplotment. I am
indebted to the work of Elaine Showalter and through her I
have gained much greater insight into the recovery of women's
art in the article by Lucy Lippard.

6. I find it essential to repeat that the critical strategy that
effaces the female signature of a text is nothing less than the
continuation of a patriarchal tradition of appropriation of the
female's work through the destruction of her signature. Cisneros
has created a female voice who writes with strength in a social
context where doing so is an act of transgression, and she
writes for "A las mujeres/To the Women" as the dedication so

poignantly states. I want to acknowledge the importance of Nancy K. Miller's article which has offered me the intellectual support for my recasting of text as texture.

7. The Spanish Latin poet Catullus in his "The Marriage of Peleus and Thetes," describes the wedding gift of the three sisters, the Fates, all dressed in white, spinning their prophecy. The allusion of the spider web in Cisneros's text also gives the three sisters not only the gift of prophecy but an emblem of the weaver of tales of aunts as "the organizers and custodians of folklore and stories" (Showalter 233). The prophecy of Cisneros's three sisters is the gift of her identity.

8. An essential point to my argument is to emphasize the importance of an open text in writing by women. Virginia Woolf's characters after *Jacob's Room* are created for the reader to develop by inference and her essays, and especially *A Room of One's Own*, are for the reader to collaborate in a dialogical relationship with the writer. The metaphor of a room of one's own is, therefore, the highly charged space that comes to be through freedom to engage her other as equal in discussion, a right, not a privilege, traditionally denied to women.

WORKS CITED

Bachelard, Gaston. *The Poetics of Reverie*. Trans. Daniel Russell. New York: Orion, 1969.

———. *The Poetics of Space*. Trans. Maria Jolas. Boston: Beacon, 1969.

Black, Naomi. *Social Feminism*. Ithaca: Cornell UP, 1989.

Catullus. *The Poems of Catullus*. Ed. William A. Aiken. New York: 1960. 164–76.

Cisneros, Sandra. *The House on Mango Street*. Houston: Arte Publico P, 1988.

———. "From a Writer's Notebook: Do You Know Me? I Wrote *The House on Mango Street*." *The Americas Review* 15:1 (1987): 77–79.

Cohn, Dorrit. "From Narration to Monologue." *Transparent Minds: Narrative Models for Presenting Consciousness in Fiction*. Princeton: Princeton UP, 1978. 173–216.

Kristeva, Julia. *Desire in Language: A Semiotic Approach to Literature and Art*. New York: Columbia UP, 1980.

————. "The System and the Speaking Subject." *The Tell-Tale Sign: A Survey of Semiotics*. Ed. Thomas A. Sebeok. Lisse, Netherlands: Ridder, 1975. 45–55.

Lippard, Lucy. "Up, Down and Across: A New Frame for New Quilts." *The Artist and the Quilt*. Ed. Charlotte Robinson. New York: Knopf, 1983.

Miller, Nancy K. "Arachnologies: The Woman, The Text and the Critic." *The Poetics of Gender*. Ed. Nancy K. Miller. New York: Columbia UP, 1986. 270–95.

Olivares, Julian. "Sandra Cisneros' *The House on Mango Street*, and the Poetics of Space." *The Americas Review* 15:3–4 (1987): 160–70.

Ricoeur, Paul. *The Rule of Metaphor*. Trans. Robert Czerny. Toronto: U Toronto P, 1977.

————. "What is a Text? Explanation and Understanding." "The Model of the Text: Meaningful Action Considered as a Text." *Hermeneutics and the Human Sciences*. Ed., trans. John B. Thomson. Cambridge: Cambridge UP, 1981. 145–64; 197–221.

Rodriguez, Juan. "*The House on Mango Street*, by Sandra Cisneros." *Austin Chronicle* (August 10, 1984). Cited in Pedro Gutierrez-Revuelta. "Genero e ideologia en el libro de Sandra Cisneros: *The House on Mango Street*." *Critica* 1:3 (1986): 48–59.

Showalter, Elaine. "Piecing and Writing." *The Poetics of Gender*. Ed. Nancy K. Miller. New York: Columbia UP, 1986. 222–47.

Smith, Sidonie. *A Poetics of Women's Autobiography*. Bloomington: Indiana UP, 1987.

Woolf, Virginia. *A Room of One's Own*. London: Harcourt Brace Jovanovich, 1929.

THE JUNGLE
(UPTON SINCLAIR)

Upton Sinclair
by Jon A. Yoder (1975)

INTRODUCTION

Upton Sinclair's *The Jungle* is a startling indictment of American greed and hypocrisy. As such, it exposes as a sham the elusive immigrant dream of coming to a new land and finding the promised peace and justice for all. Detailing how Sinclair dreamed of a socialist society where everyone would know economic equality, Jon A. Yoder shows how Sinclair critiques the American Dream, and how Sinclair's vision for America is really another version of the American Dream created by the Founding Fathers. As Yoder deduces, Sinclair "was a muckraker determined to expose the inhumanity of capitalism so that Americans could opt for an economic system more closely aligned with their accepted ideals." According to Yoder, Sinclair's idealistic vision and happy ending are "traditionally American," a testimony to the American ability to rethink what American has become and all it can be.

Yoder, Jon A. *Upton Sinclair*. New York: Ungar, 1975.

When the Statue of Liberty was dedicated in 1886, the poetic
sentiments carved on its pedestal had already achieved the status of
national mystique. But the response to the invitation went beyond the
imaginations of the Founding Fathers who had identified America
as a land offering liberty and justice for all. During the first ten years
of this century, 8,795,386 immigrants entered the United States.
Although 8,136,016 of the people came from Europe, less than a half
million were from Great Britain, whereas the number included more
than two million Italians and another two million from Austria and
Hungary. Certainly the Pilgrims, despite seeing themselves as models
to be emulated, would never have predicted that within a single
decade 1,597,306 Russians would follow their example in choosing
this New World. [1]

Since he wanted to give a current report on the state of the American experiment, Sinclair's creation of a Lithuanian immigrant family
was quite appropriate. For significant Russian immigration (including
Lithuanians) was a recent phenomenon. In 1880 only five thousand
Russians emigrated to the United States. But this number increased
steadily until 1907, one year after *The Jungle* was published, when
more than a quarter of a million Russians bet their lives that America
was their promised land. [2]

If these were new sorts of immigrants, they were coming for
traditional economic and religious reasons. And Sinclair, who never
separated his economic condition from his spiritual or psychological
state, was increasingly convinced that without socialism America
could offer these new believers in the American Dream only a night-
marish existence. In 1905, while working on *The Jungle*, he took time
to organize the Intercollegiate Socialist Society. Never again—if
people like Sinclair, Jack London, Harry Laidler, and Norman
Thomas could help it—would it be possible for someone to graduate
from a university without being aware of the socialist solution. But it
was his novel that called the attention of the world to Upton Sinclair.
For his portrayal of Lithuanian peasants who come to America vividly
suggests that our melting pot is less appetizing than the terms offered
on our Statue of Liberty.

Jurgis Rudkis and Ona Lukoszaite, whose marriage in America
constitutes the first chapter of *The Jungle*, had met in Brelovicz one
and a half years earlier. It was true love at first sight, and "without ever

having spoken a word to her, with no more than the exchange of half a dozen smiles, he found himself, purple in the face with embarrassment and terror, asking her parents to sell her to him for his wife." But Ona's father was rich and Jurgis was poor; so his application was denied. Then financial disaster struck the Lukoszaite family with the death of the father. Jurgis returned to find that "the prize was within his reach."

At the advice of Jonas, the brother of Ona's step-mother, they decide to go to America, "a place of which lovers and young people dreamed," a land where "rich or poor, a man was free." So the twelve Lithuanians—Jurgis and Ona, his father, her stepmother (and six children), Uncle Jonas, Cousin Marija—come to America, believing the advertisements about opportunities for anyone willing to work.

Throughout the first part of the book, Jurgis's response to increasing trouble is the one endorsed by Benjamin Franklin. When he finds that many of his wedding guests, especially the young ones, are abusing a time-honored custom by not contributing toward the costs of the affair he says, "I will work harder." When Ona panics at his suggestion that she take a day's honeymoon away from work "he answers her again: 'Leave it to me; leave it to me. I will earn more money—I will work harder'."

The immigrants, as Sinclair describes them, are faced with the difficult task of retaining desirable aspects of an old way of life—their music, their religion, their concept of family—within a new setting that affords, supposedly, the chance to succeed economically via personal efforts. According to scholars such as Oscar Handlin, this effort was doomed to fail from the time they got on board the boat in Europe: "The qualities that were desirable in the good peasant were not those conducive to success in the transition. Neighborliness, obedience, respect, and status were valueless among the masses that struggled for space on the way." [3]

Not only do old ways fall victim to new conditions in Sinclair's novel, but the promise of equal economic opportunity for which these old values were sacrificed turns out to be fraudulent. Again Handlin supports Sinclair's earlier analysis: "It was characteristic that, about then [1900], for every hundred dollars earned by native wage earners, the Italian-born earned eighty-four, the Hungarians sixty-eight, and the other Europeans fifty-four." [4]

Sinclair's title indicates that American society, in his analysis, had returned to the law of the jungle, where might makes right in a brutal survival of the fittest. But Sinclair was in no way one of those theorists who sought to apply the biological insights of Darwin to the realm of social relationships. John Higham has observed that "in their eagerness to convert social values into biological facts, Darwinian optimists unblinkingly read 'the fittest' to mean 'the best.'"[5]

Sinclair directly opposed this. Rather than praising competition as a healthy and natural process—with cream always rising to the top—Sinclair accepted the contradictory value of cooperation. Competition, the socially inadequate law of the jungle, turns men into brutes in his novel:

> Every day the police net would drag hundreds of them off the streets, and in the Detention Hospital you might see them, herded together in a miniature inferno, with hideous, beastly faces, bloated and leprous with disease, laughing, shouting, screaming in all stages of drunkenness, barking like dogs, gibbering like apes, raving and tearing themselves in delirium.

Those who survived the dehumanizing competition inherent in capitalism were likely to be the least fit morally. Later, in *The Goslings*, Sinclair would refer to Yale's professor of political economy, William Graham Sumner (a leading Social Darwinist), as "a prime minister in the empire of plutocratic education." And what Sumner called an objective analysis of the way society had to operate was called by Sinclair the deification of the most brutish sort of selfishness, "covered by the mantle of science." In short, the classic Social Darwinist statement of John D. Rockefeller represents quite precisely those ideas that Sinclair felt were antithetical to the American Dream:

> The growth of a large business is merely a survival of the fittest.... The American Beauty rose can be produced in the splendor and fragrance which bring cheer to its beholder only by sacrificing the early buds which grow up around it. This is not an evil tendency in business. It is merely the working-out of a law of nature and a law of God.[6]

In Sinclair's book, his version of reality, Jurgis cannot succeed financially without exchanging his high morality and willingness to work for a cynical acceptance of the need to lie, cheat, steal, and exploit others. He gets his first job in Packingtown—the name used to refer to the stockyards district of Chicago—with ease, because he stands out as a fresh young stalwart among the rest of the applicants. Having completed a tour of his new environment, he is prepared to face his first day's work with energetic enthusiasm: "He had dressed hogs himself in the forest of Lithuania; but he had never expected to live to see one hog dressed by several hundred men. It was like a wonderful poem to him, and he took it all in guilelessly."

With the whole clan contributing, Jurgis is able to put together enough money for the down payment on a home—another opportunity they would not have had in feudal Europe. But the contract is rigged so that if they ever miss a payment they will lose the house. Jurgis eventually understands this, and decides to work harder so that such a disaster will not occur. He makes the same response when he discovers that his monthly payments do not include the annual interest fee.

After one summer of work by the whole family, enough money is accumulated "for Jurgis and Ona to be married according to home traditions of decency." But the first winter brings the first death. Jurgis's father contracts a fatal disease, probably tuberculosis, from working in a filthy cellar. Stanislovas, Ona's fourteen-year-old stepbrother, is a psychological victim of the same winter. Although he continued to work at filling lard cans for five cents per hour, he "conceived a terror of the cold that was almost a mania" as a result of having seen his partner's frozen ears drop off when they were rubbed too vigorously.

The financial contribution of Marija, who earned even more than Jurgis by painting cans, stops without warning when the canning factory closes for the winter. For Jurgis, too, winter is a slack season. Although he is expected to be available at the "killing beds" all day, he is paid only for those hours when he actually works; this system often reduces his income to about thirty-five cents per day. In order to make the twelve-dollar monthly house payment, meet the extra expenses of coal and winter clothing, and feed the clan, Jurgis once again decides he will simply have to work harder.

Spring arrives, and so does a son, little Antanas. Ona develops "womb trouble" from going back to work too quickly. But "the great majority of the women who worked in Packingtown suffered in the same way, and from the same cause, so it was not deemed a thing to see the doctor about." Summer provides a chance to build up financial and physical reserves for the second Chicago winter.

The first snowstorm hits just before Christmas, making it impossible for the weakened Ona to walk to the spot on the line where she sewed hams all day. But "the soul of Jurgis rose up within him like a sleeping lion." Starting out before dawn, he carries Ona through snowdrifts that come up to his armpits, repeating the performance around eleven o'clock every night.

But chance events can confound even the most physically fit. Upon occasion a steer would break loose on the killing beds, running amuck among workers who scramble over bloody floors to get behind pillars so that when "the floor boss would come rushing up with a rifle and begin blazing away" they could be counted among the survivors. During one such adventure Jurgis sprains his ankle and is unable to stand on his feet for two weeks. To make matters worse, Jonas, the brother of Ona's stepmother, decides that personal interests weigh more than family loyalty; he disappears, reducing the total income of the household while house payments remain constant.

Jurgis goes back to work before his ankle is healed, but he cannot function, so he loses his job. Now the family must try harder; the two younger brothers of Stanislovas, aged eleven and ten, become part of America's work force by selling newspapers. During this time one of the youngest children dies, probably from eating "tubercular pork that was condemned as unfit for export," but legal fare for Europeans who had come to America.

After two months Jurgis is able to walk again, but since he is no longer a prime physical specimen the only place in Packingtown where he can get a job is the fertilizer plant.

> To this part of the yards came all the "tankage," and the waste products of all sorts; here they dried out the bones—and in suffocating cellars, where the daylight never came, you might see men and women and children bending over whirling

machines and sawing bits of bone into all sorts of shapes, breathing their lungs full of the fine dust, and doomed to die, every one of them, within a certain definite time.

Jurgis spends his third American summer there, and while he is able to make all of the house payments on time, his home falls apart. He and Ona have little to talk about, and they are generally too weary to care about each other. But remnants of old values remain. Thus when Jurgis discovers the following winter that Ona has slept with her boss in order to retain her job, he attacks the man viciously, gets himself thrown in jail for one month, and returns to find that the house is repainted—sold as new to brand-new victims.

He finally finds his family, lodged in the cheapest garret of a boardinghouse, and enters to hear the screams of Ona dying in child-birth—an eighteen-year-old worn-out woman. He discovers that because of his attack on Ona's boss he is blacklisted, unable to work anywhere in Packingtown. This is almost overwhelming, but Jurgis's hopes are raised again when he finds relatively desirable work at the Harvester plant. The job lasts nine days; then the works are closed until further notice. He moves to a steel mill, works four days, and burns his hand so severely that he is laid off for more than a week. Then little Antanas drowns in the mud of Chicago's streets, and Jurgis becomes a cynic.

All this time Jurgis had been relatively successful in withstanding the temptation to escape his environment in the way chosen by most of the workers—alcohol. Now, rather than turning to drink, he decides to escape altogether. Jurgis walks out on the rest of Ona's relatives and becomes a hobo. When a farmer refuses to give him some food, he tears up one hundred young peach trees by the roots, thus demonstrating that he has adapted to America.

Jurgis wanders around the countryside for a summer, learning much about wine and women, and then returns to Chicago in the winter to help dig freight tunnels. A fight with a bartender leads to a second short jail term. But this time he makes friends with a profes-sional thief who introduces Jurgis to the criminal underworld. Gradu-ating from theft to political illegalities, Jurgis rises quite rapidly. He becomes a "foreman," placed back on the killing beds to insure the election of selected politicians every voting day.

Then a remnant of integrity from his past arises to plague him again. He meets Ona's old boss by chance and instinctively repeats his attack. His political friends are able to help him avoid a prison sentence, but he is now of little use to them and he must return to the life of a Chicago bum—stealing cabbages from grocers, drinking cheap beer for the sake of shelter, begging for funds to finance a night in a flophouse.

While begging, he discovers the address of Cousin Marija, who has become a prostitute. He visits her, hoping for some help, and learns that Stanislovas has been killed and eaten by rats after having been locked into his factory overnight by mistake.

Back on the street, Jurgis has no particular place to go, so in order to stay warm he enters a building in which a political rally is being held. He listens to a socialist speaker who correctly predicts that the "scales will fall from his eyes, the shackles will be torn from his limbs—he will leap up with a cry of thankfulness, he will stride forth a free man at last!"

Within a week of his conversion Jurgis finds a job at a small hotel run by a socialist. He begins to work at his new life with his old diligence. He reads much socialist literature and soon has enough money to support Ona's relatives again. (Marija, however, has become a dope addict, and "chooses" to remain a prostitute.) By the end of the novel Jurgis has become a thoroughly convinced socialist, part of the social movement that he and Sinclair expected to turn Chicago into a place fit for Americans.

Sinclair's novel is remembered, and rightly so, for its graphic descriptions of working conditions in Packingtown. But only about half of the book is concerned with the meat-packing industry, and even this half is used as a vehicle for Sinclair's larger message. What had happened to the spirit of America? What devil had tempted the American mind to substitute cash for value, thus allowing this intended Garden of Eden to go to seed—nourished by the heat of industrialization into a jungle of greed and grease and despair?
[. . .]

Beneath the rhetoric of a new society based on equality and brotherhood, America had built its experiment on tried and tested foundations of competition and greed. As indicated above, Jurgis personifies the willingness to accept individual responsibility for his own situation. He sets out across an ocean to solve his own problems through his own honest efforts; he wants to work. But by the turn of the century this point of view had become a demonstration of naiveté rather than of healthy optimism. Jurgis's co-laborers had already discovered that the game was rigged to allow only a few winners. So their response is the complete negation of the American Dream; they hate to work.

> They hated the bosses and they hated the owners; they hated the whole place, the whole neighborhood—even the whole city, with an all-inclusive hatred, bitter and fierce. Women and little children would fall to cursing about it; it was rotten, rotten as hell—everything was rotten.

For Sinclair, this undesirable result was built into the very theory of competitive capitalism:

> Here was Durham's, for instance, owned by a man who was trying to make as much money out of it as he could, and did not care in the least how he did it, and underneath him, ranged in ranks and grades like an army, were managers and superintendents and foremen, each one driving the man next below him and trying to squeeze out of him as much work as possible.

Men are not essentially evil, but within capitalism immoral behavior is systematically rewarded. Continuing his authorial comment in *The Jungle*, Sinclair contended:

> You could lay that down for a rule—if you met a man who was rising in Packingtown, you met a knave . . . . The man who told tales and spied upon his fellows would rise; but the man who minded his own business and did his work—why, they would "speed him up" till they had worn him out, and then they would throw him into the gutter.

Consequently, good men turn vicious in order to survive. Jurgis, who tries desperately to retain traditional values, yields to the stronger forces of inhumanity at the death of his son, "tearing up all the flowers from the garden of his soul, and setting his heel upon them." But Jurgis's creator retains those ideals, and he is in charge of the direction of the book. In his expression of very traditional American optimism, Sinclair believes that democracy will come to American industry because right eventually triumphs:

> Those who lost in the struggle were generally exterminated; but now and then they had been known to save themselves by combination—which was a new and higher kind of strength. It was so that the gregarious animals had overcome the predaceous; it was so, in human history, that the people had mastered the kings. The workers were simply the citizens of industry, and the Socialist movement was the expression of their will to survive.

Sinclair's happy ending, the conversion of Jurgis to a rational method of social organization, is made complete and personal via a charge of emotional energy:

> The voice of Labor, despised and outraged; a mighty giant, lying prostrate—mountainous, colossal, but blinded, bound, and ignorant of his strength. And now a dream of resistance haunts him, hope battling with fear; until suddenly he stirs, and a fetter snaps—and a thrill shoots through him, to the farthest ends of his huge body, and in a flash the dream becomes an act! ... He springs to his feet, he shouts in his new-born exultation—

Nothing could be more traditionally American than the belief that this happy ending was inevitable since God was counted on the good side of the struggle. Socialism, for Sinclair, "was the new religion of humanity—or you might say it was the fulfillment of the old religion, since it implied but the literal application of all the teachings of Christ." Filtering Tom Paine through Jonathan Edwards, Sinclair preaches about the redemption of "a man who was the world's first revolutionist, the true founder of the Socialist movement. . . .Who denounced in unmeasured terms the exploiters of his own time. . . . This union carpenter! This agitator, lawbreaker, firebrand, anarchist!"

Answering the objection of those who do not believe in democratic socialism, Sinclair guaranteed the achievement of American equality through a rational distribution of wealth *without* totalitarian thought control:

There was only one earth, and the quantity of material things was limited. Of intellectual and moral things, on the other hand, there was no limit, and one could have more without another's having less; hence "Communism in material production, anarchism in intellectual," was the formula of modern proletarian thought.

Sinclair's answer to the immigrants' problem applies the old solution, democracy, to the new conditions, industrialization and the emergence of mass man. Instead of the pathetic marriage of old immigrant values and new economic frustrations, Sinclair's solution insures that the survival of the fittest will also mean the perpetuation of the best.

[. . .]

Sinclair served the public, then, as a reflector of the condition of the American liberal by recording what liberals were thinking for half a century—including both optimistic and cynical periods. In terms of his own goal, the production of liberal propaganda, few American authors have been more successful. Certainly his presentation and personification of the complex liberal dilemma remains the most exhaustive analysis on record.

NOTES

1. Samuel E. Morrison and Henry Steele Commager, *The Growth of the American Republic*, 2 (New York, 1950): 910.
2. Maldwyn A. Jones, *American Immigration* (Chicago, 1960), p. 202.
3. Oscar Handlin, *The Uprooted* (New York, 1951), p. 61.
4. Ibid., p. 76.
5. John Higham, *Strangers in the Land* (New York, 1967), p. 135.
6. Quoted by Richard Hofstadter, *Social Darwinism in American Thought* (Boston, 1955), p. 45.

LEAVES OF GRASS
(WALT WHITMAN)

❧ ☙

"Preface to *Leaves of Grass* (1855)"
by Walt Whitman,
Walt Whitman: Complete Poetry and Collected Prose (1982)

INTRODUCTION

In his famous "Preface" to the 1855 edition of *Leaves of Grass*, Whitman tells his dream of becoming the great American bard, one who can record "the greatest poem": The United States. With grand, sweeping descriptions of a diverse, democratic society, Whitman calls for a national literature. In doing so, he articulates the American Dream of living in an ideal society in which all are honored and each is free to purse liberty, life, and happiness. Such idealism marks Whitman's epic vision. In peering into the self, describing the American society, publishing his own creation, and naming his intentions, Whitman stands as one of the greatest proponents of the American Dream, a lyric voice that honors all America is and all it can be.

☙❧

Whitman, Walt. "Preface to *Leaves of Grass* (1855)." *Walt Whitman: Complete Poetry and Collected Prose.* New York: Literary Classics of the United States, 1982.

America does not repel the past or what it has produced under its forms or amid other politics or the idea of castes or the old religions . . . accepts the lesson with calmness . . . is not so impatient as has been supposed that the slough still sticks to opinions and manners and literature while the life which served its requirements has passed into the new life of the new forms . . . perceives that the corpse is slowly borne from the eating and sleeping rooms of the house . . . perceives that it waits a little while in the door . . . that it was fittest for its days . . . that its action has descended to the stalwart and well-shaped heir who approaches . . . and that he shall be fittest for his days.

The Americans of all nations at any time upon the earth have probably the fullest poetical nature. The United States themselves are essentially the greatest poem. In the history of the earth hitherto the largest and most stirring appear tame and orderly to their ampler largeness and stir. Here at last is something in the doings of man that corresponds with the broadcast doings of the day and night. Here is not merely a nation but a teeming nation of nations. Here is action untied from strings necessarily blind to particulars and details magnificently moving in vast masses. Here is the hospitality which forever indicates heroes . . . . Here are the roughs and beards and space and ruggedness and nonchalance that the soul loves. Here the performance disdaining the trivial unapproached in the tremendous audacity of its crowds and groupings and the push of its perspective spreads with crampless and flowing breadth and showers its prolific and splendid extravagance. One sees it must indeed own the riches of the summer and winter, and need never be bankrupt while corn grows from the ground or the orchards drop apples or the bays contain fish or men beget children upon women.

Other states indicate themselves in their deputies . . . but the genius of the United States is not best or most in its executives or legislatures, nor in its ambassadors or authors or colleges or churches or parlors, nor even in its newspapers or inventors . . . but always most in the common people. Their manners, speech, dress, friendships—the freshness and candor of their physiognomy—the picturesque looseness of their carriage their deathless attachment to freedom—their aversion to anything indecorous or soft or mean—the practical acknowledgment of the citizens of one state by the citizens of all other states—the fierceness of their roused resentment—their curiosity and welcome of novelty—their self-esteem and wonderful sympathy—their susceptibility to a slight—the air they have of persons who never knew how it felt to stand in the presence of superiors—the fluency of their speech—their delight in music, the sure symptom of manly tenderness and native elegance of soul . . .their good temper and openhandedness—the terrible significance of their elections—the President's taking off his hat to them not they to him—these too are unrhymed poetry. It awaits the gigantic and generous treatment worthy of it.

The largeness of nature or the nation were monstrous without a corresponding largeness and generosity of the spirit of the citizen. Not nature nor swarming states nor streets and steamships nor prosperous business nor farms nor capital nor learning may suffice for the ideal of man . . . nor suffice the poet. No reminiscences may suffice either. A live nation can always cut a deep mark and can have the best authority the cheapest . . . namely from its own soul. This is the sum of the profitable uses of individuals or states and of present action and grandeur and of the subjects of poets.—As if it were necessary to trot back generation after generation to the eastern records! As if the beauty and sacredness of the demonstrable must fall behind that of the mythical! As if men do not make their mark out of any times! As if the opening of the western continent by discovery and what has transpired since in North and South America were less than the small theatre of the antique or the aimless sleepwalking of the middle ages! The pride of the United States leaves the wealth and finesse of the cities and all returns of commerce and agriculture and all the magnitude of geography or shows of exterior victory to enjoy the breed of fullsized men or one fullsized man unconquerable and simple.

The American poets are to enclose old and new for America is the race of races. Of them a bard is to be commensurate with a people. To him the other continents arrive as contributions . . . he gives them reception for their sake and his own sake. His spirit responds to his country's spirit . . . . he incarnates its geography and natural life and rivers and lakes. Mississippi with annual freshets and changing chutes, Missouri and Columbia and Ohio and Saint Lawrence with the falls and beautiful masculine Hudson, do not embouchure where they spend themselves more than they embouchure into him. The blue breadth over the inland sea of Virginia and Maryland and the

sea off Massachusetts and Maine and over Manhattan bay and over
Champlain and Erie and over Ontario and Huron and Michigan and
Superior, and over the Texan and Mexican and Floridian and Cuban
seas and over the seas off California and Oregon, is not tallied by the
blue breadth of the waters below more than the breadth of above and
below is tallied by him. When the long Atlantic coast stretches longer
and the Pacific coast stretches longer he easily stretches with them
north or south. He spans between them also from east to west and
reflects what is between them. On him rise solid growths that offset
the growths of pine and cedar and hemlock and liveoak and locust and
chestnut and cypress and hickory and limetree and cottonwood and
tulip-tree and cactus and wildvine and tamarind and persimmon . . . .
and tangles as tangled as any canebrake or swamp . . . . and forests
coated with transparent ice and icicles hanging from the boughs and
crackling in the wind . . . . and sides and peaks of mountains . . . .
and pasturage sweet and free as savannah or upland or prairie . . . .
with flights and songs and screams that answer those of the wildpi-
geon and highhold and orchard-oriole and coot and surf-duck and
redshouldered-hawk and fish-hawk and white-ibis and indian-hen
and cat-owl and water-pheasant and qua-bird and pied-sheldrake and
blackbird and mockingbird and buzzard and condor and night-heron
and eagle. To him the hereditary countenance descends both mother's
and father's. To him enter the essences of the real things and past and
present events—of the enormous diversity of temperature and agriculture and mines—the tribes of red aborigines—the weather-beaten
vessels entering new ports or making landings on rocky coasts—the
first settlements north or south—the rapid stature and muscle—the
haughty defiance of '76, and the war and peace and formation of
the constitution . . . . the union always surrounded by blatherers
and always calm and impregnable—the perpetual coming of immigrants—the wharfhem'd cities and superior marine—the unsurveyed
interior—the loghouses and clearings and wild animals and hunters
and trappers . . . . the free commerce—the fisheries and whaling and
gold-digging—the endless gestation of new states—the convening
of Congress every December, the members duly coming up from all
climates and the uttermost parts . . . . the noble character of the young
mechanics and of all free American workmen and workwomen . . . .
the general ardor and friendliness and enterprise—the perfect equality

of the female with the male . . . . the large amativeness—the fluid movement of the population—the factories and mercantile life and laborsaving machinery—the Yankee swap—the New-York firemen and the target excursion—the southern plantation life—the character of the northeast and of the northwest and southwest—slavery and the tremulous spreading of hands to protect it, and the stern opposition to it which shall never cease till it ceases or the speaking of tongues and the moving of lips cease. For such the expression of the American poet is to be transcendant and new. It is to be indirect and not direct or descriptive or epic. Its quality goes through these to much more. Let the age and wars of other nations be chanted and their eras and characters be illustrated and that finish the verse. Not so the great psalm of the republic. Here the theme is creative and has vista. Here comes one among the wellbeloved stonecutters and plans with decision and science and sees the solid and beautiful forms of the future where there are now no solid forms.

Of all nations the United States with veins full of poetical stuff most need poets and will doubtless have the greatest and use them the greatest. Their Presidents shall not be their common referee so much as their poets shall. Of all mankind the great poet is the equable man. Not in him but off from him things are grotesque or eccentric or fail of their sanity. Nothing out of its place is good and nothing in its place is bad. He bestows on every object or quality its fit proportions neither more nor less. He is the arbiter of the diverse and he is the key. He is the equalizer of his age and land . . . . he supplies what wants supplying and checks what wants checking. If peace is the routine out of him speaks the spirit of peace, large, rich, thrifty, building vast and populous cities, encouraging agriculture and the arts and commerce—lighting the study of man, the soul, immortality— federal, state or municipal government, marriage, health, freetrade, intertravel by land and sea . . . . nothing too close, nothing too far off . . . the stars not too far off. In war he is the most deadly force of the war. Who recruits him recruits horse and foot . . . he fetches parks of artillery the best that engineer ever knew. If the time becomes slothful and heavy he knows how to arouse it . . . he can make every word he speaks draw blood. Whatever stagnates in the flat of custom or obedience or legislation he never stagnates. Obedience does not master him, he masters it. High up out of reach he stands turning a

concentrated light . . . he turns the pivot with his finger . . . he baffles
the swiftest runners as he stands and easily overtakes and envelops
them. The time straying toward infidelity and confections and persi-
flage he withholds by his steady faith . . . he spreads out his dishes . . .
he offers the sweet firmfibred meat that grows men and women. His
brain is the ultimate brain. He is no arguer . . . he is judgment. He
judges not as the judge judges but as the sun falling around a helpless
thing. As he sees the farthest he has the most faith. His thoughts are
the hymns of the praise of things. In the talk on the soul and eternity
and God off of his equal plane he is silent. He sees eternity less like
a play with a prologue and denouement . . . . he sees eternity in men
and women . . . he does not see men and women as dreams or dots.
Faith is the antiseptic of the soul . . . it pervades the common people
and preserves them . . . they never give up believing and expecting and
trusting. There is that indescribable freshness and unconsciousness
about an illiterate person that humbles and mocks the power of the
noblest expressive genius. The poet sees for a certainty how one not a
great artist may be just as sacred and perfect as the greatest artist. . . . .
The power to destroy or remould is freely used by him but never the
power of attack. What is past is past. If he does not expose superior
models and prove himself by every step he takes he is not what is
wanted. The presence of the greatest poet conquers . . . not parleying
or struggling or any prepared attempts. Now he has passed that way
see after him! there is not left any vestige of despair or misanthropy or
cunning or exclusiveness or the ignominy of a nativity or color or delusion of hell or the necessity of hell . . . . and no man thenceforward
shall be degraded for ignorance or weakness or sin.

The greatest poet hardly knows pettiness or triviality. If he breathes
into any thing that was before thought small it dilates with the grandeur and life of the universe. He is a seer . . . . he is individual . . . he
is complete in himself . . . . the others are as good as he, only he sees it
and they do not. He is not one of the chorus . . . . he does not stop for
any regulation . . . he is the president of regulation. What the eyesight
does to the rest he does to the rest. Who knows the curious mystery
of the eyesight? The other senses corroborate themselves, but this is
removed from any proof but its own and foreruns the identities of the
spiritual world. A single glance of it mocks all the investigations of
man and all the instruments and books of the earth and all reasoning.

What is marvellous? what is unlikely? what is impossible or baseless or vague? after you have once just opened the space of a peachpit and given audience to far and near and to the sunset and had all things enter with electric swiftness softly and duly without confusion or jostling or jam.

The land and sea, the animals fishes and birds, the sky of heaven and the orbs, the forests mountains and rivers, are not small themes . . . but folks expect of the poet to indicate more than the beauty and dignity which always attach to dumb real objects . . . . they expect him to indicate the path between reality and their souls. Men and women perceive the beauty well enough . . . probably as well as he. The passionate tenacity of hunters, woodmen, early risers, cultivators of gardens and orchards and fields, the love of healthy women for the manly form, seafaring persons, drivers of horses, the passion for light and the open air, all is an old varied sign of the unfailing perception of beauty and of a residence of the poetic in outdoor people. They can never be assisted by poets to perceive . . . some may but they never can. The poetic quality is not marshalled in rhyme or uniformity or abstract addresses to things nor in melancholy complaints or good precepts, but is the life of these and much else and is in the soul. The profit of rhyme is that it drops seeds of a sweeter and more luxuriant rhyme, and of uniformity that it conveys itself into its own roots in the ground out of sight. The rhyme and uniformity of perfect poems show the free growth of metrical laws and bud from them as unerringly and loosely as lilacs or roses on a bush, and take shapes as compact as the shapes of chestnuts and oranges and melons and pears, and shed the perfume impalpable to form. The fluency and ornaments of the finest poems or music or orations or recitations are not independent but dependent. All beauty comes from beautiful blood and a beautiful brain. If the greatnesses are in conjunction in a man or woman it is enough . . . . the fact will prevail through the universe . . . . but the gaggery and gilt of a million years will not prevail. Who troubles himself about his ornaments or fluency is lost. This is what you shall do: Love the earth and sun and the animals, despise riches, give alms to every one that asks, stand up for the stupid and crazy, devote your income and labor to others, hate tyrants, argue not concerning God, have patience and indulgence toward the people, take off your hat to nothing known or unknown or to any man or number of men, go freely with powerful uneducated persons and with the young and with the mothers of families, read these leaves in the open air every season of every year of your life, re-examine all you have been told at school or church or in any book, dismiss whatever insults your own soul, and your very flesh shall be a great poem and have the richest fluency not only in its words but in the silent lines of its lips and face and between the lashes of your eyes and in every motion and joint of your body . . . . The poet shall not spend his time in unneeded work. He shall know that the ground is always ready ploughed and manured . . . . others may not know it but he shall. He shall go directly to the creation. His trust shall master the trust of everything he touches . . . . and shall master all attachment.

The known universe has one complete lover and that is the greatest poet. He consumes an eternal passion and is indifferent which chance happens and which possible contingency of fortune or misfortune and persuades daily and hourly his delicious pay. What balks or breaks others is fuel for his burning progress to contact and amorous joy. Other proportions of the reception of pleasure dwindle to nothing to his proportions. All expected from heaven or from the highest he is rapport with in the sight of the daybreak or a scene of the winter woods or the presence of children playing or with his arm round the neck of a man or woman. His love above all love has leisure and expanse . . . . he leaves room ahead of himself. He is no irresolute or suspicious lover . . . he is sure . . . he scorns intervals. His experience and the showers and thrills are not for nothing. Nothing can jar him . . . . suffering and darkness cannot—death and fear cannot. To him complaint and jealousy and envy are corpses buried and rotten in the earth . . . . he saw them buried. The sea is not surer of the shore or the shore of the sea than he is of the fruition of his love and of all perfection and beauty.

The fruition of beauty is no chance of hit or miss . . . it is inevitable as life . . . . it is exact and plumb as gravitation. From the eyesight proceeds another eyesight and from the hearing proceeds another hearing and from the voice proceeds another voice eternally curious of the harmony of things with man. To these respond perfections not only in the committees that were supposed to stand for the rest but in the rest themselves just the same. These understand the law of perfection in masses and floods . . . that its finish is to each for itself and onward from itself . . . that it is profuse and impartial . . . that there is not a minute of the light or dark nor an acre of the earth or sea without it—nor any direction of the sky nor any trade or employment nor any turn of events. This is the reason that about the proper expression of beauty there is precision and balance . . . one part does not need to be thrust above another. The best singer is not the one who has the most lithe and powerful organ . . . the pleasure of poems is not in them that take the handsomest measure and similes and sound.

Without effort and without exposing in the least how it is done the greatest poet brings the spirit of any or all events and passions and scenes and persons some more and some less to bear on your individual character as you hear or read. To do this well is to compete with the laws that pursue and follow time. What is the purpose must surely be there and the clue of it must be there . . . . and the faintest indication is the indication of the best and then becomes the clearest indication. Past and present and future are not disjoined but joined. The greatest poet forms the consistence of what is to be from what has been and is. He drags the dead out of their coffins and stands them again on their feet . . . . he says to the past, Rise and walk before me that I may realize you. He learns the lesson . . . . he places himself where the future becomes present. The greatest poet does not only dazzle his rays over character and scenes and passions . . . he finally ascends and finishes all . . . he exhibits the pinnacles that no man can tell what they are for or what is beyond . . . . he glows a moment on the extremest verge. He is most wonderful in his last half-hidden smile or frown . . . by that flash of the moment of parting the one that sees it shall be encouraged or terrified afterward for many years. The greatest poet does not moralize or make applications of morals . . . he knows the soul. The soul has that measureless pride which consists in never acknowledging any lessons but its own. But it has sympathy as measureless as its pride and the one balances the other and neither can stretch too far while it stretches in company with the other. The inmost secrets of art sleep with the twain. The greatest poet has lain close betwixt both and they are vital in his style and thoughts.

The art of art, the glory of expression and the sunshine of the light of letters is simplicity. Nothing is better than simplicity . . . . nothing can make up for excess or for the lack of definiteness. To carry on the heave of impulse and pierce intellectual depths and give all subjects their articulations are powers neither common nor very uncommon. But to speak in literature with the perfect rectitude and insousiance of the movements of animals and the unimpeachableness of the sentiment of trees in the woods and grass by the roadside is the flawless triumph of art. If you have looked on him who has achieved it you have looked on one of the masters of the artists of all nations and times. You shall not contemplate the flight of the graygull over the bay or the mettlesome action of the blood horse or the tall leaning of sunflowers on their stalk or the appearance of the sun journeying through heaven or the appearance of the moon afterward with any more satisfaction than you shall contemplate him. The greatest poet has less a marked style and is more the channel of thoughts and things without increase or diminution, and is the free channel of himself. He swears to his art, I will not be meddlesome, I will not have in my writing any elegance or effect or originality to hang in the way between me and the rest like curtains. I will have nothing hang in the way, not the richest curtains. What I tell I tell for precisely what it is. Let who may exalt or startle or fascinate or soothe I will have purposes as health or heat or snow has and be as regardless of observation. What I experience or portray shall go from my composition without a shred of my composition. You shall stand by my side and look in the mirror with me.

The old red blood and stainless gentility of great poets will be proved by their unconstraint. A heroic person walks at his ease through and out of that custom or precedent or authority that suits him not. Of the traits, of the brotherhood of writers savans musicians inventors and artists nothing is finer than silent defiance advancing from new free forms. In the need of poems philosophy politics mechanism science behaviour, the craft of art, an appropriate native grand-opera, shipcraft, or any craft, he is greatest forever and forever who contributes the greatest original practical example. The cleanest expression is that which finds no sphere worthy of itself and makes one.

The messages of great poets to each man and woman are, Come to us on equal terms, Only then can you understand us, We are no better than you, What we enclose you enclose, What we enjoy you may enjoy. Did you suppose there could be only one Supreme? We affirm there can be unnumbered Supremes, and that one does not countervail another any more than one eyesight countervails another . . . and that men can be good or grand only of the consciousness of their supremacy within them. What do you think is the grandeur of storms and dismemberments and the deadliest battles and wrecks and the wildest fury of the elements and the power of the sea and the motion of nature and of the throes of human desires and dignity and hate and love? It is that something in the soul which says, Rage on, Whirl on, I tread master here and everywhere, Master of the spasms of the sky and of the shatter of the sea, Master of nature and passion and death, And of all terror and all pain.

The American bards shall be marked for generosity and affection and for encouraging competitors . . . They shall be kosmos . . . without monopoly or secrecy . . . glad to pass any thing to any one . . . hungry for equals night and day. They shall not be careful of riches and privilege . . . . they shall be riches and privilege . . . . they shall perceive who the most affluent man is. The most affluent man is he that confronts all the shows he sees by equivalents out of the stronger wealth of himself. The American bard shall delineate no class of persons nor one or two out of the strata of interests nor love most nor truth most nor the soul most nor the body most . . . . and not be for the eastern states more than the western or the northern states more than the southern.

Exact science and its practical movements are no checks on the greatest poet but always his encouragement and support. The outset and remembrance are there . . . there the arms that lifted him first and brace him best . . . there he returns after all his goings and comings. The sailor and traveler . . . the anatomist chemist astronomer geologist phrenologist spiritualist mathematician historian and lexicographer are not poets, but they are the lawgivers of poets and their construction underlies the structure of every perfect poem. No matter what rises or is uttered they sent the seed of the conception of it . . . of them and by them stand the visible proofs of souls . . . . always of their fatherstuff must be begotten the sinewy races of bards. If there shall be love and content between the father and the son and if the greatness of the son is the exuding of the greatness of the father there shall be love between the poet and the man of demonstrable science. In the beauty of poems are the tuft and final applause of science.

Great is the faith of the flush of knowledge and of the investigation of the depths of qualities and things. Cleaving and circling here swells the soul of the poet yet is president of itself always. The depths are fathomless and therefore calm. The innocence and nakedness are resumed . . . they are neither modest nor immodest. The whole theory of the special and supernatural and all that was twined with it or educed out of it departs as a dream. What has ever happened . . . . what happens and whatever may or shall happen, the vital laws enclose all . . . . they are sufficient for any case and for all cases . . . none to be hurried or retarded . . . . any miracle of affairs or persons inadmissible in the vast clear scheme where every motion and every spear of grass and the frames and spirits of men and women and all that concerns them are unspeakably perfect miracles all referring to all and each distinct and in its place. It is also not consistent with the reality of the soul to admit that there is anything in the known universe more divine than men and women.

Men and women and the earth and all upon it are simply to be taken as they are, and the investigation of their past and present and future shall be unintermitted and shall be done with perfect candor. Upon this basis philosophy speculates ever looking toward the poet, ever regarding the eternal tendencies of all toward happiness never inconsistent with what is clear to the senses and to the soul. For the eternal tendencies of all toward happiness make the only point of sane philosophy. Whatever comprehends less than that . . . whatever is less than the laws of light and of astronomical motion . . . or less than the laws that follow the thief the liar the glutton and the drunkard through this life and doubtless afterward . . . . . or less than vast stretches of time or the slow formation of density or the patient upheaving of strata—is of no account. Whatever would put God in a poem or system of philosophy as contending against some being or influence is also of no account. Sanity and ensemble characterise the great master . . . spoilt in one principle all is spoilt. The great master has nothing to do with miracles. He sees health for himself in being one of the mass . . . . he sees the hiatus in singular eminence. To the perfect shape comes common ground. To be under the general law is great for that is to correspond with it. The master knows that he is unspeakably great and that all are unspeakably great . . . . that nothing for instance is greater than to conceive children and bring them up well . . . that to be is just as great as to perceive or tell.

In the make of the great masters the idea of political liberty is indispensible. Liberty takes the adherence of heroes wherever men

and women exist . . . . but never takes any adherence or welcome
from the rest more than from poets. They are the voice and exposition of liberty. They out of ages are worthy the grand idea . . . . to
them it is confided and they must sustain it. Nothing has precedence
of it and nothing can warp or degrade it. The attitude of great poets
is to cheer up slaves and horrify despots. The turn of their necks, the
sound of their feet, the motions of their wrists, are full of hazard to
the one and hope to the other. Come nigh them awhile and though
they neither speak or advise you shall learn the faithful American
lesson: Liberty is poorly served by men whose good intent is quelled
from one failure or two failures or any number of failures, or from
the casual indifference or ingratitude of the people, or from the
sharp show of the tushes of power, or the bringing to bear soldiers
and cannon or any penal statutes. Liberty relies upon itself, invites
no one, promises nothing, sits in calmness and light, is positive and
composed, and knows no discouragement. The battle rages with
many a loud alarm and frequent advance and retreat . . . . the enemy
triumphs . . . . the prison, the handcuffs, the iron necklace and anklet,
the scaffold, garrote and leadballs do their work . . . . the cause is
asleep . . . . the strong throats are choked with their own blood . . . .
the young men drop their eyelashes toward the ground when they
pass each other . . . . and is liberty gone out of that place? No never.
When liberty goes it is not the first to go nor the second or third
to go . . . it waits for all the rest to go . . . It is the last . . . When
the memories of the old martyrs are faded utterly away . . . . when
the large names of patriots are laughed at in the public halls from the
   lips of the orators . . . . when the boys are no more christened
after the same but christened after tyrants and traitors instead . . . .
when the laws of the free are grudgingly permitted and laws for
informers and bloodmoney are sweet to the taste of the people . . . .
when I and you walk abroad upon the earth stung with compassion
at the sight of numberless brothers answering our equal friendship
and calling no man master—and when we are elated with noble joy at
the sight of slaves . . . . when the soul retires in the cool communion
of the night and surveys its experience and has much extasy over the
word and deed that put back a helpless innocent person into the gripe
of the gripers or into any cruel inferiority . . . . when those in all parts
of these states who could easier realize the true American character

but do not yet—when the swarms of cringers, suckers, doughfaces, lice of politics, planners of sly involutions for their own preferment to city offices or state legislatures or the judiciary or congress or the presidency, obtain a response of love and natural deference from the people whether they get the offices or no . . . . when it is better to be a bound booby and rogue in office at a high salary than, the poorest free mechanic or farmer with his hat unmoved from his head and firm eyes and a candid and generous heart . . . . and when servility by town or state or the federal government or any oppression on a large scale or small scale can be tried on without its own punishment following duly after in exact proportion against the smallest chance of escape . . . . or rather when all life and all the souls of men and women are discharged from any part of the earth—then only shall the instinct of liberty be discharged from that part of the earth.

LOVE MEDICINE
(LOUISE ERDRICH)

"*Love Medicine* and the American Dream"
by Margaret J. Downes,
University of North Carolina at Asheville

The Chippewa Indians in Louise Erdrich's novel *Love Medicine* often replace the common "American Dream" with another dream, one more specific to Native Americans. Although some characters in *Love Medicine*'s two main families, the Kashpaws and the Lamartines, occasionally pursue the American Dream of success, wealth, and individual prestige, many of them instead embrace the dream of *belonging*—ultimately a less illusory goal, though it too proposes a difficult and complicated quest. When these Chippewa find real happiness, they find it among family and ancestors, back home on the reservation. The characters who do leave home and their native culture to chase the American Dream of worldly success find that the fragments of that dream they do temporarily capture are ultimately unsatisfying. Albertine, for example, runs away when she's a teenager; but when "she was in the city, all the daydreams she'd had were useless . . . . She had come here for some reason, but couldn't remember what that was" (168–69). When, as an adult, she leaves again, this time to become a doctor, her cousin remarks, "She had gotten all skinny and ragged haired . . . the way she was straining her mind didn't look too hopeful" (253).

These men and women, always seeking, show us again and again just where in our challenging human condition we can find some happy moments in our constant yearning for fulfillment. Erdrich's characters' contentment, their sense of self and spirituality, comes from their identification with their cultural group, especially their families; it's in that group that they find a dream fulfilled as much as any dream *can* be fulfilled. In *Love Medicine*, we know ourselves and find most happiness when we accept and share a common identity. It doesn't matter whether we define our "group" as the all-inclusive "brotherhood of man," or as our ethnic community present and past, or as our family. As Luther Standing Bear, a Oglala Sioux Indian Chief said, "Men must be born and reborn to belong. Their bodies must be born of the dust of their forefathers' bones."

Erdrich's characters' acknowledgement of this pervasive and satisfying sense of belonging emphasizes the author's thesis: "Love heals." Love is a medicine because the people it affects believe that it is. Their acceptance of this love-connection cancels their nightmare of isolation, and heals the wounds they receive while chasing the American Dream of individual gain and power. In knowing that they belong, *Love Medicine*'s Chippewa attain the best that any human beings can have: a sense of worth, shared with and nurtured by those who love them.

But though *Love Medicine*'s Chippewa love widely and deeply, their lives and these emotions are complicated. They also sometimes despair, and some of them become vengefully angry. Erdrich is careful to keep us from simplifying her characters' existences; she doesn't present us with stereotypical American Indians. As the American Indian Culture Research Center points out:

> It must be emphasized that no one person speaks for Indian People. There are over five hundred distinct American Indian Nations in the present United States. Each has its own language and history, its own sacred places and rituals. Each is rooted in and part of the land out of which it grew. (www.bluecloud.org/dakota.html)

Yet, the spirituality of Indian Nations generally includes a sense of kinship with all creation: all natural forces, and all beings, are brothers and sisters. Erdrich's men and women, though they're portrayed as individuals, are also portrayed as Indians in this sense. They're constantly pulled together as they intricately interrelate: they marry, they have children, they leave each other, they reunite, they fight, and they love. They affect each other as parts of an organic wholeness. Their relationships are, in fact, the forces that most clearly define who they are, and thus what kind of dream they attain in life.

Even the way that Erdrich begins *Love Medicine* and organizes its chapters reflects this intricate networking of human lives. Right at the beginning, before her list of chapter titles, she presents us with a two-page chart of the Kashpaw and Lamartine family trees, whose branches are bewilderingly intermingled with multiple marriages, "sexual affair[s] or liaison[s]," and children. It's somewhat confusing, and as the reader becomes involved in the unfolding stories it becomes necessary to flip back to this diagram of the characters' relationships. Similarly, the chapters themselves are subtitled by the name (or, in mid-chapter, sometimes a second name) of the person who is narrating that section. Though Erdrich skillfully characterizes each individual, it's easy to become confused about who's who because they're all talking about each other, and all telling us the same stories, but from different points of view. Stories in the earlier chapters (for example, Marie Lazarre's bizarre experiences in the convent) are retold toward the end, or in the middle—and thus we get the impression that time for them is a wholeness rather than a linear progression. The very structure of this book reflects its author's theme that any happiness we might find comes to us through unification. *Love Medicine*'s organizational elements, like its characters' lives, overlap and pull together toward a common center and completion—toward a *home*.

The novel is framed by that very important word, *home*. The novel's opening section, describing June Kashpaw's tragic death in the deep snow, ends with this theme-setting, one-sentence paragraph: "The snow fell deeper that Easter than it had in forty years, but June walked over it like water and came home" (7). Erdrich then finishes her book with this same word, as Lipsha Morrissey, June's son, now finally acknowledged by his father, and musing about old relatives and ancient waters, says this: "The morning was clear. A good road led on. So there was nothing to do but cross the water, and bring her home." The *her* here is ambiguous: it could be his car, or, more likely in this novel about love and spiritual connectedness, it could be his mother, June. Lipsha at this point has found fulfill-ment of *his* dream by having connected with his dad, and being assured that they do truly love one another. Like June, Lipsha had left home; and like June, he finally heads for home, crossing the water— as heroes in their archetypal journeys always do, when they leave, and when they return.

The characters in *Love Medicine* (Lipsha and June included) are well aware of the attractions of the American Dream, and do sometimes chase it. They're especially proud of their cars, those major symbols of American achievement. Henry Lamartine, for example, whose spirit was devastated by his service as a U.S. Marine in Vietnam, is almost revived by his interest in his brother Lyman's car—the first convert-ible on the reservation, a red Olds (181). When Henry drowns in the river, Lyman heads that car toward the water, and watches it go under. Without his brother, even a red Olds means nothing; that prime, proud sign of the American Dream is suddenly paltry and meaning-less. Similarly, King Kashpaw loves his brand-new sports car; but even it can't overcome his sense of failure, any more than his unhappy marriage to Lynette can ("that white girl," his mother calls her [15]).

Beverly Lamartine also is unhappily married to a white woman, "a natural blond" whose family admires Beverly's "perfect tan," one of the more superficial signs of the "white man's American Dream" (111). He chases that American Dream in the Twin Cities, where "there were great relocation opportunities for Indians with a certain amount of natural stick-to-it-iveness and pride":

> He worked devilishly hard. Door to door, he'd sold children's after-school home workbooks for the past eighteen years.... Beverly's territory was a small-town world of earnest dreamers.... His son played baseball in a sparkling-white uniform stained across the knees with grass. (109-10)

But when Beverly, who's thirsting for love more than for money, returns to the reservation to claim the boy he believes is his second son, he's quickly re-enchanted by Lulu Nanapush Lamartine. Lulu is the boy's mother, Beverly's ex-lover and his brother Henry's widow; and Beverly finds he just can't leave.

Nector Kashpaw is another man enchanted by Lulu (she has many lovers, in her long and happy life). He's sometimes caught between the attractions of the American Dream, and those of love and tribal fellowship. On the reservation, he tells us, "I got everything handed to me on a plate. It came from being a Kashpaw . . . . Our family was respected as the last hereditary leaders of this tribe" (122). The White Americans wanted him, as well, but they wanted him to play the imaginary Indian roles in their version of the American Dream, where the Cowboys always win. Picked out from his high school graduating class by a talent scout, Nestor was hired as a Hollywood extra "for the wagon-train scenes" :

> I got hired for the biggest Indian part. But they didn't know I was a Kashpaw, because right off I had to die. "Clutch your chest. Fall off that horse," they directed. That was it. Death was the extent of Indian acting in the movie theater. So I thought it was quite enough to be killed the once you have to die in this life, and I quit. (123)

He was picked to play other Indian roles, too, in that American Dream. "Take off your clothes!" a "snaggle-toothed" old artist tells him, so she can paint his picture:

> *Plunge of the Brave*, was the title of it . . . . It would hang in the Bismarck state capitol. There I was, jumping off a cliff, naked of course, down into a rocky river. Certain death . . . . When I saw that the greater world was only interested in my doom, I went home. (123-24)

Nestor's most devastating involvement with the American Dream nearly causes him to lose Lulu's love forever. He's tribal chairman, his kids are educated, his wife Marie is proud that she's now solid class, thanks to his political accomplishments. But his pride in his position leads Nestor to allow the tribal council to take over Lulu's land as "the one perfect place to locate a factory" (138). Lulu's home, posted as government property, is accidentally burned to the ground; soon afterwards, the factory is built on that site. "Here were the government

Indians ordering their own people off the land of their forefathers to build a modern factory," says Lulu:

> Indian against Indian, that's how the government's money offer made us act.... To make it worse, it was a factory that made equipment of false value. Keepsake things like bangle beads and plastic war clubs. A load of foolishness, that was. Dreamstuff. (283)

She rails at the tribal council for betraying the Indian dream of having land, and for having substituted for that fulfillment the humiliating image of the Indian that's allowed in the standard American Dream:

> It was the stuff of dreams, I said. The cheap false longing that makes your money-grubbing tongues hang out. The United States government throws crumbs on the floor, and you go down so far as to lick up those dollars that you turn your own people off the land. I got mad. "What's that but *ka-ka?*" I yelled at them. "False value!" I said to them that this tomahawk factory mocked us all. (284)

Lyman Lamartine organizes that factory, hiring job applicants from the tribe's clans and families in a fair and orderly way, so as to keep the peace and assure steady production. Lulu and Marie, once arch-rivals and now feisty old friends, work side-by-side there as instructors and consultants. But their disagreement, triggered by the intensity of traditional family relationships and feuds, ultimately leads to havoc in the factory. "I felt the balance of the whole operation totter . . . away from me," Lyman says, as Marie Kashpaw grandly walks away from an insult he foolishly thrusts at her. "The factory was both light and momentous now, a house of twigs. *One slight tap,* I realized" (316). Thanks to a drunken Lipsha Morrissey, the factory blows up, and chaos descends, demolishing the whole enterprise. "It ran like a machine made to disassemble itself," Lyman remarks. "Standing among the rapid disintegrations, in a dream, I felt myself rewinding, too" (320). Quickly, then, he sinks into self-pity and alcohol.

Erdrich doesn't avoid the fact that drinking is a big problem on the reservation. While martinis may create for the white middle-class an illusion of participating in the American Dream, the grain alcohol consumed by so many of Erdrich's characters simply devastates them. Gordie Kashpaw, for example, still deeply mourning his wife June's death, "saw clearly that the setup of life was rigged and he was trapped" (220). In despair, he drinks himself into a stupor. Similarly, Henry Lamartine, who no longer can be touched (literally or figuratively) by those who love him, finds drunkenness the quickest way to escape the awful and abandoned self he had become in Vietnam.

Even the God of the Christians, the Generous Father in the American Dream, seems to have turned a deaf ear to the Chippewa. "HAIL MARIE FULL OF GRACE," yells old Nestor Kashpaw at church. "God don't hear me otherwise," he says, and his grandson Lipsha realizes there is terrible truth in this: "I knew this was perfectly right and for years not one damn other person had noticed it. God's been going deaf . . . . Our Gods aren't perfect," he points out, "but at least they come around. They'll do a favor if you ask them right. You don't have to yell. But . . . to ask proper was an art that was lost to the Chippewas once the Catholics gained ground" (236).

"Maybe," Lipsha realizes, "we got nothing but ourselves. And that's not much." Immediately upon that realization, Lipsha thinks of things he wants to do to help his family, "to help some people like my Grandpa and Grandma Kashpaw get back some happiness within the tail ends of their lives" (237). The "love medicine" he prepares for them then works. Although Lipsha knows it's fake, even after Grandpa Kashpaw's death from choking on the medicine, he refuses to leave his wife, whose love keeps him present. "Love medicine ain't what brings him back to you, Grandma," Lipsha says. "It's true feeling, not no magic" (257). That fragile web of love in life, with all its twists and turns, ends up stronger than death. Rather than the elusive American Dream, it is the Chippewas' life-giving, love-based dream, forged in the torments and trials of life, that fulfills Erdrich's characters. When old Nestor dies, "[a]ll the blood children and the took-ins, like me," says Lipsha, "came home from Minneapolis and Chicago . . . . The family kneeling down turned to rocks in a field. It struck me how strong and reliable grief was, and death. Until the end of time, death would be our rock" (253). Death is very much a part of life, and even the dead are reminded that their people are their *home*. Lulu, still mourning her drowned son Henry, affirms that faith: "I broke custom very often and spoke Henry Junior's name, out loud, on my tongue. I wanted him to know, if he heard, that he still had a home" (295).

Part of the American Dream is the Frontier Dream, the dream of being a strong individual who can get past all the fences of convention and tradition, and can make it alone. It's an American concept, a sense that it is our birthright to recreate ourselves as the men and women that we want to be: to transform ourselves into new and improved beings, unencumbered by our pasts. For *Love Medicine*'s Chippewa, however, the American Dream of moving to someplace far away is a nightmare, a bad dream that some in their tribe were forced into by the Federal Government. Although *all* the land once belonged to the Indians, they realize, the Government takes what it wants, and pushes the Indians west. As Albertine points out, "When allotments were handed out[,] . . . most were deeded parcels far off, in Montana" (18).

Yet these Chippewa can sometimes grab (or almost grab) a piece of the "American Pie." King Kashpaw, frustrated with his life in the Twin Cities, says, "Every time I work my way up—say I'm next in line for the promotion—they shaft me . . . . Entry level. Stuck down at the bottom with the minnows." But he's convinced that he'll make it: "I'm gonna rise," he says. "One day I'm gonna rise. They can't keep down the Indians" (346).

Interestingly, *Love Medicine* offers us two roads to that rising in life. One way, a way into the American Dream, is discovered by Lyman after his Indian souvenir factory is destroyed. He declares:

> It was time, high past time the Indians smartened up and started using the only leverage they had—federal law . . . . *Bingo! Bingo!* Not only that, go on from there. Try gambling casino . . . . Gambling fit into the old traditions, chance was kind of an old-time thing . . . . Jazz these hand games up with lights and clinkers and you put in shag carpet and you got a Chippewa casino . . . . Money was the key to assimilating, so Indians were taught. Why not make a money business out of money itself? . . . . He saw the future, and it was based on greed and luck. (326-28)

The other way to rise (and a way to have a second chance to win, if the casinos fail) is the dream that's realized in the life that Lulu's boys have found and that all the Chippewa know about: "Lulu's boys had grown into a kind of pack. They always hung together," Erdrich writes:

> Clearly they were of one soul. Handsome, rangy, wildly various, they were bound in total loyalty, not by oath but by the simple, unquestioning belongingness of part of one organism. (118)

The "belongingness" is the secret to the Chippewa dream. Albertine Johnson failed to make the American Dream come true, and for a time she came back to the reservation. During her time at home she's happy and content as she works alongside her mother and aunt, making "beautiful pies—rhubarb, wild Juneberry, apple, and gooseberry, all fruits preserved by Grandma Kashpaw or my mother or Aurelia" (13). The Chippewa in *Love Medicine* keep coming home. They find the rewards of belongingness sometimes are flawed, but its dream makes them happy. Far more happy, Erdrich shows us, than their chasing the mythical and elusive American Dream.

WORKS CITED AND BIBLIOGRAPHY

American Indian Culture Research Center. http://www.bluecloud.org/dakota.html

Bancroft-Hunt, Norman, Werner Forman, photog. *People of the Totem: The Indians of the Pacific Northwest.* Norman: U of Oklahoma P, 1979.

Basil, Johnston. *Ojibway Heritage.* Lincoln: U of Nebraska, 1990.

Benedict, Ruth F. *The Concept of the Guardian Spirit in North America.* 1923, rpt. New York: Kraus Reprinting, 1970.

Brown, Dee. *Bury My Heart at Wounded Knee: An Indian History of the American West.* New York: Henry Holt, 1970.

Brown, Joseph Epes, and Nicholas Black Elk. *The Sacred Pipe.* Norman: U of Oklahoma P, 1953; Baltimore: Penguin, 1971.

Brown, Joseph Epes. *The Spiritual Legacy of the American Indian.* Lebanon, PA: Sowers, 1970.

Densmore, Frances. *Chippewa Customs.* Minnesota Historical Society P, 1979.

Erdrich, Louise. *Love Medicine.* New York: Henry Holt, 1984.

Luther Standing Bear. http://www.powersource.com/gallery/people/luther.html

Mails, Thomas E. *Dog Soldiers, Bear Men, and Buffalo Women: A Study of the Societies and Cults of the Plains Indians*. Englewood Cliffs: Prentice-Hall, 1973.

Native Languages of the Americas: Native American Cultures. http://www. native-languages.org/home.htm#links

Native Web. http://www.nativeweb.org/

Ojibwe History. http://www.tolatsga.org/ojib.html

OF MICE AND MEN
(JOHN STEINBECK)

❧

Of Mice and Men
by Peter Lisca,
in *The Wide World of John Steinbeck* (1958)

INTRODUCTION

Of Mice and Men, John Steinbeck takes a hard look at America, the land of dreams, and shows not only how those of lowly estate dream of a better tomorrow but also how they suffer in modern American society. In focusing on Lennie's dream of the farm, Peter Lisca provides a thorough examination of *Of Mice and Men,* exploring Steinbeck's articulated intentions, the book's realistic elements, its allegorical nature, and formal patterns. Lisca shows how the American Dream is embodied in the book's characters and how this dream, forever elusive, is a source of American tragedy.

☙

Concerning the book's theme, Steinbeck wrote his agents, "I'm sorry that you do not find the new book as large in subject as it should be. I probably did not make my subjects and my symbols clear. The micro-

Lisca, Peter. "*Of Mice and Men.*" *The Wide World of John Steinbeck.* New Brunswick, NJ: Rutgers UP, 1958. 130–43.

cosm is rather difficult to handle and apparently I did not get it over—
the earth longings of a Lennie who was not to represent insanity at
all but the inarticulate and powerful yearning of all men . . ." To Ben
Abramson he wrote a similar comment on the book's theme: " . . . it's
a study of the dreams and pleasures of everyone in the world." (JS-BA,
ca. September, 1936).

Such words as "microcosm," "of all men," and "everyone in the
world" indicate that the problems he has set himself in *Of Mice and
Men* was similar to that he had solved in his previous novel, *In Dubious
Battle*. But whereas in the earlier work the de-personalized protagonists were easily absorbed into a greater pattern because that pattern
was physically present in the novel, in *Of Mice and Men* the protagonists are projected against a very thin background and must suggest or
create this larger pattern through their own particularity. To achieve
this, Steinbeck makes use of language, action, and symbol as recurring
motifs. All three of these motifs are presented in the opening scene,
are contrapuntally developed through the story, and come together
again at the end.

The first symbol in the novel, and the primary one, is the little spot
by the river where the story begins and ends. The book opens with
a description of this place by the river, and we first see George and
Lennie as they enter this place from the highway to an outside world.
It is significant that they prefer spending the night here rather than
going on to the bunkhouse at the ranch.

Steinbeck's novels and stories often contain groves, willow thickets
by a river, and caves which figure prominently in the action. There are,
for example, the grove in *To a God Unknown*, the place by the river
in the Junius Maltby story, the two caves and a willow thicket in *The
Grapes of Wrath*, the cave under the bridge in *In Dubious Battle*, the
caves in *The Wayward Bus*, and the thicket and cave in *The Pearl*. For
George and Lennie, as for other Steinbeck heroes, coming to a cave or
thicket by the river symbolizes a retreat from the world to a primeval
innocence. Sometimes, as in *The Grapes of Wrath*, this retreat has
explicit overtones of a return to the womb and rebirth. In the opening
scene of *Of Mice and Men* Lennie twice mentions the possibility of
hiding out in a cave, and George impresses on him that he must
return to this thicket by the river when there is trouble.

While the cave or the river thicket is a "safe place," it is physically impossible to remain there, and this symbol of primeval innocence becomes translated into terms possible in the real world. For George and Lennie it becomes "a little house an' a couple of acres." Out of this translation grows a second symbol, the rabbits, and this symbol serves several purposes. Through synecdoche it comes to stand for the "safe place" itself, making a much more easily manipulated symbol than the "house an' a couple of acres." Also, through Lennie's love for the rabbits Steinbeck is able not only to dramatize Lennie's desire for the "safe place," but to define the basis of that desire on a very low level of consciousness—the attraction to soft, warm fur, which is for Lennie the most important aspect of their plans.

This transference of symbolic value from the farm to the rabbits is important also because it makes possible the motif of action. This is introduced in the first scene by the dead mouse which Lennie is carrying in his pocket (much as Tom carries the turtle in *The Grapes of Wrath*). As George talks about Lennie's attraction to mice, it becomes evident that the symbolic rabbits will come to the same end—crushed by Lennie's simple, blundering strength. Thus Lennie's killing of mice and later his killing of the puppy set up a pattern which the reader expects to be carried out again. George's story about Lennie and the little girl with the red dress, which he tells twice, contributes to this expectancy of pattern, as do the shooting of Candy's dog, the crushing of Curley's hand, and the frequent appearances of Curley's wife. All these incidents are patterns of the action motif and predict the fate of the rabbits and thus the fate of the dream of a "safe place."

The third motif, that of language, is also present, in the opening scene. Lennie asks George, "Tell me—like you done before," and George's words are obviously in the nature of a ritual. "George's voice became deeper. He repeated his words rhythmically, as though he had said them many times before." The element of ritual is stressed by the fact that even Lennie has heard it often enough to remember its precise language: "*An' live off the fatta the lan'* . . . . An' have *rabbits*. Go on George! Tell about what we're gonna have in the garden and about the rabbits in the cages and about . . . ." This ritual is performed often in the story, whenever Lennie feels insecure. And of course it is while Lennie is caught up in this dream vision that George shoots him, so that on one level the vision is accomplished—the dream never interrupted, the rabbits never crushed.

The highly patterned effect achieved by these incremental motifs of symbol, action, and language is the knife edge on which criticism of *Of Mice and Men* divides. For although Steinbeck's success in creating a pattern has been acknowledged, criticism has been divided as to the effect of this achievement. On one side, it is claimed that this strong patterning creates a sense of contrivance and mechanical action,[1] and on the other, that the patterning actually gives a meaningful design to the story, a tone of classic fate.[2] What is obviously needed here is some objective critical tool for determining under what conditions a sense of inevitability (to use a neutral word) should be experienced, as mechanical contrivance, and when it should be experienced as catharsis effected by a sense of fate. Such a tool cannot be forged within the limits of this study; but it is possible to examine the particular circumstances of *Of Mice and Men* more closely before passing judgment.

Although the three motifs of symbol, action, and language build up a strong pattern of inevitability, the movement is not unbroken. About midway in the novel (chapters 3 and 4) there is set up a countermovement which seems to threaten the pattern. Up to this point the dream of "a house an' a couple of acres" seemed impossible of realization. Now it develops that George has an actual farm in mind (ten acres), knows the owners and why they want to sell it: "The ol' people that owns it is flat bust an' the ol' lady needs an operation." He even knows the price—"six hundred dollars." Also, the old workman, Candy, is willing to buy a share in the dream with the three hundred dollars he has saved up. It appears that at the end of the month George and Lennie will have another hundred dollars and that quite possibly they "could swing her for that." In the following chapter this dream and its possibilities are further explored through Lennie's visit with Crooks, the power of the dream manifesting itself in Crooks's conversion from cynicism to optimism. But at the very height of his conversion the mice symbol reappears in the form of Curley's wife, who threatens the dream by bringing with her the harsh realities of the outside world and by arousing Lennie's interest.

The function of Candy's and Crooks's interest and the sudden bringing of the dream within reasonable possibility is to interrupt, momentarily, the pattern of inevitability. But, and this is very important, Steinbeck handles this interruption so that it does not actually reverse the situation. Rather, it insinuates a possibility. Thus, though working against the pattern, this countermovement makes that pattern more credible by creating the necessary ingredient of free will. The story achieves power through a delicate balance of the protagonists' free will and the force of circumstance.

In addition to imposing a sense of inevitability, this strong patterning of events performs the important function of extending the story's range of meanings. This can best be understood by reference to Hemingway's "fourth dimension," which has been defined by Joseph Warren Beach as an "aesthetic factor" achieved by the protagonists' repeated participation in some traditional "ritual or strategy,"[3] and by Malcolm Cowley as "the almost continual performance of rites and ceremonies" suggesting recurrent patterns of human experience.[4] The incremental motifs of symbol, action, and language which inform *Of Mice and Men* have precisely these effects. The simple story of two migrant workers' dream of a safe retreat, a "clean well-lighted place," becomes itself a pattern of archetype which exists on three levels.

There is the obvious story level on a realistic plane, with its shocking climax. There is also the level of social protest, Steinbeck the reformer crying out against the exploitation of migrant workers. The third level is an allegorical one, its interpretation limited only by the ingenuity of the audience. It could be, as Carlos Baker suggests, "an allegory of Mind and Body."[5] Using the same kind of dichotomy, the story could also be about the dumb, clumsy, but strong mass of humanity and its shrewd manipulators. This would make the book a more abstract treatment of the two forces of *In Dubious Battle*—the mob and its leaders. The dichotomy could also be that of the unconscious and the conscious, the id and the ego, or any other forces or qualities which have the same structural relationship to each other that do Lennie and George. It is interesting in this connection that the name Leonard means "strong or brave as a lion," and that the name George means "husbandman."

The title itself, however, relates the whole story to still another level which is implicit in the context of Burns's poem.

But, Mousie, thou art no thy lane,
In proving foresight may be vain:

The best laid schemes o' mice an' men
Gang aft a-gley
An' lea'e us nought but grief an' pain
For promis'd joy.

In the poem, Burns extends the mouse's experience to include that
of mankind; in *Of Mice and Men*, Steinbeck extends the experience
of two migrant workers to the human condition. "This is the way
things are," both writers are saying. On this level, perhaps the most
important, Steinbeck is dramatizing the non-teleological philosophy
which had such a great part in shaping *In Dubious Battle* and which
would be fully discussed in *Sea of Cortez*. This level of meaning is
indicated by the title originally intended for the book—"Something
That Happened."[6] In this light, the ending of the story is, like the
ploughman's disrupting of the mouse's nest, neither tragic nor brutal,
but simply a part of the pattern of events. It is amusing in this regard
that a Hollywood director suggested to Steinbeck that someone else
kill the girl, so that sympathy could be kept with Lennie. (JS-MO,
3/?/38)

In addition to these meanings which grow out of the book's
"pattern," there is what might be termed a subplot which defines
George's concern with Lennie. It is easily perceived that George, the
"husbandman," is necessary to Lennie; but it has not been pointed
out that Lennie is just as necessary to George. Without an explanation of this latter relationship, any allegory posited on the pattern
created in *Of Mice and Men* must remain incomplete. Repeatedly,
George tells Lennie, "God, you're a lot of trouble. I could get
along so easy and so nice if I didn't have you on my tail." But this
getting along so easy never means getting a farm of his own. With
one important exception, George never mentions the dream except
for Lennie's benefit. That his own "dream" is quite different from
Lennie's is established early in the novel and often repeated: "God
a'mighty, if I was alone I could live so easy. I could go get a job an'
work, an' no trouble. No mess at all, and when the end of the month
come I could take my fifty bucks and go into town and get whatever
I want. Why, I could stay in a cat house all night. I could eat any
place I want, hotel or anyplace, and order any damn thing I could
think of. An' I could do all that every damn month. Get a gallon

whiskey, or set in a pool room and play cards or shoot pool." Lennie has heard this from George so often that in the last scene, when he realizes that he has "done another bad thing," he asks, "Ain't you gonna give me hell? . . . Like, 'If I didn't have you I'd take my fifty bucks—'."

Almost every character in the story asks George why he goes around with Lennie—the foreman, Curley, Slim, and Candy. Crooks, the lonely Negro, doesn't ask George, but he does speculate about it, and shrewdly—"a guy talkin' to another guy and it don't make no difference if he don't hear or understand. The thing is, they're talkin' . . . ." George's explanations vary from outright lies to a simple statement of "We travel together." It is only to Slim, the superior workman with "God-like eyes," that he tells a great part of the truth. Among several reasons, such as his feeling of responsibility for Lennie in return for the latter's unfailing loyalty, and their having grown up together, there is revealed another: "He's dumb as hell, but he ain't crazy. An' I ain't so bright neither, or I wouldn't be buckin' barley for my fifty and found. If I was even a little bit smart, I'd have my own little place, an' I'd be bringin' in my own crops, 'stead of doin' all the work and not getting what comes up outa the ground."

This statement, together with George's repeatedly expressed desire to take his fifty bucks to a cat house and his continual playing of solitaire, reveals that to some extent George needs Lennie as a rationalization for his failure. This is one of the reasons why, after the body of Curley's wife is discovered, George refuses Candy's offer of a partnership which would make the dream a reality and says to him, "I'll work my month an' I'll take my fifty bucks an' I'll stay all night in some lousy cat house. Or I'll set in some poolroom till ever'body goes home. An' then I'll come back an' work another month an' I'll have fifty bucks more." The dream of the farm originates with Lennie and it is only through Lennie, who also makes the dream impossible, that the dream has any meaning for George. An understanding of this dual relationship will do much to mitigate the frequent charge that Steinbeck's depiction of George's attachment is concocted of pure sentimentality. At the end of the novel, George's going off with Slim to "do the town" is more than an escape from grief. It is an ironic and symbolic twist to his dream.

NOTES

1. Mark Van Doren, "Wrong Number," *The Nation*, 144 (March 6, 1937). p. 275; also, Joseph Wood Krutch, *American Drama Since 1918* (New York, 1939), p. 396.

2. Stark Young, "Drama Critics Circle Award," *The New Republic*, 94 (May 4, 1938), p. 396; also, Frank H. O'Hara, *Today in American Drama* (Chicago, 1939), p. 181.

3. "How Do You Like It Now, Gentlemen?" *Sewanee Review*, 59 (Spring, 1953.), pp. 311–328.

4. "Introduction," *The Portable Hemingway* (New York, 1944).

5. Carlos Baker, "Steinbeck of California," *Delphian Quarterly*, 23 (April, 1940), 42.

6. Toni Jackson Ricketts [Antonia Seixas], "John Steinbeck and the Non-Teleological Bus," *What's Doing on the Monterey Peninsula*, 3. (March, 1947). This article is now available in *Steinbeck and His Critics*, ed. by E. W. Tedlock, Jr., and C. V. Wicker (Albuquerque, 1957).

MY ÁNTONIA
(WILLA CATHER)

❧ ❧

"*My Ántonia* and the American Dream"
by James E. Miller, Jr.,
in *Prairie Schooner* (1974)

INTRODUCTION

In "*My Ántonia* and the American Dream," James Miller considers Willa Cather's novel as a work appreciated for the wrong reasons. He explains that *My Ántonia* reveals much about the disparity between the American Dream and the American experience as pioneers settled westward during the late nineteenth century. Miller contends that Cather's novel shares the concerns of F. Scott Fitzgerald's *The Great Gatsby* and William Carlos Williams' epic poem *Paterson*. These works all question how and when Americans lost touch with the dream for a better world. Jim Burden, the narrator and protagonist of *My Ántonia*, has attained material success and achieved the American Dream, yet he continues to look back to his time on the prairie, seeking the vitality he lost in his quest for prosperity. Like Fitzgerald and Williams, Cather meditates upon the sense of incompleteness, feelings of loss, and lack of

---

Miller, James E., Jr. "*My Ántonia* and the American Dream." *Prairie Schooner* 48, no. 2 (Summer 1974): 112–23.

fulfillment that often plague those who strive for worldly success.

∽⨯∾

Some books in our literature, like Walt Whitman's *Leaves of Grass* and Herman Melville's *Moby-Dick*, like F. Scott Fitzgerald's *The Great Gatsby* and Ernest Hemingway's *The Sun also Rises*, assume a greater importance in our culture than their literary merit seems (at least at first glance) to justify. These are usually books that appear to reveal more about ourselves, our dreams and our despairs, than we had ever before recognized. Frequently these books are neglected on first appearance, or valued for reasons quite other than those that give them their later fame. It is quite possible that the authors wrote out of intense personal feeling and passion that had very little, at least on the conscious level, to do with the meanings we have come to recognize as the chief and enduring value of the books.

I would like to examine Willa Cather's *My Ántonia*[1] as a book of this kind, offering perhaps an explanation for the way it often clings tenaciously in the mind, and even comes to haunt the reader long after he has put it down. Like the Fitzgerald and Hemingway novels, *My Ántonia* is, I believe, a commentary on the American experience, the American dream, and the American reality. It is the novel, after *Alexander's Bridge*, *O Pioneers!*, and *The Song of the Lark*, in which Willa Cather hit her stride in her own native material, and, in it, she penetrated more deeply, I think, into the dark recesses of the American psyche than in any of her later novels—though some of them might be more richly and complexly woven.

I would like to begin with an aspect of *My Ántonia* that helps burn it into the memory. Willa Cather in effect commented on the technique within the book, when she had Jim Burden say near the end, after his final visit to Ántonia on the Nebraska prairie: "Ántonia had always been one to leave images in the mind that did not fade—that grew stronger with time. In my memory there was a succession of such pictures, fixed there like the old woodcuts of one's first primer" (pp. 352–53). It takes little imagination to transfer this statement to the novel itself, as we recall the strong and vivid images that it creates over and over again, usually in a few simple and seemingly effortless strokes.

One of these brilliant images stands in the heart of the book, and comes at the end of "The Hired Girls," the idyl placed near the end of Book II. That this episode represents also the emotional heart of the book is suggested by its derivation from the earlier 1909 story, "The Enchanted Bluff"—a story which, as Mildred Bennett has pointed out in her Introduction to *Willa Cather's Collected Short Fiction, 1892–1912*, filters with emotional intensity through much of Cather's fiction. Jim Burden and the girls have spent the day out on the embankment of the prairie river, and as they seat themselves on a height overlooking the lands that have both threatened and succored them, they begin to talk about the future and the past. They fall slowly silent: "The breeze sank to stillness. In the ravine a ringdove mourned plaintively, and somewhere off in the bushes an owl hooted" (p. 244). Gradually the land itself becomes transfigured before their very eyes:

> Presently we saw a curious thing: There were no clouds, the sun was going down in a limpid, gold-washed sky. Just as the lower edge of the red disk rested on the high fields against the horizon, a great black figure suddenly appeared on the face of the sun. We sprang to our feet, straining our eyes toward it. In a moment we realized what it was. On some upland farm, a plough had been left standing in the field. The sun was sinking just behind it. Magnified across the distance by the horizontal light, it stood out against the sun, was exactly contained within the circle of the disk; the handles, the tongue, the share—black against the molten red. There it was, heroic in size, a picture writing on the sun.
>
> Even while we whispered about it, our vision disappeared; the ball dropped and dropped until the red tip went beneath the earth. The fields below us were dark, the sky was growing pale, and that forgotten plough had sunk back to its own littleness somewhere on the prairie. [P. 245]

Most readers of *My Ántonia* have that black plow silhouetted against the red sun deeply etched in their minds. And they are likely to remember its heroic size and its hieroglyphic nature as a "picture writing on the sun"—as though left by some primitive race of giants who lived long ago in a heroic age and left their enigmatic mark and their obscure meaning in a scrawl on the heavenly body that served as their deity. But you will have noticed that I have quoted the paragraph that follows this vivid and suggestive imagery, describing simply the disappearance of the "vision." The plow that was a moment before so heroic and full of hidden meaning suddenly sinks back "to its own littleness somewhere on the prairie," and becomes "forgotten."

Too often, I suspect, we remember only that hieroglyphic plow etched into the sun, and forget Willa Cather's description of its swift shrinkage and disappearance, both from sight and from memory. In these succeeding images, we are, I want to suggest, near the heart not only of the book but of its hieroglyphic meaning. The novel is, in some sense, about a national experience—the frontier or pioneer experience—and its rapid diminishment and disappearance from the national memory. But more than an experience is involved and at stake. Obscurely related to the experience and its consequences is the American dream. Was it a trivial or mistaken impulse all along, magnified in the imagination beyond its possibilities? Was it a reality that was in some blundering way betrayed by us all? Or was it, perhaps, an illusion, created out of nothing, and, finally, disappearing into nothing, and well forgotten. I do not want to suggest that *My Ántonia* provides precise answers for these questions, inasmuch as it is a novel and not a tract. But I do want to indicate that the novel evokes these questions and explores them dramatically, leaving the reader to struggle with his own answers.

The image of the plow first magnified and then shrunken and then obliterated may stand as a paradigm for a recurrent pattern in *My Ántonia*, embodied most strikingly in the narrator, Jim Burden. For Jim the book might be described as a search for that lost and forgotten plow, or better, perhaps, a quest for understanding the experience that caused the plow to magnify into a brilliant presence, and then to fade into insignificance and triviality. In brief, Jim is in search of the American past, his past, in an attempt to determine what went wrong, and perhaps as well what was right, with the dream. His is an attempt to read that "picture writing on the sun," and unravel the reasons for his own, and his country's anguished sense of loss. His loss is personal, because he, like the plow, once glowed in the sun and felt the expansion of life within him, life with all its promise and possibilities. But by the time we encounter him as the nostalgic narrator of *My Ántonia*, his life has diminished and faded, and he himself seems to feel the dark descend.

But of course no one with the name of Jim Burden could be a totally *un*allegorical figure. He carries with him not only his acute sense of personal loss but also a deep sense of national unease, a *burden* of guilt for having missed a chance, for having passed up an opportunity, for having watched with apathy as the dream dissipated in the rapidly disappearing past. The social burden may be all the heavier for Jim Burden because he has assigned himself the task of spokesman in the quest for what went wrong, or, better, what was missed, at a crucial moment of the national history. With him as the narrator of the book, we find out nearly everything about his past, but almost nothing about his present. The novel's "Introduction" provides one glimpse into his current unhappy state, given by his long-time friend and fellow Nebraskan: "Although Jim Burden and I both live in New York, I do not see much of him there. He is legal counsel for one of the great Western railways and is often away from his office for weeks together. That is one reason why we seldom meet. Another is that I do not like his wife. She is handsome, energetic, executive, but to me she seems unimpressionable and temperamentally incapable of enthusiasm. Her husband's quiet tastes irritate her, I think, and she finds it worth while to play the patroness to a group of young poets and painters of advanced ideas and mediocre ability. She has her own fortune and lives her own life. For some reason, she wishes to remain Mrs. James Burden" (p. viii).

Although the glimpse is brief, it is sufficient to reveal an empty marriage, an artificial, even superficial, and trivialized life. Mrs. James Burden is destined to remain a shadowy character throughout the novel, but even so an important if only hovering presence, contrasting sharply in her vacuous super-sophistication with the women of the novel's action, and particularly with Jim's—or "my"—Ántonia. For it is she, the writer of the "Introduction" tells us, who has come to mean "the country, the conditions, the whole adventure" of their childhood. Thus as Jim recreates the story of his and, in part, the country's past, he envisions it through the disillusion of his—and, in part, his country's—unhappy present. It is, perhaps, only such disillusionment that enables Jim to recount the past without falsifying the brutalizing nature of the pioneer experience. All the first book of *My Ántonia*,

entitled "The Shimerdas," is filled with animal imagery which suggests
the diminishment of the lives of the people who have left their coun-
tries, their civilizations, their cultures behind and who have been
reduced to confronting a hostile environment much as the animals
confront it, scratching and scrabbling for the barest necessities of life
itself. If the plow silhouetted against the sun somehow encompasses
the free and open spirit embodied in Ántonia, it must be remembered
that that plow also was the lure and background that ended in the
suicide of old Mr. Shimerda and which turned Mrs. Shimerda into
an envious scold and soured Ántonia's brother, Ambrosch, into a
sullen sneak and brute. Many other lesser characters were demeaned
and hardened by their cruel experiences. The entire first part of *My
Ántonia* is remarkable for nostalgically evoking the past without blurring its harshness and its brutalizing weight. Ántonia is thus all the
more remarkable for preserving her free and generous spirit in the face
of all the crushing blows of the virgin prairie experience.

Thus *My Ántonia* does not portray, in any meaningful sense, the
fulfillment of the American dream. By and large, the dreams of the
pioneers lie shattered, their lives broken by the hardness of wilderness
life. Even those who achieve, after long struggle, some kind of secure
life are diminished in the genuine stuff of life. For example, in one of
his accounts that reach into the future beyond the present action, Jim
Burden tells us of the eventual fate of the vivacious Tiny Soderball,
one of the few to achieve "solid worldly success." She had a series of
exciting adventures in Alaska, ending up with a large fortune. But
later, when Jim encountered her in Salt Lake City, she was a "thin,
hard-faced woman . . . . She was satisfied with her success, but not
elated. She was like someone in whom the faculty of becoming interested is worn out" (pp. 301–302).

One of the major material successes of the book is Jim Burden, and
in many ways the novel traces his rise in position and wealth. As most
of the characters of the book travel west, his is a journey east, and, in
the process, the acquisition of education, wealth, social position. In
short, Jim has all the appearances of one who has lived the American
dream and achieved fulfillment. But the material fulfillment has not
brought the happiness promised. The entire novel is suffused with his
melancholy at the loss of something precious—something that existed
back in the hard times, now lost amidst comfort and wealth. The

whole promise of the dream has somehow slipped through his fingers right at the moment it appeared within his grasp. Why? The question brings us around to a central problem in the novel: Why has Jim, so appreciative of the vitality and freedom represented by the hired girls, ended up in a marriage so empty of meaning?

Perhaps Jim's melancholy itself tells us the reason. The book in a way represents his confession, a confession of unaware betrayal of the dream. In looking back from his vantage point in time, Jim can come to the full realization of what the hired girls (especially such as Ántonia Shimerda and Lena Lingard) represented and what they have come to symbolize: simply all that is best, all that survives of worth, of the faded dream. Some critics have seen in Jim's obtuseness in his male–female relationship with Ántonia and Lena a defect in the book's construction. On the contrary, this theme is very much a part of the book's intention. Jim looking back from the wisdom of his later years and the unhappiness of his meaningless marriage can come to a much sharper awareness of precisely what he missed in his ambitious movement eastward and upward.

In Book II, "The Hired Girls," we are in a way witness to the dream turning sour: "The daughters of Black Hawk merchants had a confident, unenquiring belief that they were 'refined,' and that the country girls, who 'worked out,' were not" (p. 199). "The country girls were considered a menace to the social order. Their beauty shone out too boldly against a conventional background. But anxious mothers need have felt no alarm. They mistook the mettle of their sons. The respect for respectability was stronger than any desire in Black Hawk youth" (p. 201–202). Jim Burden remembered his roaming the streets of Black Hawk at night, looking at the "sleeping houses": "for all their frailness, how much jealousy and envy and unhappiness some of them managed to contain! The life that went on in them seemed to me made up of evasions and negations; shifts to save cooking, to save washing and cleaning, devices to propitiate the tongue of gossip. This guarded mode of existence was like living under a tyranny. People's speech, their voices, their very glances, became furtive and repressed. Every individual taste, every natural appetite, was bridled by caution" (p. 219).

"Respect for respectability" is, perhaps, the cancer battening at the heart of the dream (a theme that William Faulkner was to emphasize later in his Snopes trilogy), and the reader may wonder to what extent Jim Burden himself had been infected, especially in view of the brittle wife he had acquired at some stage in his rise to the top. Moreover, Jim was strongly attracted to the vitality of the hired girls, consciously and unconsciously, as revealed in a recurring dream he had: "One dream I dreamed a great many times, and it was always the same. I was in a harvest-field full of shocks, and I was lying against one of them. Lena Lingard came across the stubble barefoot, in a short skirt, with a curved reaping-hook in her hand, and she was flushed like the dawn, with a kind of luminous rosiness all about her. She sat down beside me, turned to me with a soft sigh and said, 'Now they are all gone, and I can kiss you as much as I like'" (pp. 225–26). After this remarkable sexual revelation, Jim adds: "I used to wish I could have this flattering dream about Ántonia, but I never did." Sister-like Ántonia cannot be transfigured, even in dream, to sexual figure. Her role in the book, and in Jim's psyche, is destined to be more idealized, more mythic.

But Lena Lingard is the subject of an entire book of *My Ántonia*. And that book works out metaphorically the meaning of the novel's epigraph from Virgil as well as the specific personal relation of Jim and Lena, this latter through symbolic use of a play they both attend, Dumas's *Camille*. The epigraph for *My Ántonia* is drawn from Virgil's *Georgics*, and reads: "*Optima dies ... prima fugit.*" This phrase comes into the novel in Book III, after Jim has entered the University of Nebraska and begun his study of Latin, translating the phrase "the best days are the first to flee." As Lena Lingard, now with a dress-making shop in Lincoln, brings to mind for Jim all the vitality of the hired girls of Black Hawk, he makes the connection between them and the haunting phrase from Virgil: "It came over me, as it had never done before, the relation between girls like those and the poetry of Virgil. If there were no girls like them in the world, there would be no poetry. I understand that clearly, for the first time. This revelation seemed to me inestimably precious. I clung to it as if it might suddenly vanish" (p. 270).

But if Lena (along with Ántonia and the others) is equated with poetry, she is also a breathing physical reality to Jim, and Book III brings Jim as close physically to one of the hired girls as the novel permits. A large part of the Book is taken up with a description of

Jim's and Lena's attendance at a performance of *Camille*, the senti-
mental but highly effective drama by Dumas *fils*. As Jim remarks:
"A couple of jack-rabbits, run in off the prairie, could not have been
more innocent of what awaited them than were Lena and I" (p. 272).
Although some critics see the long account of theatre-going as a kind
of inserted story or intrusion, in fact it provides a kind of sophisticated mirror image in literature for the thematic dilemma posed in
the novel itself—and particularly the dilemma Jim faces in his attraction to Lena. Only a few pages before this episode, he has come to
the insight equating the hired girls, in all their vitality and freedom,
with poetry. Now he is confronted with the physical presence of one
for whom he feels a strong attraction.

The hired girls are not, of course, Camilles, but they have some
of the same kind of magic, poetry, freedom, love of life that attracted
Armand to Camille—and that attract Jim to Lena. As Jim and Lena
find themselves drawn closer and closer together in Lincoln, their
conversation turns more and more to marriage—but only obliquely
do they hint of anything deeper than friendship between themselves. Lena, pressed by Jim about her future, says she will never
marry, that she prefers to be "lonesome," that the experience of
marriage as she has witnessed it is even repellent. Jim answers, "'But
it's not all like that.'" Lena replies: "'Near enough. It's all being
under somebody's thumb. What's on your mind, Jim? Are you afraid
I'll want you to marry me some day?'" Jim's immediate remark after
this, to the reader, is: "Then I told her I was going away" (p. 292).
The moment has passed, the future for Jim has been, in a sense,
determined. Lena will go on her successful, "lonesome" way; Jim
will go on to his considerable achievement and position—and his
disastrous marriage.

What happened to the dream—to Jim's dream of Lena, to the
larger dream of personal fulfillment? Was his failure in not seeing
some connection between the dreams? Was Jim's destiny in some
obscure sense a self-betrayal? And is this America's destiny, a self-
betrayal of the possibilities of the dream? There are many literary
texts that could be cited for parallels, but I want to limit myself to
two that will, I hope, prove suggestive. The first is F. Scott Fitzgerald's novel, *The Great Gatsby*. There is, of course, a wide gulf between
Jay Gatsby and Jim Burden (and in many ways Jim's function more

nearly parallels Nick Carroway's), but Gatsby and Burden share in common a profound innocence and also, perhaps, a colossal illusion, a dream. And within themselves they carry the seeds of their own disaster or defeat. Gatsby's Daisy is not worthy of his dream, while Jim's Ántonia is perhaps worth more than his: but the point to be made is that both women are transfigured in the imagination to mythic dimensions, and become embodiments of the dream that is somehow, in the progress of both fictions, betrayed. At the end of *The Great Gatsby*, Nick Carroway sits on Gatsby's lawn meditating on Gatsby's life and death. In the deepening darkness he envisions the place as it must have looked to the first explorers and settlers: "Its vanished trees, the trees that had made way for Gatsby's house, had once pandered in whispers to the last and greatest of all human dreams; for a transitory enchanted moment man must have held his breath in the presence of this continent, compelled into an aesthetic contemplation he neither understood nor desired, face to face for the last time in history with something commensurate to his capacity for wonder."[2] The problem with Gatsby, Nick realizes, is that he did not know that his dream "was already behind him, somewhere back in that vast obscurity beyond the city, where the dark fields of the republic rolled on under the night."

William Carlos Williams's *Paterson* is, as an epic poem, far different in structure and effect from either *My Ántonia* or *The Great Gatsby*. But thematically it touches on some of the same vital matters. The protagonist of the poem is in search throughout for *Beautiful Thing*, whether in the historical Paterson, New Jersey, or in the modern industrial city that shows all the signs of the contemporary waste land. Only gradually does the reader come to realize that the search for Beautiful Thing is destined—probably—to be futile, because it has disappeared with the very past itself. A full understanding of the poem and the phrase will carry the reader back to Williams's earlier book, *In the American Grain*, and his inclusion of one of Columbus's accounts of his discovery of the New World. The account ends: "On shore I sent the people for water, some with arms, and others with casks; and as it was some little distance, I waited two hours for them. During that time I walked among the trees which was the most *beautiful thing* which I had ever seen."[3]

This same short passage is quoted by Williams some twenty-five years later, in *Paterson*. The protagonist of *Paterson* is in quest of that lost promise of the New World which Columbus found in the wilderness—among the trees—some centuries before.

Early in my discussion, I described one of Willa Cather's basic techniques as imagistic, and cited the example of the plow that stands out sharply etched, and then disappears. Such images cluster near the end of *My Ántonia*, one of them characterizing Ántonia herself—or rather Ántonia as transfigured by Jim Burden's imagination. When, after many years have passed, Jim pays Ántonia his final visit—in Book V, "Cuzak's Boys,"—Ántonia takes Jim out to see her fruit cave, and there Jim witnesses all her children dash out of the cave: "a veritable explosion of life out of the dark cave into the sunlight" (p. 339). This image of affirmation and vitality remains with Jim as somehow symbolic of all that Ántonia stands for—and all that he himself has somehow missed.

But the final image to be etched on the mind of the reader comes at the end of the book, as Jim wanders over the prairie after his final parting from Ántonia. It is a "bit of the first road that went from Black Hawk out to the north country"; "this half-mile or so within the pasture fence was all that was left of that old road which used to run like a wild thing across the open prairie." Jim begins to follow the road as far as he can: "On the level land the tracks had almost disappeared—were mere shadings in the grass, and a stranger would not have noticed them. But wherever the road had crossed a draw, it was easy to find. The rains had made channels of the wheel-ruts and washed them so deeply that the sod had never healed over them. They looked like gashes torn by a grizzly's claws, on the slopes where the farm-wagons used to lurch up out of the hollows with a pull that brought curling muscles on the smooth hips of the horses. I sat down and watched the haystacks turn rosy in the slanting sunlight" (pp. 370–71).

This road is not, of course, simply Jim's and Ántonia's road. It is America's road, leading not into the future, but into the past, fast fading from the landscape, fast fading from memory. Like Gatsby's dream that lies somewhere out there already lost in the vastness of the continent, like *Paterson*'s Beautiful Thing that appeared only for a brief moment as Columbus walked among the New World trees—the

road beckons but eludes simultaneously. It is Jim's and Ántonia's—
and perhaps America's—"road of Destiny":

> This was the road over which Ántonia and I came on that
> night when we got off the train at Black Hawk and were
> bedded down in the straw, wondering children, being taken
> we knew not whither. I had only to close my eyes to hear the
> rumbling of the wagons in the dark, and to be again overcome
> by that obliterating strangeness. The feelings of that night were
> so near that I could reach out and touch them with my hand. I
> had the sense of coming home to myself, and of having found
> out what a little circle man's experience is. For Ántonia and for
> me, this had been the road of Destiny; had taken us to those
> early accidents of fortune which predetermined for us all that
> we can ever be. Now I understood that the same road was to
> bring us together again. Whatever we had missed, we possessed
> together the precious, the incommunicable past. [Pp. 371–72]

As Americans who have dreamed the dream, we might say with
Jim: "Whatever we have missed, we possess together the precious, the
incommunicable past." In some dark sense, Jim's experience is the
American experience, his melancholy sense of loss also his country's,
his longing for something missed in the past a national longing.

The lost promise, the misplaced vision, is America's loss—our
loss—and it haunts us all, still.

NOTES

1. First published by Houghton Mifflin Company in 1918. All
   page references are to the Sentry Edition (Boston: Houghton
   Mifflin, 1961).
2. F. Scott Fitzgerald, *The Great Gatsby* (New York: Charles
   Scribner's Sons, 1925), p. 182.
3. *In the American Grain: Essays by William Carlos Williams*
   (Norfolk, Conn.: New Directions, 1956), p. 26.

NARRATIVE OF THE LIFE OF FREDERICK DOUGLASS (FREDERICK DOUGLASS)

"Frederick Douglass"
by Harriet Beecher Stowe,
in *The Lives and Deeds of Our Self-Made Men* (1872)

INTRODUCTION

In the following essay, abolitionist and novelist Harriet Beecher Stowe praises Frederick Douglass and his ascendancy to political and literary prominence. She succinctly defines the myth of self-ascendancy that lies at the heart of the American Dream: by following a good work ethic, adhering to Christian notions of morality, and being properly ambitious, any individual can overcome the humblest of circumstances to achieve prosperity. After recounting parts of Douglass' remarkable story of emancipation, Stowe describes his role as a lecturer in the abolitionist movement, holding up his story as both an exemplary manifestation of the American Dream coming to fruition and as "a comment on the slavery system which speaks for itself."

Stowe, Harriet Beecher. "Frederick Douglass." *The Lives and Deeds of Our Self-Made Men*. Chicago, IL: M.A. Parker & Co.,1872.

The reader will perceive, in reading the memoirs which we have collected in the present volume, that although they give a few instances of men who have risen to distinction from comfortable worldly circumstances, by making a good use of the provision afforded them by early competence and leisure, yet by far the greater number have raised themselves by their own unaided efforts, in spite of every disadvantage which circumstances could throw in their way.

It is the pride and the boast of truly republican institutions that they give to every human being an opportunity of thus demonstrating what is in him. If a man is a man, no matter in what rank of society he is born, no matter how tied down and weighted by poverty and all its attendant disadvantages, there is nothing in our American institutions to prevent his rising to the very highest offices in the gift of the country. So, though a man like Charles Sumner, coming of an old Boston family, with every advantage of Boston schools and of Cambridge college, becomes distinguished through the country, yet side by side with him we see Abraham Lincoln, the rail-splitter, Henry Wilson, from the shoemaker's bench, and Chase, from a New Hampshire farm. But there have been in our country some three or four million of human beings who were born to a depth of poverty below what Henry Wilson or Abraham Lincoln ever dreamed of. Wilson and Lincoln, to begin with, owned nothing but their bare hands, but there have been in this country four or five million men and women who did not own even their bare hands. Wilson and Lincoln, and other brave men like them, owned their own souls and wills—they were free to say, "Thus and thus I will do—I will be educated, I will be intelligent, I will be Christian, I will by honest industry amass property to serve me in my upward aims." But there were four million men and women in America who were decreed by the laws of this country not to own even their own souls. The law said of them—They shall be taken and held as chattels personal to all intents and purposes. This hapless class of human beings might be sold for debt, might be mortgaged for real estate, nay, the unborn babe might be pledged or mortgaged for the debts of a master. There were among these unfortunate millions, in the eye of the law, neither husbands nor wives, nor fathers nor mothers; they were only chattels personal. They could no more contract a legal marriage than a bedstead can marry a cooking-stove, or a plough be wedded to a spinning wheel. They were week after week advertised in public prints to be sold in company with horses, cows, pigs, hens, and other stock of a plantation.

They were forbidden to learn to read. The slave laws imposed the same penalty on the man who should teach a slave to read as on the man who wilfully put out his eyes. They had no legal right to be Christians, or enter the kingdom of heaven, because the law regarded them simply as personal property, subject to the caprice of an owner, and when the owner did not choose to have his property be a Christian, he could shut him out from the light of the gospel as easily as one can close a window shutter.

Now if we think it a great thing that Wilson and Lincoln raised themselves from a state of comparatively early disadvantage to high places in the land, what shall we think of one who started from this immeasureable gulf below them?

Frederick Douglass had as far to climb to get to the spot where the poorest free white boy is born, as that white boy has to climb to be president of the nation, and take rank with kings and judges of the earth.

There are few young men born to competence, carried carefully through all the earlier stages of training, drilled in grammar school, and perfected by a four years' college course, who could stand up on a platform and compete successfully with Frederick Douglass as an orator. Nine out of ten of college educated young men would shrink even from the trial, and yet Frederick Douglass fought his way up from a nameless hovel on a Maryland plantation, where with hundreds of others of the young live stock he shivered in his little tow shirt, the only garment allowed him for summer and winter, kept himself warm by sitting on the sunny side of out buildings, like a little dog, and often was glad to dispute with the pigs for the scraps of what came to them to satisfy his hunger.

From this position he has raised himself to the habits of mind, thought and life of a cultivated gentleman, and from that point of sight has illustrated exactly what slavery WAS, (thank God we write in the past tense,) in an autobiography which most affectingly presents what it is to be born a slave. Every man who struck a stroke in our late great struggle—every man or woman who made a sacrifice for it—every one conscious of inward bleedings and cravings that never shall be healed or assuaged, for what they have rendered up in this great anguish, ought to read this autobiography of a slave man, and give thanks to God that even by the bitterest sufferings they have been permitted to do something to wipe such a disgrace and wrong from the earth.

[. . .]

About this time Douglass became deeply awakened to religious things, by the prayers and exhortations of a pious old colored slave who was a drayman. He could read and his friend could not, but Douglass, now newly awakened to spiritual things, read the Bible to him, and received comfort from him. He says, "He fanned my already intense love of knowledge into a flame by assuring me that I was to be a useful man in the world. When I would say to him, how can these things be, his simple reply was, '*trust in the Lord.*' When I told him that I was a *slave* FOR LIFE, he said: 'The Lord can make you free, my dear. All things are possible with him, only have faith in God. If you want your liberty, ask the Lord for it in faith, and HE WILL GIVE IT TO YOU.'" Cheered by this advice, Douglass began to offer daily and earnest prayers for liberty.

With reference to this he began to turn his thoughts towards acquiring the art of writing. He was employed as waiter in a ship yard, and watching the initial letters by which the carpenters marked the different parts of the ship, and thus in time acquired a large part of the written alphabet. This knowledge he supplemented by getting one and another boy of his acquaintance on one pretence or other, to write words or letters on fences or boards. Then he surreptitiously copied the examples in his little master's copybook at home, when his mistress was safely out of the house, and finally acquired the dangerous and forbidden gift of writing a fluent, handsome current hand. He had various reverses after this as he grew in age and developed in manliness. He was found difficult to manage, and changed from hand to hand like a vicious intractable horse. Once a celebrated negro breaker had a hand upon him, meaning to break his will and reduce him to the condition of a contented animal, but the old story of Pegasus in harness came to pass. The negro breaker gave him up as a bad case, and finally his master made a virtue of necessity, and allowed him to hire his own time. The bargain was that Douglass should pay him three dollars a week, and make his own bargains, find his own tools, board and clothe himself. The work was that of caulker in a ship yard.

This, he says, was a hard bargain; for the wear and tear of clothing, the breakage of tools and expenses of board made it necessary to earn at least six dollars a week, to keep even with the world, and this percentage to the master left him nothing beyond a bare living.

But it was a freeman's experience to be able to come and go unwatched, and before long it enabled him to mature a plan of escape, and the time at last came when he found himself a free colored citizen of New Bedford, seeking employment, with the privilege of keeping his wages for himself. Here, it was that reading for the first time the Lady of the Lake, he gave himself the name of Douglass, and abandoned forever the family name of his old slaveholding employer. Instead of a lazy thriftless young man to be supported by his earnings, he took unto himself an affectionate and thrifty wife, and became a settled family man.

He describes the seeking for freeman's work as rapturous excitement. The thought "I can work, I can earn money, I have no master now to rob me of my earnings," was a perfect joyous stimulus whenever it arose, and he says, "I sawed wood, dug cellars, shoveled coal, rolled oil casks on the wharves, helped to load and unload vessels, worked in candle works and brass foundries, and thus supported myself for three years. I was, he says, now living in a new world, and wide awake to its advantages. I early began to attend meetings of the colored people, in New Bedford, and to take part in them, and was amazed to see colored men making speeches, drawing up resolutions, and offering them for consideration."

His enthusiasm for self-education was constantly stimulated. He appropriated some of his first earning to subscribing for the Liberator, and was soon after introduced to Mr. Garrison. How Garrison appeared to a liberated slave may be a picture worth preserving, and we give it in Douglass' own words.

"Seventeen years ago, few men possessed a more heavenly countenance than William Lloyd Garrison, and few men evinced a more genuine or a more exalted piety. The Bible was his text book—held sacred, as the word of the Eternal Father—sinless perfection—complete submission to insults and injuries—literal obedience to the injunction, if smitten on one side to turn the other also. Not only was Sunday a Sabbath, but all days were Sabbaths, and to be kept holy. All sectarism false and mischievous—the regenerated, throughout the world, members of one body, and the HEAD Jesus Christ. Prejudice against color was rebellion against God. Of all men beneath the sky, the slaves, because most neglected and despised, were nearest and dearest to his great heart. Those ministers who defended slavery from the Bible, were of their 'father the devil;' and those churches which fellowshipped slaveholders as Christians, were synagogues of Satan, and our nation was a nation of liars. Never loud or noisy—calm and serene as a summer sky, and as pure. 'You are the man, the Moses, raised up by God, to deliver his modern Israel from bondage,' was the spontaneous feeling of my heart, as I sat away back in the hall and listened to his mighty words; mighty in truth—mighty in their simple earnestness."

From this time the course of Douglass is upward. The manifest talents which he possessed, led the friends of the Anti-Slavery cause to feel that he could serve it better in a literary career than by manual labor.

In the year 1841, a great anti-slavery convention was held at Nantucket, where Frederick Douglass appeared on the stage and before a great audience recounted his experiences. Mr. Garrison followed him, and an immense enthusiasm was excited—and Douglass says: "That night there were at least a thousand Garrisonians in Nantucket." After this the general agent of the Anti-Slavery Society came and offered to Douglass the position of an agent of that society, with a competent support to enable him to lecture through the country. Douglass, continually pursuing the work of self-education, became an accomplished speaker and writer. He visited England, and was received with great enthusiasm. The interest excited in him was so great that several English friends united and paid the sum of one hundred and fifty pounds sterling, for the purchase of his liberty. This enabled him to pursue his work of lecturer in the United States, to travel unmolested, and to make himself every way conspicuous without danger of recapture.

He settled himself in Rochester, and established an Anti-Slavery paper, called Frederick Douglass' Paper, which bore a creditable character for literary execution, find had a good number of subscribers in America and England.

Two of Frederick Douglass' sons were among the first to answer to the call for colored troops, and fought bravely in the good cause.

Douglass has succeeded in rearing an intelligent and cultivated family, and in placing himself in the front rank among intelligent and cultivated men. Few orators among us surpass him, and his history from first to last, is a comment on the slavery system which speaks for itself.

ON THE ROAD
(JACK KEROUAC)

❧ ⚜ ☙

"Alternative Routes along the Road: Kerouac and the Multifaceted American Dream"
by Jeff Williams,
Universidad Nacional de La Rioja

Pressure to conform to a common ideology dominated the cultural and political landscape of the United States during World War II, and became even more pronounced during the Cold War that followed. The Beat Generation, a budding counterculture, reacted strongly against this forced conformity. The Beats

> were a loosely affiliated arts community—one that encompassed two or three generations of writers, artists, activists, and nonconformists who sought to create a new alternative culture that served as a bohemian retreat from the dominant culture, as a critique of mainstream values and social structures, as a force for social change, and as a crucible for art. (Skerl 2)

Beginning in the 1940s and lasting until the 1960s, these "mainstream values and social structures" were propagated in popular culture, including novels, magazines, radio shows, film and television. Many of these mainstream values make up the American Dream, such as the idea that anyone can attain success, where success means a university education, a traditional family with at least two children, a house, a car, and a well-paying job that offers opportunities for advancement.

Though the concept of the American Dream has its origins in the colonial period of the United States, where the "New World" was seen as a land of destiny and opportunity, the actual phrase was created by James Truslow Adams in 1931. In *The Epic of America*, Adams describes America as a land where all individuals can improve their life, and where opportunities exist for all, depending on their achievements and abilities Adams (404). The American Dream took on a different dimension during the post-World War II years, when the GI Bill allowed open access to any university of choice to all war veterans. These educational opportunites led to a narrower definition of the American Dream in the mid-1940s and early 1950s. During this epoch the American dream became the dream of the average citizen living in the United States, and not just immigrants looking for a better life. But in reality, not everyone, no matter how great the effort, can become a business success, create a happy family, and prosper. Success and failure is not always controlled by the person struggling and fighting to succeed. Pulling one's self up by one's own bootstraps often involves outside help. Discrimination—racial, gender, and class prejudices—often worked against American dreamers. Some of these burdens of reality are portrayed in Jack Kerouac's *On the Road*.

The events in Kerouac's novel take place between 1947 and 1949; the book was written in 1951 and published in 1957. The published work is actually Kerouac's memoir in novel form; where the real characters' names were replaced with fictional names and the original format—a single paragraph with minimal punctuation—was altered to fit more traditional reading expectations. The main characters, Sal Paradise (Jack Kerouac) and Dean Moriarty (Neal Cassidy), travel back and forth (but not always together) across the U.S. and into Mexico, experiencing the underside of the American landscape and searching for an unattainable "IT."

This "IT" could signify various desires and wishes, from the Buddhist nirvana to a muse to inspire poetry, writing, and bebop. Dean recognizes "IT" outside a jazz club while watching Rollo Greb (Kerouac 118). The "IT" is also "the last thing," as Dean explains, "[t]hat last thing is what you can't get, Carlo. Nobody can get to that last thing. We keep on living in hopes of catching it once and for all" (43). This unattainable goal is reminiscent of the American Dream. In *On the Road* there are countless characters, and they are often happy and satisfied even though their lives are far outside of mainstream America. When one travels the road, a broad vista opens, with "[g]reat beautiful clouds . . . overhead, valley clouds that [make] you feel the vastness of old tumbledown holy America from mouth to mouth and tip to tip" (140).

This "vastness" creates the possibility for multiple dreams. There is no single dream in Kerouac's world. The American dream is a bright pearl with as many shining reflections as there are individuals. It becomes a road of many roads with a variety of hero travelers. Most of the heroes that populate Kerouac's novel are migrant workers, hoboes, drifters, jazz musicians, jazz aficionados, prostitutes, and thieves. They are members of mainstream America, but they all have individualistic traits and/or were once drifters, hoboes, or hitchhikers. Their travels and dreams are evocative of Walt Whitman's poem "Song of the Road," which celebrates a diverse America. In "Song of the Road," the marginal and mainstream explore life together with non-materialistic contentment and celebration of diversity: "[t]o know the universe itself as a road—as many roads—as roads / for traveling souls" (Whitman 177). Sal's first lesson on his first day out to hitchhike across the country is that in America, it is impossible to travel only one road. Sal is fascinated with the idea of taking a single road most of the way to Denver: "I'd been pouring over maps of the United States in Paterson for months, even reading books about the pioneers and savoring names like Platte and Cimarron and so on, and on the roadmap was one long red line called Route 6 that led from the tip of Cape Cod clear to Ely" (9). But during his first night out, while stuck in the rain waiting for a ride, he discovers he has made a mistake: "[i]t was my dream that screwed up, the stupid hearthside idea that it would be wonderful to follow one great red line across America instead of trying various roads and routes" (10).

The different roads symbolize the different lives and people that Sal encounters. Two significant groups make up these "traveling souls" in *On the Road*. One is the population of the disenfranchised, "the poor lost sometimeboy[s]" (97). This group lives in "the wilderness of America" (97) and experiences Kerouac's reality:

> [i]sn't it true that you start your life as a sweet child believing in everything under your father's roof? Then comes the day of the

Laodiceans, when you know you are wretched and miserable
and poor and blind and naked, and with the visage of a
gruesome grieving ghost you go shuddering through nightmare
life. (97)

For this group the traditional American Dream is "the mad dream—
grabbing, taking, giving, sighing, dying, just so they could be buried
in those awful cemetery cities beyond Long Island City" (98). Sal's
first trip, to San Francisco and back to New York, contains a variety
of these non-conformist characters, and in their personality traits we
can understand the American Dream as Kerouac sees it.

In starting this first journey to Denver, Sal meets up with a couple
of truck drivers and gets a ride from one along the now famous Route
66. The trucker, "a great big tough truckdriver with popping eyes
and a hoarse raspy voice who just slammed and kicked at everything
and got his rig under way and hardly paid any attention to me" (13),
yells his stories and knows various tricks in order to avoid the police
(13). For the trucker, the law represents authority in general, and his
rebellion against it makes him a kindred spirit on the road, despite his
lack of hipster sensibilities. Farmers (14), an ex-hobo cowboy (16), an
old man with a "weird crazy homemade Nebraska trailer," an old ex-
hitchhiker (19), some North Dakota farmer boys, city boys who play
high school football, and Minnesota farm boys (22)—all befriend Sal
on his journey and offer rides and assistance. Sal meets Mississippi
Gene (a hobo and old acquaintance of Old Bill Lee) and Montana
Slim (21) on a flatbed truck; Mississippi Gene tells a story about Big
Slim Hazzard, who as a child sees an old hobo and decides to become
a hobo when he grows up (24). The next-to-last ride, which takes Sal
to the outskirts of Denver, is from a young painter whose father is an
editor (31). These diverse collections of people that Sal meets along
the way reveal the existence of an underground culture, a population
following their own dreams of simply surviving and traveling the
world. At the very least, these travelers are living a dream that is the
opposite of "the mad dream." Even when Sal encounters an exception to this underground culture, in the form of a mainstream Denver
businessman, the novel still revels in the unconventional. Instead of
going directly into the city, the businessman takes Sal through the
town's outskirts, into a landscape usually not described with accep-

tance nor praise in popular culture: "there were smokestacks, smoke, railyards, red-brick buildings, and here I was in Denver. He let me off at Larimer Street. I stumbled along with the wicked grin of joy in the world, among the old bums and beat cowboys of Larimer Street" (32).

Sal takes a bus for his journey from San Francisco to Denver, for a stay that ends disastrously in a broken friendship (70-71). He leaves the same way he came in, drinks beer with some bums in a saloon and takes two rides to get to Bakersfield, the first "with a burly blonde kid in a souped-up rod" (73). Leaving Bakersfield Sal meets Terry, a Mexican girl, on a bus to Los Angeles, where "[t]he beatest characters in the country swarmed the sidewalks . . . .You could smell tea, weed, I mean marijuana, floating in the air together with the chili beans and beer" (80). Los Angeles is where Sal hears the mix of sounds, "[t]hat grand wild sound of bop floated from beer parlors; it mixed with every kind of cowboy and boogie-woogie in the American night" (80). And it is in Los Angeles that Sal sees the most diverse mix of marginal cultures:

> Everybody looked like Hassel. Wild Negroes with bop caps and goatees came laughing by; then longhaired brokendown hipsters straight off Route 66 from New York; then old desert rats, carrying packs and heading for a park bench at the Plaza; then Methodist ministers with raveled sleeves, and an occasional Nature Boy saint in beard and sandals. I wanted to meet them all, talk to everybody, but Terry and I were too busy trying to get a buck together. (80)

A full range of life in the peripheries is described, celebrated, and honored. Los Angeles serves as an initiation; Sal experiences a different culture and savors his new found love, Terry. His experience deepens when after failed attempts to earn enough money to hitch-hike together to New York, he eventually ends up working picking grapes (88-90). At the end of fifteen days, Sal heads back to New York. Similar adventures take place on the return trip; bus rides, a ride on an apple truck, and another ride in a big rig (95). Sal arrives in New York after his first trip out west, thinking "[t]here is something brown and holy about the East; and California is white like washlines and emptyheaded." (72).

The sub-cultures Sal meets on his first trip to San Francisco indicate that there were many non-conformists living outside mainstream culture, who were not following "the mad dream." The second group that exists in *On the Road* offers a closer look at individual non-conformists. This group is comprised of the close-knit friends that formed around Paradise and Moriarity: Remi Boncoeur, Big Ed Dunkle, Tim Gray, Elmer Hassle, Chad King, Jane Lee, Old Bull Lee (William Burroughs), Roland Major, Marylou, and Carlo Marx (Allen Ginsberg), among others. Unlike the diverse non-conformists Sal met on the road, this is mostly a group of Beats, and the novel describes in detail their idiosyncrasies and how each lives his own version of the American Dream. Some of the most interesting of these individuals include Chad, Major, Remi, Old Bull, Carlo, and of course, Dean and Sal.

Chad is fascinated with the Plains Indians, weaves Indian baskets at a local museum and goes on expeditions for Indian artifacts in the mountains (33). Even though he is part of Sal's circle of friends, he and others are ignoring Dean. A "war" was brewing, where Chad aligned with Tim and Major in order to ignore Dean and Carlo. This war has social overtones; Dean is the son of a wino, associated with a poolhall gang and had arrest records for stealing cars (34). Therefore, the others did not consider him an intellectual. Even within the Beats, class consciousness had not been completely erased. Major is also a part of the separate group. Major writes Hemingway-esque short stories, loves good wine, wears a silk dressing gown, and does not approve of hopping trains (36). He thinks that "[t]he arty types were all over America sucking up its blood," but did not consider Sal an arty type (36). Later, Major shows up drunk at a restaurant and crashes a dinner part that Remi and his father are having for Sal. This incident wrecks the friendship between Sal and Remi.

Of the other members of this group, Remi is more of a non-conformist. He lives in Mill City. He "was an old prep-school friend, a Frenchman brought up in Paris and a really mad guy . . ." (8). Remi lives in a shack and works as a night guard for barracks housing overseas construction workers (58). He has one of the greatest laughs in the world and he steals his groceries from the barracks cafeteria as a way to live according to Truman's injunction, "we must cut down on the cost of living" (64). Remi steals because he feels the world owes him something, and he steals as a way to make it the best way one can (64). He enjoys his life and at times works on ships in order to travel the globe (292).

Old Bull is another eccentric Beat. Critical and anti-everything (7), he lives in a "house outside of town near the river levee. It was on a road than ran across a swampy field. The house was a dilapidated old heap with sagging porches running around and weeping willows in the yard; the grass was a yard high, old fences leaned, old barns collapsed" (132). He is anti-authoritarian and "[h]is chief hate was Washington bureaucracy; second to that, liberals; then cops" (135). Sal relates the story in which someone commented on an ugly picture on the wall and Old Bull replied that he liked it because it was ugly; Sal ends the story with the comment that "[a]ll his life was in that line" (134). Old Bull experiments with heroine addiction, has traveled widely, and is the acknowledged teacher of the group. Most of the Beats have sat at his feet at one time or another, including Jane, Dean, Carlo, and Sal (135).

Alongside Old Bull, the key members of the small circle of friends are Carlo, Dean, and Sal. *On the Road* actually chronicles Sal's initiation into beat culture, and within the story the three are interlinked, with Sal and Dean's relationship as the main focus. Sal relates that

> [a] tremendous thing happened when Dean met Carlo Marx. Two keen minds that they are, they took to each other at the drop of a hat. Two piercing eyes glanced into two piercing eyes—the holy con man and the shining mind, and the sorrowful poetic con-man with the dark mind that is Carlo Marx. (5)

Carlo lives in Denver in a basement apartment where he recites poetry and where he and Dean have their talk sessions: "[t]hey sat on the bed crosslegged and looked straight at each other . . . . They began with an abstract thought, discussed it; reminded each other of another abstract point forgotten in the rush of events . . ." (43). The two would continue like this for hours on end, leaving Sal with the thought that they would both go crazy (45). Dean has a shady past, and constantly cons Sal and thinks only of himself; but still Sal cannot help but respect Dean's beatness, his crazy and wild nature. They travel together to Mexico and take in all the beautiful people and respect the simplicity of life. Dean remains the same throughout the story, but Sal, a college student on the GI Bill, finishes his first novel and then begins his three-year odyssey into membership in the Beat's world and culture.

Kerouac broke new ground in *On the Road*. For the first time, representatives of a marginal population were portrayed in a novel with respect and dignity; they are in fact the heroes of the novel. In addition, the reader also sees up-close the lives of that slice of mainstream America who simply try to subsist. These hard-working people are disenfranchised from the traditional dream; their idea of the American Dream is simply the ability to survive from day to day, but they are happy and content with their life. *On the Road* includes additional variations on the American Dream that are legitimized through the lifestyles of the participants, where living the dream meant relishing the celebratory feeling of stealing cars and driving fast; living a life of heroine addiction; traveling aimlessly as a hitchhiker or hobo; working just enough to go from one day to the next while enjoying simple pleasures; engaging in night long talk sessions; searching for an unattainable "IT"; pursuing a career in writing, playing jazz, or simply listening to jazz; living a life creating art or poetry; or simply living wild and crazy without purpose. Seeking experiences for the sake of feeling the experience comprises another facet of the "IT," Dean's American dream. "He [Dean] and I suddenly saw the whole country like an oyster for us to open; and the pearl was there, the pearl was there. Off we roared south" (129). But in this case, the pearl is neither wealth, stability, nor worldly ambition. It does not represent the common American Dream inherent in a capitalistic society; it is not Adams' American Dream or the redefined American Dream of the 1940s and 1950s. This "IT" is more in line with Whitman's notion of the American Dream as expressed in "Song of the Road." All of these visions and aspirations become legitimate expressions of the pursuit of the American Dream. Contentment and success can be expressed in the anti-dream of an anti-establishment culture. Feeling the joy and exuberance of life is the dream, and traveling "the road" requires putting job security and monetary goals in the background (or even disregarding them completely). Throughout the novel and at every turn in the road, the Beats, and to a lesser degree the others who populate side streets, jazz cafes, and outskirts of town across the United States, engage in a pro-active rebellion against "the mad dream" of living for money and material success.

WORKS CITED

Adams, James Truslow. *The Epic of America*. Boston: Little, Brown & Company, 1931.

Kerouac, Jack. *On the* Road. 1957. New York: Penguin, 1999.

Skerl, Jennie, ed. *Reconstructing the Beats*. Basingstoke, Hampshire: Palgrave Macmillan, 2004.

Whitman, Walt. *Leaves of Grass*. Ed. David McKay. Sherman: Philadelphia, 1900.

A RAISIN IN THE SUN
(LORRAINE HANSBERRY)

"Discrimination and the American Dream in Lorraine Hansberry's *A Raisin in The Sun*"
by Babacar M'Baye,
Kent State University

The scholar Joseph Wilson argued that "The history of the Afro-American people is a mosaic woven into the fabric of the history of labor in America" (vii). *A Raisin in the Sun* (1959) validates this observation and helps us understand the challenges that confronted African-American workers in Chicago from the 1920s to the 1950s. The play discusses the impact of labor and housing discrimination on the American dreams of these black populations through the experiences of two generations of the Younger family. First, *Raisin* suggests the distinct impact of job discrimination in the life of Big Walter Lee, who is Mama's deceased husband. Second, the play reveals the frustrations that complicate the Younger family's dreams for success and admissibility into mainstream American society of the 1950s. Although a few members of the Younger family finally achieve a part of their dreams, they do so while remembering the trials and tribulations that have led them to such a well-deserved victory.

When *Raisin* was first produced in 1959 the critical reaction was ambivalent. As Steven Carter points out, the early honors bestowed on Hansberry brought about some controversy in the white intellectual community:

When the New York Drama Critics Circle gave *A Raisin*
their 1959 award for Best Play of The Year over such fine
contenders as Eugene O'Neill's *A Touch of The Poet*, Tennessee
Williams's *Sweet Bird of Youth*, and Archibald Macleish's *J.B.*,
several critics expressed dismay, claiming that the choice of
such a young black playwright's work could only be based on
liberal bias. (19)

In the same vein, Harold Cruse, a prominent black critic, claimed
that:

A Raisin in The Sun demonstrated that the Negro playwright
has lost the intellectual and, therefore, technical and creative,
ability to deal with his own special ethnic group materials
in dramatic form. The most glaring manifestation of this
conceptual weakness is the constant slurring over, the blurring,
and evasion of the internal facts of Negro ethnic life in terms of
class and social caste divisions, institutional and psychological
variations, political divisions, acculturation variables, clique
variations, religious divisions, and so forth. (281)

Such negative commentary from a leading black scholar created doubt
and frustration about the way black people in general received the
play. As Loften Mitchell observed in 1967, "There were Negroes who
became angry because critics said the play really said nothing about
the Negro plight" (182).

Since the 1980s, however, *Raisin* has generally been highly
praised. In his review of a 1986 revival of the play, David Richards of
the *Washington Post* acknowledged that *Raisin* is "a milestone—the
first play by a black woman ever to be produced on Broadway" (D1).
He continues, "What is important is that Lorraine Hansberry gave us
a work that miraculously continues to speak to the American experience" (D1). Amiri Baraka echoed this optimism when he declared,
also in 1986, that *Raisin* is "the quintessential civil rights play" and
"probably the most widely appreciated black play (particularly by
Afro-Americans)" (F1; 3). In a similar vein, Nicole King described
Raisin as one of the black literary representations that "saw and
promoted group solidarity against the diverse manifestations of white

racism and discrimination as important, viable, and as cemented by a working class rather than a middle-class ideology" (214).

The above comments acknowledge the radical and subversive nature of *Raisin*'s struggle against racism. But they do not address the important role that the African-American dream of admissibility and equality has in this struggle. Regardless of whether they praised or condemned *Raisin*, the early commentators on the play had one thing in common: they tended to be more concerned with the racial background of the dramatist than with the complex work she created. When a film of *Raisin* appeared in 1961, it immediately drew attention away from the text version of the play. On the other hand, it is probable that very little would have been said about *Raisin* if the play had never been staged on Broadway. If one values what the critics say about the play more than what the text itself discloses, *Raisin* loses its authenticity. One way to balance the critical comments on *Raisin* and the play's serious purpose is to explore the work through its political, social, and cultural messages.

In the early twentieth century, in response to increasing levels of violence and political and economic oppression in the South, thousands of African Americans, eager to find jobs that would create a better life for themselves and their families, moved to northern industrial cities such as Chicago, New York, Saint Louis, Cleveland, Pittsburgh, and Philadelphia. Yet hostile white populations frequently discriminated against the black migrants searching for homes. As Leonard Dinnerstein notes: "The worst housing in the cities was reserved for the black migrants coming from the South. Owners preferred to rent to white immigrants rather than to blacks, and the black families sometimes encountered violence when they tried to move outside their growing ghettos" (162). In Chicago, Carl Hansberry, Lorraine Hansberry's father, encountered an infamous case of housing segregation that impelled him to stand up for his rights. According to Steven R. Carter, "In 1938, when Lorraine was eight, her father risked jail to challenge Chicago's real estate covenants, which legally enforced housing discrimination, by moving his family into an all-white neighborhood near the University of Chicago" (9). These actual historical events show that *Raisin* is far more than an abstract comment on black life in mid-twentieth-century America. The play is based on actual events that affected Hansberry's own family, as well as many blacks in Chicago and in other northern cities of the 1940s and 1950s. Philip Johnson, a former Lutheran minister in Salem parish on the South Side of Chicago, relates a similar case:

> On Wednesday, July 27, 1949 rioting broke out in the 7200 block of South St. Lawrence Avenue. Arthur Jordan, a Ph.D. candidate had moved into the block, the first Negro to venture south of Seventy-first street in the quiet respectable neighborhood of Park Manor. For days the rioting went on. Women cursed, children jeered, teen-agers hurled bricks and bottles, and men snarled angrily, "Burn the b- b- out"(2).

While such events surely influenced Hansberry to write *Raisin*, the title of the play comes from a famous poem by Langston Hughes, "Harlem" (89-90). Written in 1951, and included in Hughes's *Montage of a Dream Deferred*, "Harlem" explores the destiny of the African-American dream:

What happens to a dream deferred?

> Does it dry up
> like a raisin in the sun?
> Or fester like a sore—
> And then run?
> Does it stink like rotten meat?
> Or crust and sugar over—
> like a syrupy sweet?
>
> Maybe it just sags
> like a heavy load.
>
> *Or does it explode?* (426)

Hughes's poem raises serious questions about the fulfillment of the American ideal of justice and equality that continues to be postponed by racist actualities against African Americans. He asks whether the ideal will "dry up" and not become realized, or "fester" like an old and painful wound, or "explode" into a nightmare of violence. In asking these questions, Hughes represents the African-American dream of success, equality, and freedom as an ambiguous process. On the one hand, this dream seems to be feasible and full of possibilities—like the hopeful image of an exploding raisin with "crust and sugar over." Yet, as suggested in the image of a drying raisin that could "fester like an old sore and run," this dream is hard to attain when forces of segregation, racism, intolerance, and violence defer it. In making the American Dream be an faint reality, Hughes captures the essence of the American Dream of African Americans that critic David Jarraway eloquently describes as "the willed mystery, the uncertainty, the indeterminacy" or "the deferred Otherness" of "black experience" (823).

In *Raisin*, the dim reality of the American dream of African Americans is apparent in the harsh working conditions of Chicago blacks of the 1920s. These conditions are represented through the experience of Big Walter Lee, which is told through Mama's voice. First Mama depicts Big Walter as a courageous man who fought all his life to secure a happy future for his family. She states: "That man worked hisself [himself] to death like he done. Like he was fighting his own war with this here world . . . ."(45). Big Walter's life was a constant struggle against a personal sorrow and a hostile economic and social world that discriminated against him. Mama emphatically insists that the money she receives from Big Walter's death is not worth the value of the man.

> *(She holds the check away from her, still looking at it. Slowly her face sobers into a mask of unhappiness)* Ten thousand dollars. (*She hands it to RUTH*) Put it away somewhere, Ruth. (*She does not look at RUTH; her eyes seem to be seeing something somewhere very far off*) Ten thousand dollars they give you. Ten thousand dollars. (69)

Mama's frustration suggests that she is disappointed by the way Big Walter's life and American dream have been unjustly valued at a mere ten thousand dollars. In the 1950s, ten thousand dollars was quite a lot of money. Still, this amount of money cannot replace the worth that Big Walter had in Mama's life and in society. Besides, as the estimated worth of lifelong work and struggle, the insurance money reflects the low professional status that Big Walter and other Chicago blacks had in the 1920s. In *The Negro Family in The United*

States, Frazier notes: "In the North the black worker was confined to domestic and personal service" (334). Hansberry does not tell us what kind of job Big Walter had, but the situation in which the Youngers live makes it obvious that Big Walter was not rich. Moreover, Mama emphasizes that her husband hated domestic jobs:

> My husband always said being any kind of a servant wasn't a fit thing for a man to have to be. He always said a man's hands was made to make things, or to turn the earth with—not to drive nobody's car for 'em—or—(she looks at her own hands) carry them slop jars. (103)

Farming and rural life or the idea of being a skilled craftsman appealed to Big Walter. His ideal of work reflects an idealized nostalgia for a lost tradition of American agrarian pastoralism. Like Thomas Jefferson, Big Walter acknowledges the humanizing virtue of agriculture. According to Lawrence Levine, Jefferson had "assured his country of its destined power and influence at the same time that he urged it to retain its purity and simplicity by remaining a nation of agrarians"(191). We can see in Mama's appearance and hear in her critique of degrading domestic work that she had been forced to spend a lifetime supporting Big Walter's urban struggle for decent work and dignity by carrying "slop jars." Although both of them are industrious and ambitious, Mama and Walter have been relegated to the demeaning roles of servants, dependents, and unskilled workers. Mama's contribution to family support through menial jobs continues even after Big Walter's death. She plans to take a new job: "I could maybe take on a little day work again, few days a week"(44). Mama's support exemplifies her dogged determination to take care of the Younger family, which remains heavily dependent on her. She takes low-paying jobs, plays a domestic role in the house and hopes for the day when her children will be able to achieve more in life than she did.

In the 1920s, most Chicago blacks were domestic workers. Moreover, as Franklin Frazier remarks in *The Negro Family in the United States*, that in 1920, New York City, Chicago, and Philadelphia were cities where "a fifth of employed Negro men were in semi-skilled industrial occupations, while nearly 30 per cent were engaged in similar occupations in Detroit" (336). Indeed, in the 1920s Chicago blacks were often unemployed. Harold M. Baron explains: "There was a slackening of the demand for black labor when post-war demobilization caused heavy unemployment. In Chicago, where as many as 10,000 black laborers were out of work, the local Association of Commerce wired to Southern chambers of commerce: 'Are you in need of Negro labor'" (196).

Furthermore, in the period following the Great Migration of the 1920s, blacks like Big Walter rarely received respect or decent jobs in urban settings because white Americans commonly denied blacks their humanity, dignity, and value. As Thomas F. Gossett points out, "American thought of the period 1880-1920 generally lacks any perception of the Negro as a human being with potentialities for improvement" (286). Big Walter's predicament was a direct effect of the educational, economic, and social discrimination that confronted African Americans in the first half of the twentieth century. This discrimination was an insurmountable barrier to the development of a strong African American community. Barry Bluestone writes:

> Denied the educational resources and the physical infrastructure necessary to develop technical skills and provide an efficient means of production, while at the same time denied access to the corporate sector through discriminatory practices in housing, in the schools, on the job, and in the capital market, the ghetto has been forced to rely upon its one remaining resource: cheap labor. (231)

Job and housing discrimination were interrelated consequences of educational and economic discrimination against African Americans in Chicago. The result of such discrimination in Big Walter's life is exhaustion, poverty, anger, and despair. These feelings are perceptible in Mama's words:

> I seen ... him ... night after night ... come in ... and look at that rug ... and then look at me ... the red showing in his eyes ... the veins moving in his head ... I seen him grow thin and old before he was forty ... working and working and working like somebody's old horse ... killing himself. (129)

The repetitions and the ellipses in Mama's assertion suggest that Big Walter's work was a dreary cycle of hardships and self-sacrifice. These hardships were present in both his family life and his workplace, where violence against blacks was very common. In an essay exploring the challenges that confronted black workers in Chicago in the early twentieth century, the critic William M. Tuttle states:

> As racial friction mounted with the heat in the spring and summer of 1919, whites and blacks battled on the city's streetcars and in its parks and schools. Several Negroes were murdered in mob assaults, and both blacks and whites armed themselves for the riot that numerous Chicagoans feared would erupt at any moment . . . . This riot was also the result of longstanding discord between white and black job competitors in the Chicago labor market. (87)

The intensity of violence shattered the vision of a peaceful and economically secure life that black Southern migrants such as the Youngers had hoped to have as they fled from oppression in the South to seek jobs and justice in the North. Mama tells Walter: "In my time we was worried about not being lynched and getting to the North if we could and how to stay alive and still have a pinch of dignity too" (74). However, Mama's American dream for peace in the North is compromised by the rampant segregation that her family faces in being compelled not to buy a house from the white neighborhood of the Clybourne Park Improvement Association. Shortly after Mama arranges to buy the house, she receives the visit from Mr. Karl Lindner, the white spokesperson of the Clybourne Park Improvement Association. As Lindner explains, the purpose of his visit is to convince the Youngers not to move to Clybourne Park: "It is a matter of the people of Clybourne Park believing, rightly or wrongly, as I say, that for the happiness of all concerned that our Negro families are happier when they live in their *own* communities" (118). Lindner acts like a judge who gives a last sentence after having heard the arguments of every interested party. He assumes that he and the rest of the Clybourne Park people know what is best for the Youngers. He presumes that a black person moving into a white neighborhood cannot be happy. When he finds that his segregationist strategy has not altered the Youngers' determination to move, Mr. Lindner attempts to arrange a financial settlement: "Our association is prepared, through the collective effort of our people, to buy the house from you at a financial gain to your family"(118). This proposal shows that the C.P.I.A. as an organization is prepared to use its economic power to maintain its racist policies. Such racist behavior was not uncommon in reality. The practice of buying out the houses of prospective black residents was pervasive in American society during the 1950s.

Raisin also depicts the fundamental ways in which job discrimination affects the generation represented by Mama and Big Walter's son Walter and his wife Ruth. Walter belongs to the black working class in Chicago of the 1950s. Early in the play, he voices his dissatisfaction with his work. He tells Mama:

> A job. (*Looks at her*) Mama, a job? I open and close car doors all day long. I drive a man around in his limousine and I say, "Yes, sir; no, sir; very good, sir; shall I take the Drive, sir?" Mama, that ain't no kind of job ... that ain't nothing at all. (*Very quietly*) Mama, I don't know if I can make you understand. (73)

Walter minimizes the position of a car driver because to him it diminishes his manhood and his sense of individual worth. In his own view, his work as a chauffeur places him in a boring and humiliating relationship of servitude to white Americans. Walter wants a work life that is far better than that of his parents. According to Harold M. Baron, in the 1920s and 1930s, blacks used to perform vast quantities of "common labor; heavy, hot, and dirty work; pouring crucibles; work in the grinding room; and so on" (197). Compared to these occupations, the position of a car driver may be, in some ways, better. Certainly, it involves less strenuous physical labor. However, in Walter's view, this position reflects the same demeaning, humiliating, and alienating quality that exists in any type of menial job. Walter's problem in finding a decent job is a result of his illiteracy and his lack of business skills, but race prejudice and discrimination are crucial factors in his inability to acquire them. When combined with segregation and race prejudice, illiteracy and lack of business skills create a terrible dilemma for the black man. In 1901, W.E.B. Du Bois wrote an article depicting the detrimental effect that a lack of skills, along with prejudice and discrimination, had on the life of the black man:

> Young colored men can seldom get positions above menial grade, and the training of the older men unfits them for competitive business. Then always the uncertain but ever present factor of racial prejudice is present to hinder or at least make more difficult the advance of the colored merchant or businessman. (107)

Du Bois emphasized the importance of strong educational training to promote the development of a talented black leadership that could help develop America. In "Careers Open to College-Bred Negroes," written in 1898, Du Bois stated that the educated black man should be a man "who, by rational methods and business sense, with a knowledge of the world market, the methods of transportation, and the possibilities of the soil, will make this land of the South to bloom and blossom" (Huggins 834).

In *Raisin*, Du Bois's idea of an educated black leadership is challenged by Mrs. Johnson, a neighbor of the Younger family, who asserts that she always "thinks like Booker T. Washington said that time—'Education has spoiled many a good plow hand—'"(103). Here, Hansberry presents Mrs. Johnson's essentially Southern and old-fashioned viewpoint as a source of ridicule. Her unsupported comment represents just the kind of outmoded thinking that Hansberry wanted blacks to reject in the 1950s. First, in Mrs. Johnson's view, education is not very important for the salvation of the black man. This position is decisively rejected in *Raisin*, as evidenced from the great emphasis that the Youngers give to the education of Beneatha and Travis. Second, Mrs. Johnson's comment centers on agricultural employment, something that is not relevant to Walter's dream of a business career. It even appears that Mrs. Johnson misunderstands Washington, because her statement infers that Washington was totally against the education of the black man, which is not true. As Jeanne Noble has pointed out, Washington "sought to build an educational blueprint for further developing skills by founding Tuskegee Institute in Alabama" (Noble 58). Washington emphasized that black people needed marketing skills in order to be "able to perfect themselves in the industries at their doors and in securing property"(60). While his educational strategy differed sharply from that of the Harvard-trained intellectual, like Du Bois, Washington recognized that black men needed to possess the skills that would enable them to navigate in the American economy.

Walter lacks basic business skills. Unable to handle his poverty and his frustration with the economic system, he leaves his position as a driver. Ruth complains about this: "Walter, you ain't been to work for three days . . . . You're going to lose your job"(105). Walter responds with a sense of futility and resignation: "That's right . . . [*He turns on the radio*]" (105). His defeatism leaves him vulnerable to the charge that he is an irresponsible husband and that he actually contributes to the economic trouble of the Youngers. When Ruth chastises Walter—"Oh, Walter, and with your mother working like a dog every day" (105) —he responds with a real sadness: "That's sad too—Everything is sad" (105). Walter's skepticism stems from his feeling of being left out of a privileged world that requires basic skills and a solid business sense, all things that he lacks. Walter is probably literate, but he does not have the kind of experience that would really equip him for the success he imagines. Unlike Walter's, the economic situation of many young black men in the Chicago of the 1950s was not totally desperate. In a remarkable study of civil rights activism in Chicago written in 1993, James R. Ralph pointed out that

> In the 1950s the image of the city as a promised land, cultivated in the early years of the twentieth century, still retained some of its lustre among blacks. In 1957, a leading black entrepreneur could still write a booklet of a hundred pages entitled "Chicago: City of Progress and Opportunity." By 1960 the median black family income approached $5,000, far higher than the national black average, and though the black unemployment rate tended to run roughly three times as high as the fluctuating figure for whites during the 1950s, most blacks could secure jobs. (13)

Ralph's comment is uninformed by the sense of Walter's frustration. It suggests that, in the 1950s, there was some work, literacy, and hope available in the black community. However, Ralph fails to mention that many black men, like Walter, were left out of economic advancement because they lacked basic business skills. Clearly, Ralph's allusion to the "lustre" that blacks retained from the image of Chicago as a "promised land" does not reflect the sense of the Youngers' sub-standard economic and work conditions. For example, when she talks about her boss, Ruth points out the precariousness of the jobs available to black workers and the humiliations that they engendered: "She'd be calling up the agency and screaming at them, 'My girl didn't come in today—send me somebody!'" (42). Ruth is usually exhausted since, in addition to her outside employment, she is married and has her own domestic job. As Friedman Sharon pointed out in her 1984 study of Feminism in American drama, "The condition of women forced to work at subsistence wages and relegated to domestic labor is epitomized by Hansberry in her portrayal of the black domestic who must clean the kitchen of white women as well as her own" (85).

At the end of *Raisin*, the future labor prospects of Hansberry's characters provide grounds for both optimism and pessimism. The future work possibilities for Ruth seem bleak. Unlike Beneatha and George, Ruth has less chance to find a decent job because she is not going to school. Indeed, in one sense, Ruth and Walter face some-what similar problems. Due to their lack of education, neither seems a likely candidate for success in a professional career. Walter will succeed financially because he abandons his frustration and becomes more reasonable. Walter says, "Mama. You always telling me to see life like it is . . . You know it's all divided up . . . Between the takers and the taken. [He laughs] I've figured it out finally" (141). This is a positive sign that suggests a new strength in Walter's mind and understanding of life. As he insists, Walter now understands that life is not about having a dream, but doing your best in order to achieve it. He knows that his success in the American economy will depend on his strength and his ability to stand strong and take risks. Studies of work and education in the post-World War II era suggest that, in the late 1950s and early 1960s, blacks had achieved substantial economic progress. In a 1965 essay on the employment patterns of African Americans, Professor Ray Marshall pointed out that:

> Significant gains were made by nonwhites in the 1955-1962 period in such professional categories as hospital, medical, and other health services, welfare and religious institutions, and

business and repair services. The relative increase of nonwhites in these occupations was 70 per cent, about twice that of whites. Nonwhites also have gained relatively faster than whites in the educational services field and in government employment. (4)

Marshall's comment suggests that in the late 1950s and beginning of the 1960s, well-educated African Americans did find significant opportunities to move into professional occupations. As a prospective student of medicine, Beneatha will be lucky to find a job after her education; so too will be George. The positive change in work opportunities that Beneatha and George gained was, in some way, an effect of the increasing level of education among Blacks that started in the 1940s. As the critic Karl E. Taeuber pointed out in a 1972 essay on the life of blacks in American cities, between 1940 and 1950, the educational level of African Americans substantially increased (169). In 1960, one year after *Raisin* was published, the job market opened widely for African Americans through social welfare programs. As Nicholas Lemann pointed out in a 1991 history: "Black employment in public social welfare programs increased by 850,000 from 1960 to 1976 (a period during which the black middle class tripled in size), and many new government jobs were also created for blacks outside the social welfare sphere, for example in local transportation authorities and law enforcement agencies" (201). This remarkable change in work opportunity is, in one way, a realization of the dream of economic success and middle-class status that Hansberry fosters in *Raisin*. She envisioned the dream and knew that it would eventually "explode success" "like a raisin in a sun."

Raisin discusses the labor conditions of African Americans in the 1920s and 1950s, when they confronted job discrimination and poor economic conditions. The play reflects in Big Walter's work experience the frustration and the enduring pain that blacks suffered from poor employment and life quality in the 1920s. Like Big Walter, Walter Lee, who represents the generation of blacks of the 1950s, faces difficulties in achieving economic advancement. This predicament is caused not only by his dissatisfaction with menial jobs, but also by a lack of support from the rich middle class that George represents. *Raisin* transcends this hopelessness by suggesting that Walter and Beneatha will eventually achieve their dream of success. The family moves to Clybourne Park, marking their new membership to the black middle class. At the end of the play, Hansberry clearly does suggest that the Younger family, as a whole, has legitimate grounds for hope for improvement in their employment opportunities and economic situation. Thanks to their education, George and Beneatha may succeed financially by moving into the increasing number of professional occupations that were becoming available to African Americans in the late 1950s.

WORKS CITED

Abramson, Doris E. *Negro Playwrights in the American Theatre*. New York: Columbia UP, 1969.

Baraka, Amiri. "*Raisin in The Sun*'s Enduring Passion." *Washington Post*. November 16, 1986. F1, 3.

Barclay. Ed. *Racial Conflict, Discrimination and Power: Historical and Contemporary Studies*. New York: AMS, 1970.

Bloom, Harold. *Black American Women Poets and Dramatists*. New York: Chelsea House, 1996.

Bluestone, Barry. "Black Capitalism: The Path to Black Liberation" in William

Carter, Steven R. *Hansberry's Drama: Commitment amid Complexity*. Urbana: U of Illinois P, 1991.

Cheney, Anne. *Lorraine Hansberry*. Boston: Twayne, 1984.

Cottingham, Clement. "Blacks in Transition: An Overview of Afro-Americans" *The Social Reality of Ethnic America*. Ed. Rudolph Gomez. Lexington: Heath, 1974.

Cruse, Harold. *The Crisis of The Negro Intellectual: A Historical Analysis of The Future of Black Leadership*. New York: Quill, 1984.

Dinnerstein, Leonard and alii. *Natives and Strangers: Blacks, Indians, and Immigrants in America*. New York: Oxford UP, 1990.

Du Bois, W.E.B. "Keeping Down The Black Man Now Will Haunt Us Later." *New York Times Magazine*. April 14, 1996, 107.

Frazier, E Franklin. *The Negro Family in The United States*. Chicago: U. of Chicago P, 1966.

Friedman, Sharon. "Feminism as Theme in Twentieth Century American Women Drama." *American Studies*. 25.1 (1984): 69-89.

Gossett, Thomas F. *Race: The History of an Idea in America*. New York: Schocken, 1967.

Greenberg, Edward S. *The Struggle For Democracy*. New York: Harpercollins, 1992.

Hansberry, Lorraine. *Lorraine Hansberry Speaks Out: Art and The Black Revolution*. Cassette. Ed. Robert Nemiroff. Caedmon, 1970.

———. *A Raisin in The Sun*. 1959. New York: Vintage, 1994.

———. *To Be Young, Gifted and Black: Lorraine Hansberry in Her own Words*. Englewood Cliffs: Prentice, 1969.

Huggins, Nathan Irvin. *Du Bois, W.E.B. Writings*. New York: Viking Press, 1986.

Hughes, Langston. "Harlem." *The Collected Poems of Langston Hughes*. Eds. Arnold Rampersad and David Roessel. New York: Vintage Books, 1994, 426.

Jarraway, David R. "Montage of an Otherness Deferred: Dreaming Subjectivity in Langston Hughes." *American Literature* 68.4 (December 1996): 819-847.

Johnson, Philip A. *Call Me Neighbor, Call Me Friend: The Case of the Integration of a Neighborhood on Chicago's South Side*. New York: Doubleday, 1965.

Keppel, Ben. *The Work of Democracy: Ralph Bunche, Kenneth B. Clark, Lorraine Hansberry, and the Cultural Politics of Race*. Cambridge: Harvard UP, 1995.

King, Nicole. " 'You Think Like You White:' Questioning Race and Racial Community Through the Lens of Middle-Class Desire(s)." *Novel: A Forum on Fiction* 35.2/3 (Spring - Summer, 2002): 211-230.

Lemann, Nicholas. *The Promised Land: The Great Migration of Blacks and How It Changed America*. New York: Alfred A. Knopf, 1991.

Marshall, Ray. "The Job Problems of Negroes" in Northrup, Herbert R. Ed. *The Negro and Employment Opportunity: Problems and Practices*. Ann Arbor: U of Michigan, 1965.

Mitchell, Loften. *Black Drama: The Story of The American Negro in Theatre*. New York: Hawthorne Books, 1967.

Nemiroff, Robert. Ed. *To Be Young, Gifted and Black: Lorraine Hansberry in Her own Words*. Englewood Cliffs: Prentice, 1969.

Noble, Jeanne. *Beautiful, Also, Are The Souls of My Black Sisters: A History of The Black Woman in America*. Englewood Cliffs: Prentice Hall, 1978.

Persons, Stow. *Ethnic Studies at Chicago: 1905-45*. Urbana: U of Illinois P. 1987.

Ralph, James R. *Northern Protest: Martin Luther King, Jr., Chicago, and The Civil Rights Movement*. Cambridge: Harvard UP, 1993.

Richards, David. "Shining 'Raisin in The Sun': At The Eisenhower, a Powerful Production of a Great American Play." *Washington Post*. November 17, 1986, D1.

Taeuber, Karl E. *Negroes in Cities: Residential Segregation and Neighborhood Changes*. New York: Atheneum, 1972.

Tuttle, William M. "Labor Conflict and Racial Violence: The Black Worker in Chicago: 1894-1917." Milton Cantor. Ed. *Black Labor in America*. Westport: Negro UP, 1970.

Wilkerson, Margaret B. "The Dark Vision of Lorraine Hansberry: Excerpt from a Literary Biography." *The Massachusetts Review*. 28; 4, 1987, 642-50.

Wilson, Joseph. *Black Labor in America, 1865-1983: A Selected Annotated Bibliography*. New York: Greenwood Press, 1986.

Wright, Kathleen. *The Other Americans: Minorities in American History*. Greenwich, Conn.: Fawcett Book, 1969.

"SELF-RELIANCE"
(RALPH WALDO EMERSON)

❧ ❧

"Emerson as an American"
Julian Hawthorne,
in *The Genius and Character of Emerson* (1885)

INTRODUCTION

In this appreciation of Emerson, Julian Hawthorne (Nathaniel's son) meditates upon what it means to be American, both literally and spiritually. According to Hawthorne, America is set apart from European cultures and nations by its foundation in revolutionary ideas, or as Hawthorne phrases it, by its being "born after the spirit" rather than the "flesh." America, for Hawthorne, is primarily an open mental construct rather than a demarcated physical space. This implies that our cultural experiences are founded upon a spiritual realm of ideas. In this context, Hawthorne contends that Emerson is the quintessential American intellectual; one who gives voice to intuitions that enlarge our understanding of humanity and nature without succumbing to the temptations of constraining, systematic thought. Although not focused specifically on "Self-Reliance," Hawthorne's analysis addresses the autonomy of the self and the related responsibilities of the State that "Self-Reliance" extols.

❧

Hawthorne, Julian. "Emerson as an American." *The Genius and Character of Emerson*. F.B. Sanborn ed. Boston: James R. Osgood, 1885.

It might be said, both that the time has passed, and that it is not yet come, to assign Emerson his place among the thinkers of the world; but it can never be out of place to remark that his bent and genius were profoundly and typically American. So far as his thoughts and opinions had color, it was that of his native soil. He believed in our great experiment; he was not disheartened by our mistakes; he had faith that the goodness and wisdom of humanity would, in the long run, prove more than equal to the goodness and wisdom of any possible man; and that men would, at last, govern themselves more nobly and successfully than any individual monarch could govern them. He speaks, indeed, of Representative Men; but he was no hero-worshipper, like Carlyle. A hero was, to him, not so much a powerful and dominating personality, as a relatively impersonal instrument of God for the accomplishment of some great end. It would follow from this that humanity is the greatest hero of all; and Emerson, perhaps, believed—in this sense if not otherwise—that God has put on human nature. In the American Republic he saw the most promising field for the unhampered working out of this Divine inspiration within us.

But he was American not by determination only, but by the constitution of his mind. His catholic and unflinching acceptance of what truth soever came to him was in accordance with the American idea, though not, unfortunately, with the invariable American practice. As our land is open to the world to come and inhabit it, so was his mind open to all vigorous and progressive ideas, be their hue and parentage what they might. It were rash to predict how soon America will reach his standard of her ideal; but it is encouraging to remember that nothing in her political construction renders its final attainment impossible.

It is not with us as with other peoples. Our position seems vague, because not primarily related to the senses. I know where England or Italy is, and recognize an Englishman or an Italian; but Americans are not, to the same extent, limited by geographical boundaries. America did not originate as did European nations: they were born after the flesh, but we after the spirit. Their frontiers must be defended, and their race kept distinct; but highly though I esteem our immeasurable East and West, North and South, our Pacific and our Atlantic and our Gulf of Mexico, I cannot help deeming these a secondary matter. If America be not more than these United States, then the United States are little better than a penal colony. It is convenient, no doubt, that a great idea shall find a suitable stage and incarnation; but it depends not upon these things. It was accidental, or I would rather say providential, that the Puritans came to New England, or that Columbus discovered the continent for them; but the body is instrumental merely: it enables the spirit to take hold of its mortal affairs, just as the hilt enables us to grasp the sword. Had the Puritans not come to New England, still their spirit would have lived, and somehow made its place. How many Puritans, indeed, for how many previous ages, had been trying, and failing, to get foothold in the world! They were known by many names; their voice was heard in many tongues: the hour for them to touch their earthly inheritance had not yet struck. But the latent impetus meanwhile accumulated, and the "Mayflower" was driven across the Atlantic by it at last!

And the "Mayflower" sails still between the Old World and the New. Day by day it brings new settlers, if not to Boston Bay, and Castle Garden, and the Golden Gate, at any rate to our mental ports and wharves. I cannot take up a European newspaper without finding an American idea in it. Many of us make the trip to Europe every summer; but we come back, and bring with us many more who come to stay. I do not specify the literal emigrants in the steerage; they may or may not be Americans. But England and the Continent are full of Americans who were born and may die there, and who may be better Americans than the Bostonian or the New Yorker who votes the Republican, or the Democratic, or even the Independent ticket. Whatever their birthplace or residence, they belong to us, and are with us. Broadway and Washington Street, New Hampshire and Colorado, extend all over Europe. Russia tries to banish them to Siberia, but in vain. Are mountains and prairies solid facts?—the geography of the mind is more stubborn! I dare say there are oblique-eyed, pig-tailed New Englanders in the Celestial Empire. Though they may never have visited these shores, or heard of Kearney, they think our thought, have apprehended our idea, and by and by they or their heirs will cause it to prevail.

It is useless to hide our heads in the grass, and shun to rise to the height of our occasion. We stand as the fulfillment of prophecy; we attest a new departure in moral and intellectual development,—or which of us does not, must suffer annihilation. If I deny my birthright as an American, I vanish and am not missed; an American takes my place. The position is not altogether luxurious: you cannot sit and hold your hands. Hard and unpleasant things are expected of you, which you neglect at your peril. It is like the fable of the mermaid: she loved a mortal youth, and in order to win his affection prayed for the limbs and feet of a human maiden. Her prayer was answered, and she met her prince; but each step she took was as if she trod on razors. So it is fine to sit at ease and reflect on being American; but when we must arise and do an American's duty, how sharp the razors are!

We do not always stand the test; flesh and blood do not differ essentially on different sides of the planet. Possibly we are too numerous. It were strange if here and there among fifty millions, one were not quite a hero. Possibly, indeed, that little original band of "Mayflower" Pilgrims has not greatly multiplied since their disembarkation, so far as their spiritual progeny are concerned. We do not find a succession of Winthrops and Endicotts in the chair of the Governor and on the floor of the Senate. Bridget serves us in the kitchen; but Patrick, more helpful yet, enters the Legislature and serves the State. But turn and turn about is fair play; and we ought once in a while to take off our coat and do unto Patrick as he does unto us.

When we get in a tight place we are apt to slip out under a plea of European precedent; but was it not to avoid European precedents that we came here? America should take the highest ground in her political and commercial relations. Why must the President of the Western Union, for instance, or a late Governor of Massachusetts, be cited as typical Americans? The dominance of such men has effects out of proportion with their personal acts. What they may do is of small import: the mischief is in their inclining us to believe (as Emerson puts it) in two gods. They make the morality of Wall Street and the White House seem a different thing from that of the parlor and nursery. "He may be a little shady on Change," we say, "but a capital fellow when you know him." But if I am a capital fellow when you know me, I can afford to be shady in my business. I can endure public opprobrium so long as it remains public: it is the private cold looks that trouble me.

In short, we have two Americas,—the street-corner and newspaper America, and the ideal America. At present, the former makes the most noise; but the latter has made the former possible. A great crowd is drawn together for some noble purpose,—to declare a righteous war, or to pass a just decree. But there are persons on the outskirts unable to hear the orators, and with time hanging idle on their hands, who take to throwing bricks, smashing hats, or perhaps picking pockets. They may have assembled with virtuous and patriotic intentions; under favorable circumstances they might themselves have been the orators. Virtue and patriotism are not private property; at certain times any one may possess them. And, on the other hand, how often do we see persons of high respectability and trust turn out sorry scamps! We vary according to our company and the event: the outlook maybe sordid today, but during the Civil War the air was full of heroism. So the real and the ideal America, though far apart in one sense, are, in another, as near as our right hand to our left. They exist side by side in each one of us. But civil war comes not every day; nor do we desire it, even to show us once more that we are worthy of our destiny. Some less expensive and quieter method must remind us of that. And of such methods none, perhaps, is better than to review the lives of Americans who were truly great: to ask what their country meant to them; what they asked of her; what virtues and vices they detected in her. Passion may be generous, but cannot last, and coldness and indifference follow; but in calm moods reason and example reach us, and their lesson abides.

Although many a true American is born and dies abroad, Emerson was born and died here. In the outward accidents of generation and descent, he could not have been more American than he was. Of course, one prefers that it should be so. A rare gem should be fitly set. It helps us to believe in ourselves to know that Emerson's ancestry was not only Puritan but clerical; that through his heart ran the vital thread of the idea that created us. We have many traits not found in him; but nothing in him is not a sublimation and concentration of something in us; and such is the selection and grouping of the elements that he is a typical figure. Indeed, he is all type; which is the same as to say there is nobody like him. And, mentally, he is all force; his mind acts without natural impediment or friction,—a machine that runs unhindered by the contact of its parts. As he was physically lean and slender of figure, and his face but a welding together of features, so there was no adipose tissue in his thought. It is pure, clear, and accurate, and has the fault of dryness, but often moves with exquisite beauty. It is not adhesive; it sticks to nothing except to the memory, nor anything to it. After ranging through the philosophies of the world, it emerges clean and characteristic as ever. It has many affinities, but no adhesion; it is not always self-adherent. There are in any of his essays separate statements presenting no logical continuity; but though this may cause anxiety to disciples of Emerson, it never troubled him. Wandering at will in the garden of moral and religious philosophy, it was his part to pluck such blossoms as he saw were good and beautiful,—not to discover their botanical relationship. He might, for art or harmony's sake, arrange them according to their hue or fragrance; but it was not his affair to go further in their classification.

This intuitional method, how little soever it satisfies those who want their thinking done for them,—who want not only all the cities of the earth, but straight roads to connect them,—carries its own justification. "There is but one Reason," is Emerson's saying; and we confess again and again that the truth he asserts is true indeed. Even his divergences from the truth, when he is betrayed into them, confirm the rule; for these are seldom intuitions at first hand, but intuitions from previous intuitions,—deductions. They are from Emerson, instead of from the Absolute; tinted, instead of colorless. They show a mental bias, redeeming him back to humanity. We love him the more for them, because they imply that for him, too, was a choice of ways, and that he struggled and watched to choose the right.

We are so wedded to systems, and so prone to connect a system with a man, that Emerson's absence of system strikes us as a defect. But truth has no system, nor has the human mind. We cannot bear to be illogical, and enlist, some under this philosopher's banner, some under that; and so sacrifice to consistency at least half the truth. We cross-examine our intuitions, and ask them, not whether they are true in themselves, but what are their tendencies. If they would lead us to stultify some past conclusion to which we stand committed, we drop them like hot coals. This, to Emerson, was the nakedest personal vanity. Recognizing his finiteness, he did not covet consistency. One thing was true to-day: to-morrow, its opposite. Was it for him to elect which should have the preference? To reject either was to reject all: it belonged to God to reconcile such contradictions. Between Infinite and finite can exist no ratio; and the Creator's consistency implies the inconsistency of the creature.

Emerson's Americanism, therefore, was Americanism in its last and purest analysis,—which is giving him praise, and to America hope. But let me not pay him, who was so full of modesty and humility, the ungrateful compliment of holding him up as our permanent ideal. It is his tendency, his quality, that are valuable, and only in a minor degree his actual results. All human results are limited, and according to the epoch. Emerson does not solve for all time the problem of the universe. He solves nothing; but, what is more useful, he gives impetus and direction to lofty endeavor. He does not anticipate the lessons of the ages; but be teaches us so to deal with circumstance as to secure the good instead of the evil issue. New horizons opening before us will carry us beyond the scope of Emerson's surmise; but we shall not easily improve upon his aim and attitude. In spaces beyond the stars are marvels such as it has not entered into the mind of man to conceive; but there, as here, the right aspiration will still be upward, and the right conduct still be humble and charitable.

I spoke of Emerson's absence of system; yet his writings have coherence by virtue of their single-hearted motive. Those with whom, in this tribute to our beloved poet and sage, I have the honor to be associated, will doubtless notice, as I do, how the whole of Emerson illustrates every aspect of him. Whether your subject be his religion, his ethics, his social aspects, or what not, your picture gains color and form from each page that he has written. All that he is permeates all that he has done. His books cannot be indexed, and he can treat no topic without incorporating in his statement the germs at least of all his thought and belief. In this respect he illustrates the definition of light,—the presence of the general at the particular. And, to say truth, I am somewhat loath to diffract this pure ray to the arbitrary end of my special theme. Why speak of him as an American? He was American because he was himself. But America gives less limitation than other nationalities to a generous and serene personality.

Emerson's "English Traits" perhaps reveal his American traits more than most that he has written. We are described by our criticisms of others: the exceptions we take are the mould of our own figures. So this volume affords valuable glimpses of Emerson's contours. And it is almost as remarkable a work for him to write, as a volume of his essays would be for any one else; it is to his other books as flesh and blood to spirit. Emersonian flesh and blood, it is true, and semi-translucent; but it completes the man for us: without it, he would have been too problematical. Those who never personally knew him may here finish and solidify their impressions of him. His sympathy with England and the English is beyond our expectation of the mind that evolved "Nature" and "The Over-Soul." The grasp of his hand, I remember, was firm and stout, and we perceive those qualities in the cordiality of "English Traits." And it is an objective book; it affords a unique basis for comparing his general human faculty with that of other men. He relents from the airy heights he treads so easily, and descends to measure himself against all comers. He means only to report their stature, leaving himself out of the story; but their answers reveal the questioner. We suspect (though he did not) that his English friends were put to it to keep the pace of their clear-faced, penetrating, attentive visitor.

He has seldom said of his own countrymen such comfortable things as he vouchsafes to the English: as a father who is severe with his own children will freely admire others, for whom he is not responsible. Emerson is stern towards what we are, and arduous indeed in his estimate of what we ought to be. He intimates that we are not quite worthy yet of our continent,—have not yet lived up to our blue china. In America the geography is sublime, but the men are not. Even our more presentable public acts are due to the money-making spirit. The benefaction derived in the great West from railroads vastly exceeds any intentional philanthropy on record. He will not celebrate the Forty-niners, though admitting that California gets civilized in this immoral way; and is fain to suppose that, just as there is a use in the world for poisons, so the world cannot move without rogues. Huge animals (like America) nourish huge parasites, and the rancor of the disease attests the strength of the constitution. He ridicules our unsuspecting provincialism. "Have you seen the dozen great men of New York and Boston? Then you may as well die!" He does not spare our tendency to declamation; quotes a shrewd foreigner's remark that whatever we say has a little the air of a speech, and proceeds to ask whether the American forest has refreshed some weeds of old Pietish barbarism just ready to die out. He finds the especial foible of American youth to be—pretension; and remarks, suggestively, that we talk about the key of the age, but the key of all ages is imbecility! He will not be reconciled to the mania for travel: there is a restlessness in our people that argues want of character; can we never extract this tape-worm of Europe from our brains? Yet he concedes that we go to Europe to be Americanized, and has faith that one day we shall cast out the passion for Europe by the passion for America. As for our political doings,—politics is an after-word, a poor patching: we shall learn to supersede politics by education. He sympathizes with Lovelace, and holds that freedom and slavery are inward, not outward, conditions. Slavery is not in fetters, but in feeling; you cannot by external restrictions eradicate the irons; and the way to emancipate the slave is to make him comprehend his inviolable dignity and freedom as a human being. Amelioration of outward circumstances will be the effect, but can never be the means, of mental and moral improvement. Nothing, he affirms, is more disgusting than the crowing about liberty by slaves, as most men are, and the flippant mistaking for freedom of some paper preamble, like a Declaration of Independence, or the statute right to vote. Our America has a bad name for superficialness. Great men and great nations have not been boasters and buffoons, but perceivers of the terrors of life, and have nerved themselves to face it. Nor will he be deceived by the clamor of blatant reformers. "If an angry bigot assumes the bountiful cause of Abolition, and comes to me with his last news from Barbadoes, why should I not say to him, 'Go, love thy infant; love thy woodchopper; be good-natured and modest; have *that* grace, and never varnish your hard, uncharitable ambition with this incredible tenderness for black folk a thousand miles off!'"

He does not shrink from questioning the validity of some of our pet institutions,—universal suffrage, for instance. In old Egypt the vote of a prophet was reckoned equal to one hundred hands, and was much underestimated. Shall we, then, he asks, judge a country by the majority, or by the minority? By the minority, surely! 'Tis pedantry to estimate nations by the census, or by square miles of territory, or other than by their importance to the mind of the time. The majority are unripe, and know not yet their own opinion. Yet he would not counsel organic alteration in this respect, believing that with the progress of enlightenment such coarse constructions of human rights will adjust themselves. He concedes the sagacity of the Fultons and Watts of politics, who, noticing that the opinion of the million was the terror of the world, grouped it on a level, instead of piling it into a mountain, and so contrived to make of this terror the most harmless and energetic form of a State. But, again, he would not have us regard the State as a finality, or as relieving any man of his individual responsibility for his actions and purposes. Confide in God, and not in your money, nor in the State because it is the guard of it. The Union itself has no basis but the good pleasure of the majority to be united. The wise and just men impart strength to the State, not receive it; and if all went down, they and their like would soon combine in a new and better constitution. Yet let us not forget that only by the supernatural is man strong,—nothing so weak as an egotist. We are mighty only as vehicles of a truth before which State and individual are alike ephemeral. In this sense we, like other nations, shall have our kings and nobles,—the leading and inspiration of the best; and he who would become a member of that nobility must obey his heart.

Government, which has been a fossil, must, he says, become a plant: statute law should express, not impede, the mind of mankind. Feudalism succeeds monarchy, and this, again, is followed by trade; the good and evil of which is, that it would put everything in the market,—talent, beauty, virtue, and man himself. Trade has done its work; it has faults, and will end, as the others. We need not fear its aristocracy, because, not being entailed, it can have no permanence. In the time to come we shall, he hopes, be less anxious to be governed: government without governors will, for the first time, be adamantine; each man shall govern himself in the interests of all. These are radical views, but Emerson asks whether every man is not sometimes a radical in politics? Men are conservative when they are least vigorous or most luxurious; for Conservatism stands on man's limitations, Reform on his infinitude.

But the age of the quadruped is going out; the age of brain and heart is coming in. We are still too pettifogging and imitative in our legislative conceptions; our Legislature should become more catholic and cosmopolitan than any other. Strong natures are inevitable patriots; let us be strong enough to trust in humanity. The time, the age,—what is that but a few prominent persons and a few active persons who epitomize the times? There is a bribe possible for any finite will; but the pure sympathy with universal ends is an infinite force, and cannot be bribed or bent. The world wants saviors and religions: society is servile from want of will; but there is a destiny by which the human race is guided,—the race never dying, the individual never spared; its law is, you shall have everything as a member, nothing to yourself. Referring to the various communities so much in vogue some years ago, he holds them valuable, not for what they have done, but for the indication they give of the revolution that is on the way. Communities place faith in mutual support; but only as a man puts off from himself external support is he strong, and will he prevail. He is weaker by every recruit to his banner. A man ought to compare advantageously with a river, an oak, or a mountain. He must not shun whatever comes to him in the way of duty: the only path of escape is—performance! He must rely on Providence, but not in a timid or ecclesiastical spirit; no use to dress up that terrific benefactor in the clean shirt and white neckcloth of a student of divinity. We shall come out well, despite whatever personal or political disasters; for here, in America, is the home of man. After deducting our pitiful politics,—shall John or Jonathan sit in the chair and hold the purse?—and making due allowance for our frivolities and insanities, there still remains an organic simplicity and liberty, which, when it loses its balance, redresses itself presently, and which offers to the human mind opportunities not known elsewhere.

Whenever Emerson touches upon the fundamental elements of social and rational life, it is always to enlarge and illuminate our conceptions of them. We are not wont, for example, to question the propriety of the sentiment of patriotism. We are to swear by our own *Lares* and *Penates*, and stand by the American eagle, right or wrong. But Emerson instantly goes beneath this interpretation, and exposes its crudity. The true sense of patriotism is almost the reverse of the popular sense. He has no sympathy with that boyish egotism, hoarse with cheering for our side, for our State, for our town: the right patriotism consists in the delight which springs from contributing our peculiar and legitimate advantages to the benefit of humanity. Every foot of soil has its proper quality; the grape on two sides of the fence has new flavors; and so every acre on the globe, every family of men, every point of climate, has its distinguishing virtues. This admitted, Emerson yields in patriotism to no one; he is only concerned that the advantages we contribute shall be as many instead of as few as possible. This country, he says, does not lie here in the sun causeless; and, though it may not be easy to define its influence, men feel already its emancipating quality in the careless self-reliance of the manners, in the freedom of thought, in the direct roads by which grievances are reached and redressed, and even in the reckless and sinister politics,—not less than in purer expressions. Bad as it is, this freedom leads onward and upward to a Columbia of thought and art, which is the last and endless end of Columbus' adventure. Nor is this poet of virtue and philosophy ever more truly patriotic, from his spiritual standpoint, than when he casts scorn and indignation upon his country's sins and frailties:—

> "But who is he that prates of the vulture of mankind?
> Go, blindworm, go,—behold the famous States harrying Mexico
> With rifle and with knife!
>
> "Or who, with accent bolder, dare praise the freedom-loving mountaineer?
> I found by thee, O rushing Contoocook, and in thy valleys, Agiochook,
> The jackals of the negro-holder!
> . . . .
> "What boots thy zeal, O glowing friend, who wouldst indignant rend
> The northland from the south!
> Wherefore? to what good end? Boston Bay and Bunker Hill would serve things still;—things are of the snake!
> . . . .
> 'Tis the day of the chattel,—web to weave, and corn to grind;
> Things are in the saddle, and ride mankind!"

It is worth noting that he, whose verse is uniformly so abstractly and intellectually beautiful, kindles to passion whenever his theme is America. The loftiest patriotism never found more ardent and eloquent expression than in the hymn sung at the completion of

Concord Monument, on the 19th of April, 1836. There is no rancor in it, no taunt of triumph,—

"The foe long since in silence slept,"—

but throughout there resounds a note of pure and deep rejoicing at the victory of justice over oppression, which Concord Fight so aptly symbolized. In "Hamatreya" and "The Earth-Song" another chord is struck, of calm, laconic irony. Shall we too, he asks,—we Yankee farmers, descendants of the men who gave up all for freedom,—go back to the creed outworn of feudalism and aristocracy, and affirm of the land that yields us produce,

"'Tis mine, my children's, and my name's"?

Earth laughs in flowers at our boastfulness, and asks,—

"How am I theirs,
If they cannot hold me,
But I hold them?"

Or read "Monadnoc," and mark the insight and power wherewith the significance of the great facts of Nature is stated:—

"Complement of human kind, having us at vantage still,
Our sumptuous indigence, O barren mound, thy plenties fill!
We fool and prate; thou art silent and sedate.
To myriad kinds and times one sense the constant mountain doth dispense;
Shedding on all its snows and leaves; one joy it joys, one grief it grieves.
Thou seest, O watchman tall, our towns and races grow and fall,
And imagest the stable good for which we all our lifetime grope,
And though the substance us elude, we in thee the shadow find.
        .   .   .   .

Thou dost supply the shortness of our days,
And promise, on thy Founder's troth, long morrow to this
mortal youth!"

No other poet with whom I am acquainted has caused the very spirit of the land—the mother of men—to express itself so adequately as Emerson has done.

Emerson is continually urging us to give heed to this, grand voice of hills and streams, and to mould ourselves upon its suggestions. The difficulty and anomaly consist in the fact that we are not native; that England, quite as much as Monadnoc, is our mother; that we are heirs of memories and traditions reaching far beyond the times and boundaries of the Republic. We cannot assume the splendid childlikeness of the great primitive races, and exhibit the hairy strength and unconscious genius that the poet longs to find in us. He remarks somewhere that the culminating period of good in Nature and the world is at just that moment of transition, when the hairy juices still flow plentifully from Nature, but their astringency and acidity is got out by ethics and humanity.

It was at such a period that Greece attained her apogee; but our experience, I think, must needs be different. Our story is not of birth, but of regeneration,—a far more subtle and less obvious transaction. The Homeric California, of which Bret Harte is the reporter, is not, in the closest sense, American. "A sturdy lad from New Hampshire or Vermont," says Emerson, "who in turn tries all the professions,—who teams it, farms it, peddles, keeps a school, preaches, edits a newspaper, goes to Congress, buys a township, and so forth, in successive years, and always, like a cat, falls on his feet,—is worth a hundred of these city dolls. He walks abreast with his days, and feels no shame in not studying a 'profession,' for he does not postpone his life, but lives it already."

That is poignantly said; and yet few of the Americans whom we recognize as great have had such a history; nor, had they had it, would they on that account be any the more American. On the other hand, the careers of men like Jim Fiske and Jay Gould might serve well as illustrations of the above sketch. If we must wait for our national character until our geographical advantages and the absence of social distinctions manufacture it for us, we are likely to remain a long time in suspense. When our foreign visitors begin to evince a keener interest in Beacon Hill and Fifth Avenue than in the Mississippi and the Yellowstone, we may infer that we are assuming our proper stature relative to our physical environment. "The Land," says Emerson, "is a sanative and Americanizing influence, which promises to disclose new virtues for ages to come." Well, when we are virtuous we may, perhaps, spare our own blushes by allowing our topography symbolically to celebrate us, and when our admirers would worship the purity of our intuitions, refer them to Walden Pond; or to Mount Shasta, when they would expatiate upon our lofty idealism. Meanwhile, it is perhaps true that the chances of leading a decent life are greater in a palace than in a pigsty.

But this is holding the poet too strictly to the letter of his message; and at any rate the Americanism of Emerson is better than anything that he has said in its vindication. He is the champion of the Republic; he is our future living in our present, and showing the world, by anticipation, what sort of excellence we are capable of. A nation that has produced Emerson, and can recognize in him flesh of her flesh and bone of her bone,—and, still more, spirit of her spirit,—that nation may look forward with security. But be has done more than to prophesy of his country: he is electric, and stimulates us to fulfil our destiny. To use a phrase of his own, we cannot hear of personal vigor of any kind—great power of performance—without fresh resolution. Emerson helps us most in provoking us to help ourselves. After Concord Fight, it is Emerson who has made Concord's reputation,— or, rather, its reputation has been he. More victorious even than the embattled farmers of a century ago, he attracted invaders instead of repelling them. No one can take his place, now that he is gone; but the memory of him, and the purity and vitality of the thoughts and of the example with which he has enriched the world, will abide longer than many lifetimes, and will renew again and again, before an ever-widening audience, the summons to virtue and the faith in immortality which were the burden and the glory of his song.

The pleasantest kind of revenge is that which we can sometimes take upon great men in quoting of themselves what they have said of others. It is easy to be so revenged upon Emerson, because he has been so broadly generous and cordial in his appreciation of human worth. "If there should appear in the company," he observes, "some gentle soul who knows little of persons and parties, of Carolina or Cuba, but who announces a law that disposes these particulars, and so certifies me of the equity which checkmates every false player, bankrupts every self-seeker, and apprises me of my independence on any conditions of country, or time, or human body,—that man liberates me. I am made immortal by apprehending my possession of incorruptible goods." Who can state the mission and effect of Emerson more tersely and aptly than in those words?

But he does not need eulogiums, and it seems half ungenerous to force them upon him now that he can no longer defend himself. So I will conclude by repeating a passage, characteristic of him both as a man and as an American, which perhaps conveys a sounder and healthier criticism, both for us and for him, than any mere nerveless admiration. For great men are great only in so far as they liberate us; and in courting their tyranny we undo their work. The passage runs thus:—

> "Let me remind you that I am only an experimenter. Do not set the least value on what I do, or the least discredit on what I do not,—as if I pretended to settle anything as true or false. I unsettle all things: no facts to me are sacred, none profane. I simply experiment,—an endless Seeker, with no Past at my back!"

SONG OF SOLOMON
(TONI MORRISON)

~~~

"Toni Morrison's *Song of Solomon* and the American Dream"
by Aimable Twagilimana, Buffalo State College

Believers in the American Dream assume that America is a land of opportunity where, if one is virtuous and works hard, one will achieve wealth and success. The history of the United States, however, shows that the principles of equality and inalienable rights as set forth in the Declaration of Independence and the U.S. Constitution did not apply to a good portion of the New World's inhabitants. For a long time after their promulgation, these founding ideals were not extended to women, African Americans (both during and after slavery), or Native Americans.

For Africans who were removed from their motherland to be enslaved and exploited in the Americas, what was a dream for the slave owners was a long nightmare for the enslaved. The stories African Americans have told and written from the eighteenth century to the present are often harrowing stories of displacement, alienation, humiliation, suffering, violence, and death. Phillis Wheatley, Frederick Douglass, William Wells Brown, Harriet Jacobs, and thousands of other slaves who escaped and spoke of or wrote about their experiences could only dream of escaping completely from the shadow of slavery. Through slavery they had experienced not only the exploitation of their bodies and untold psychological damage, but also lost their connection to their ancestral land. It is therefore not surprising that African-American narratives have often expanded the American dream to include reconnecting to a land of origins.

Toni Morrison's third novel, *Song of Solomon*, reflects the aspiration of African Americans for a return "home," best captured in her use of the myth of Flying Africans. Morrison's epic novel recalls a body of other twentieth-century American texts, such as F. Scott Fitzgerald's *The Great Gatsby*, Arthur Miller's *Death of a Salesman*, Lorraine Hansberry's *A Raisin in the Sun*, and Norman Mailer's *An American Dream*, that question tenets of the American Dream. The rush to riches in twentieth-century America, these texts suggest, had drastically shifted the national focus from Franklin's values of perfectibility, industry, frugality, and humility to excess, selfishness, and vanity.

African American writers also recalibrated the meaning and direction of the quest for success. Even when Frederick Douglass, in his 1845 *Narrative of the Life of Frederick Douglass, an American Slave*, and Booker T. Washington, in his 1901 memoir *Up From Slavery*, use Benjamin Franklin's secular autobiographical formula of the American success story, they seem to regard success not as wealth or professional achievement, but as achieving qualities often assumed by other Americans: equality, life, freedom, and a sense of identity. Even though Booker T. Washington documents his success from a short life in slavery to greatness as a black leader in the segregationist, racist, and violent Post-Reconstruction period, many other African American writers decried the nightmares that blacks continued to be subjected to, even after the passage of the Thirteenth, Fourteenth, and Fifteenth amendments to the U.S. Constitution. Washington's contemporary and his harshest critic, W. E. B. Du Bois, spoke of African Americans living behind a veil and being caught in a "double-consciousness," a metaphor for an identity crisis caused by their being part of two worlds, one that rejects them (the American side) and another that they cannot quite fathom (the African side). For them, the doors of opportunity are shut, an idea later dramatized in such novels as James Weldon Johnson's *Autobiography of an Ex-Colored Man* (1912) and Ralph Ellison's landmark novel, *Invisible Man* (1952), whose unnamed protagonists go through life behind a veil, lamenting their alienation. In a manner that prefigures the journey of Toni Morrison's Milkman to the South, the protagonist in

James Weldon Johnson's novel excitedly undertakes a journey south to collect black heritage materials and reconnect with his roots. He arrives only to witness a lynching, which convinces him to go back to New York City and pass as a white man, since he cannot tolerate the "unbearable shame" of "being identified with a people that could with impunity be treated worse than animals" (499).

In *Song of Solomon*, Morrison presents two diametrically opposed views of the world, one informed by the ideology of the American Dream and the other by the quest for African American identity. The destructive nature of the American Dream is embodied by Macon Dead II throughout the novel and by his son Milkman (Macon Dead III) in the first part, whereas the redemptive aspects of one's history and cultural identity are reflected in the character of Pilate throughout the novel. Milkman finds a kind of redemption during his epic journey to the south. There he reconnects with his southern roots and eventually with the "home" of Africa, if only symbolically, in his and Pilate's merging with the mythical universe of the Flying Africans, who flew back to Africa to escape slavery in the Americas. Morrison suggests that to the African American, the American Dream that seeks the excesses of wealth at the expense of family and cultural heritage is not worth pursuing. In Morrison's novel, the quest for identity is more important than the attainment of wealth. The moment Sing Bird convinces Jake to keep the name "Dead," which was mistakenly bestowed upon him by a drunken Yankee soldier, by arguing that it would make him forget his past, he inaugurates a genealogy of Deads, people with no connection to the past, a past that includes the horrors of slavery, but also a history and culture that goes beyond slavery. At Sing Bird's behest, Jake kills the "ancestor" as well as the future generations of Deads. For Morrison, ancestors are "timeless people whose relationships to the characters are benevolent, instructive, and protective . . . who provide a certain kind of wisdom" ("Rootedness," 343). Redemption comes at the end of Milkman's quest when he reconnects himself, his aunt Pilate, and perhaps his entire black generation with their ancestor, Solomon. Like an Odysseus reaching his home in Ithaca, Milkman and Pilate return symbolically to Africa.

The reader's first glimpse into the Dead family reveals that they are set apart from most African American families in the community by their material wealth. Milkman has the distinction to be the first "colored baby . . . born inside Mercy" (9), because his maternal grand-father, Dr. Foster, works in the hospital, the first colored doctor to do so. Milkman's father himself, Macon Dead II, owns property in Southside, Michigan. Both men are financially successful, but give a bad name to the idea of success. Dr. Foster's arrogance and loathing of fellow African Americans, whom he calls "cannibals," underscores the misguided nature of his success. Many African Americans were still illiterate in the 1930s, so Dr. Foster's attainment of a medical degree is indeed a great achievement, and the black community worships him for that. But his success is marred by his racism, which does not spare his own granddaughters, First Corinthians and Magdalene, whom he checks to determine whether they are light-skinned (like himself and his daughter) when they are born.

Because Macon Dead II is "at twenty-five . . . . Already a colored man of property" (23), he can "approach the most important Negro in the city. To lift the lion's paw knocker, to entertain thoughts of marrying the doctor's daughter was possible because each key repre-sented a house which he owned at the time" (22). Traumatized by witnessing the murder of his father, Macon Dead I (Jake), by whites who wanted his property back in the South, Macon Dead II is obsessed with property just for the sake of ownership. Having inher-ited his name "Dead" from his father, Macon Dead II becomes the very incarnation of emotional death—the only exception occurs when memories of his childhood are invoked or when he is surreptitiously listening to the songs coming from his sister Pilate's house. Other-wise, he is heartless with his wife, children, and tenants, showing no kindness to widows, orphans, or the poor.

Ruth Foster, Dr. Foster's only child, develops a bizarre emotional attachment to her father, as she continues to demand the same affec-tion that a child expects of parents at an age when most girls seek the company of the opposite sex. Her childish devotion to her father becomes a concern to him (23). The sexual overtone of Ruth's demand suggests that, emotionally, she has not grown beyond the Freudian Oedipus Complex or the Electra Complex. Since her mother is already dead, she does not need to wish for her death anymore and can readily demand her father's exclusive love, which Dr. Foster does not discourage.

According to the story Macon Dead tells his son Milkman, the bizarre relationship between Ruth and her father does not stop when she gets married. In spite of Macon Dead II's objection, Dr. Foster delivers Ruth's babies. Macon Dead II thinks that "nothing could be nastier than a father delivering his own daughter's baby . . . . [Ruth] had her legs wide open and he was there. I know he was a doctor and doctors are not supposed to be bothered by things like that, but he was a man before he was a doctor" (71). Macon Dead believes there is a continuing conspiracy between his wife and her father, since "they'd ganged up on [him] forever—the both of them—and no matter what [he] did, they managed to have things their way" (71).

Dr. Foster refuses to lend Macon money to buy a piece of land that he is convinced would bring good dividends. Furthermore, Ruth refuses to intervene on his behalf, arguing that it is her father's decision, leading him "to wonder who she was married to—me or him" (72). Macon claims to catch his wife in a questionable act after Dr. Foster's death, "laying next to him. Naked as a yard dog, kissing him. Him dead and white and puffy and skinny, and she had his fingers in her mouth" (73). Pressing his story to Milkman, he continues: "I'm not saying that they had contact. But there's lots of things a man can do to please a woman, even if he can't fuck. Whether or not, the fact is she was in that bed sucking his fingers, and if she do that when he was dead, what'd she do when he was alive?" (74).

Unable to get sex from her husband, she channels her repressed sexual desires to breastfeeding her son until past the normal age. The afternoon breastfeeding has all the trappings of a sexual transaction (14-15). Ruth is the most extreme example of how alienation, dysfunction, and emptiness plagues the Dead family: isolated from their black community and unhappy in a big house that feels more like prison than home, their lives are filled with shame and trauma, which they superficially deal with by wearing what Bouson has called a "mantle of false class pride"(76).

Macon Dead II's shameless pursuit of property is also reflected in the novel's gold symbolism. The relentless pursuit of gold by men in general leads to the betrayal of fundamental human values of love, family, community, and friendship. Macon Dead's suggestion that a sack hanging in his sister's house is a bag of gold, and his conspiracy with his son Milkman and friend Guitar leads to the two of them stealing her "green sack hanging from the ceiling" (97). The reader knows Pilate's intervention leads to the conception of Milkman. When Macon Dead tries to force Ruth to abort the child, Pilate intervenes again to save the child by threatening Macon Dead II. As Ruth tells her son Milkman, "Pilate was the one brought you here in the first place" (124). After years without any lovemaking between Ruth and her husband, Pilate gives her roots—"some greenish-gray grassy-looking stuff to put in his food"(125)—that make him come to her. When he discovers her pregnancy, he forces her to do a number of things to abort the fetus, including potions and violence. At this time, she runs to Pilate, who uses her knowledge of traditional medicine to save her and the baby. Later, Pilate goes to her brother's office, has a few words with him, and places a small doll on his chair. He does not try to lay his hand on Ruth again.

Pilate is the very opposite of Macon Dead I, Macon Dead II, and Dr. Foster, and her role is pivotal in Milkman's quest. Literally existing differently than everyone else in the world—she does not have a navel—Pilate lives a simple life unencumbered by modern, urban amenities: there is no electricity, gas, or running water in her house. She and her daughter Reba and her granddaughter Hagar spend a lot of time singing songs that occasionally soothe even Macon Dead II's hard soul, as he listens to them surreptitiously. Pilate's house lies at the periphery of the community, but her marginality allows her more freedom than anyone else in the novel. Her possessions consist of a sack filled with a dead man's bones, a geography book, and a collection of rocks, all of which connect her to her past. Pilate has plenty of love to give to her daughter and granddaughter, to Milkman and Guitar. At the end of the novel, she wishes she had known and loved more people (336). Pilate's non-human characteristics, including her goodness, make her appear to be a mythic ancestor, a goddess of sorts.

From this perspective, Milkman's robbery in the pursuit of gold is a strong indictment of the heartless pursuit of materialism. It is as if Milkman betrays his "creator." Guitar, Milkman's best friend (at least in the first half of the novel), attempts to kill him when he suspects that Milkman is trying to cheat him of his share of the gold. The gold never materializes in the novel anyway, an indication that it is used only to illustrate the fallacy that wealth brings happiness. Macon Dead II's fate also underscores the fact that the pursuit of wealth for its own sake is pointless and destructive. He is not a good man, and he is vain in many respects. He owns luxurious cars that contrast with the poor emotional quality of life within his own family and the poverty of the black community at large. His capitalistic ideology strangely mimics the slaveowner's mentality. He tells his son: "Own things. And let the things you own own other things. Then you'll own yourself and other people too" (55). The futility of his quest for wealth affects his family. Morrison alludes to this by associating artificial roses with First Corinthians and Lena: they are not making real roses, which usually symbolize beauty and love; instead, their empty, middle-class lives are sterile, boring, and depressing.

Morrison uses the backdrop of Macon's pointless quest for wealth to launch her protagonist on a journey for a more meaningful goal: redemption through reconnection with ancestors. Alienated by his father's mindless pursuit of wealth and his family's dysfunctional emotional life, and progressively in open disagreement with Guitar (another alienated character), and having betrayed his aunt Pilate, Milkman Dead undertakes a journey south. It begins as a search for gold, but it turns into a quest for his ancestral origins.

The novel becomes then a palimpsest of genres: it is at the same time a Bildungsroman, an initiation story, a mystery narrative, a gothic story, a novel of magical realism, and an epic narrative. The common denominator of these narrative models in the novel is that orality becomes the main medium of transformation, growth, discovery, and knowledge. Milkman's quest starts to change when he listens to Reverend Cooper, Circe, Sweet, the elders who initiate him to hunting, and the children's rhyme in Shalimar about "Solomon don't leave me here," a version of a blues song "O Sugarman don't leave me here" that he has heard Pilate sing. It is important to realize that all these people using the oral medium belong to different generations, but they all converge, in one way or another, on the history of Solomon, his flight back to Africa, and the wife and children he left behind. The centrality of orality in Milkman's quest affirms the epic dimension of the novel. Epic narratives such as the *Iliad, Odyssey, Aeneid, Mahabharata*, and *Sundjata* were originally oral traditions passed from generation to generation. When he travels south, Milkman becomes aware of his mythic origins through stories about his ancestor Solomon as well as stories about Pilate and Macon Dead II's early life in the South. Even though he has known Pilate, an ancestor (according to the definition), since he was twelve, Milkman feels the presence of his mythic ancestor, Solomon, as he stands on Solomon's Leap. This reconnection with his ancestry gives Milkman wisdom and the strength to surrender to the air and "ride it" to confront Guitar.

It is worth noting that Milkman achieves wisdom after he has shed off the belongings that connected him with wealth and excess. As he ventures into the Pennsylvania woods looking for the cave where the gold he seeks is supposed to be, he has to walk, he loses his watch and cigarettes, he falls into a creek and his suit is soaked, and his city shoes are no help at all. In addition, there is no gold in the cave. For the hunting initiation in Shalimar, he puts on new clothes because his city ones are not adequate. In the woods, he learns to use his natural sense—he forgoes Calvin's lamp in order to "look at what it was possible to see" (276). This new way of knowing helps him to survive Guitar's attack in the dark. The hunting party rewards him with the bobcat's heart. Another indication of Milkman's dramatic transformation occurs when he later goes to Sweet, the first woman he makes love to unselfishly or treats with respect and equality. This brief relationship with Sweet makes him aware of his lack of respect for the women in his life up north: his mother, his sisters, his aunt Pilate, and his former lover Hagar, who died because of his neglect. This realiza-tion ends Milkman's alienation from his family and community. It marks an irreversible rejection of the tenets of the American Dream as practiced by his father.

Structurally, Milkman's journey recalls Robert Stepto's theory of the African American narrative. In *From Being the Veil*, Stepto distinguishes between two types of narratives: the narrative of ascent and the narrative of immersion. In the former, the individual, in order to escape slavery and oppression in the real or symbolic South, leaves his or her family, friends, and community and embraces a life of isolation and alienation. He or she acquires literacy, an impor-tant step toward freedom and survival. As an individual, he or she heads to the real or symbolic North, getting help if necessary but trusting noone. The hero or heroine of the narrative of ascent is quintessentially a solitary person, as exemplified by Linda Brent in Harriet Jacobs's *Incidents in the Life of a Slave Girl*. She spends seven years in a crawl space in her grandmother's attic waiting for a good opportunity to go north. On the other hand, the narrative of immersion involves a movement to the real or symbolic South. The hero or heroine seeks tribal literacy and knowledge. Less individualistic, he or she moves into the community, embracing its traditions and ways of life. *Song of Solomon* combines both of these narrative movements: the first part of the novel is largely a narrative of ascent, characterized by alienation and solitude, amplified by Macon Dead II's relentless quest for wealth, which his son Milkman also embraces. In the second part, the novel becomes a narrative of immersion.

In adopting this type of structure for her quest-hero, Morrison subverts the traditional initiation hero, an individual who stands out from the group because he has achieved greatness by doing something mostly through his own heroic acts. Milkman, prompted by the possibility of finding gold, living an independent life, and escaping the vain life of the Deads, undertakes a journey to the real South, back into the community and its values, which save him from the destructive, pointless, and alienating pursuit of wealth. In offering an African American hero with mythic proportions, Morrison warns her generation of African Americans that "[i]f we don't keep in touch with the ancestor . . . we are in fact, lost. When you kill the ancestor, you kill yourself. I want to point out the dangers, to show that nice things don't happen to the totally self-reliant if there is no conscious historical connection" ("Rootedness," 344).

WORKS CITED

Bouson, J. Brooks. *Quiet as it's Kept: Shame, Trauma, and Race in the Novels of Toni Morrison*. Albany: SUNY Press, 2000.

Morrison, Toni. *Song of Solomon*. New York: Penguin Group, 1987.

———. "Rootedness: The Ancestor as Foundation." *Black Women Writers (1950–1980): A Critical Evaluation*. Ed. Mari Evans. New York: Doubleday, 1984. 339–45.

Johnson, James Weldon. *The Autobiography of an Ex-Colored Man*. In *Three Negro Classics*. Intr. by John Hope Franklin. New York: Avon Books, 1965: 391–511.

Stepto, Robert B. *From Behind the Veil: A Study of Afro-American Narrative*. Urbana, IL.: University of Illinois Press, 1979.

WALDEN
(HENRY DAVID THOREAU)

"Thoreau's *Walden* and the American Dream: Challenge or Myth?"
by Michaela Keck,
I-Shou University

The interconnectedness between civilization and nature is as central to Thoreau's thought as the interconnectedness of mind and body, the ideal and the real. *Walden* is about both culture and nature, transcendent philosophy and textual body, dream and the exploration thereof. And in fulfillment of the American Dream, *Walden* embodies both success and failure.

Even those who have never read *Walden* are familiar with Thoreau, the nature lover on the one hand, and Thoreau, the social critic on the other, calling for "Simplicity, simplicity, simplicity!" (395). The juxtaposition of his ascetic life with the overflowing abundance of Walden Pond's microcosmos is another pivotal interconnectedness at the heart of *Walden*. Taking up the ancient discourse of *humilitas* versus *vanitas*, Thoreau turns the American work ethic of the time upside down, and deliberately flouts the American Dream's focus on material gain, worldly status, and success. In fact, Thoreau's paradigm of riches runs counter to what James Truslow Adams in the twentieth century defined as "that dream of a land in which life should be better and richer and fuller for every man, with opportunity for each according to his ability or achievement" (*The Epic of America* 404). Likewise, Thoreau's "notion of use value is the opposite" (Buell 12) of that of his readers. Thoreau is concerned with those riches to which material wealth poses a serious threat: "Most of the luxuries, and many of the so called comforts of life, are not only not indispensable, but positive hinderances [sic] to the elevation of mankind" (334). His credo is "to *do*, or rather [. . .] to *be*" (341) instead of to *have*, to lead "a life of simplicity, independence, magnanimity, and trust" (334) rather than to amass material riches.

Thoreau's repeated exhortations to return to a state of "nakedness" (352) in which "our lives must be stripped" (353) are yet another means of freeing himself from all that "imprison[s]" (349), or "anchor[s]" (366) or "harnesse[s]" (375) him to material achievements and super-fluous comforts. In spite of his admiration of the spirit of "enterprise and bravery" (417) inherent in commerce, he shuns business as best he can and strives for "voluntary poverty" (334). Thoreau's experiment at Walden Pond goes well beyond economic self-sufficiency. He advo-cates independence from any kind of attachment—not only physical, but also intellectual and social: "[. . .] the man who goes alone can start to-day; but he who travels with another must wait till that other is ready, and it may be a long time before they get off" (379). This atti-tude has often been interpreted as epitomizing rugged individualism. Behind Thoreau's radical departure from all that is familiar and dear to him lies the sincere attempt to uncover his own path and purpose in life, as well as his own original voice and creativity from under the many layers of familial, literary, philosophical, and religious heritage that characterize his times and culture:

> Let us [. . .] work and wedge our feet downward through the mud and slush of opinion, and prejudice, and tradition, and delusion, and appearance, that alluvion which covers the globe, [. . .] through church and state, through poetry and philosophy and religion, till we come to a hard bottom and rocks in place, which we can call *reality*, and say, This is, and no mistake; . . . . (400)

By stripping away the complex, superfluous layers of nineteenth-century life and actively distancing himself from the expectations, conventions, and traditions of society and culture, Thoreau follows in the footsteps of the "ancient philosophers" (334). He combines various cultural philosophies and mystic traditions into "a complex and bicultural concept" (Cheng 218). While continuing on the path of such radical New England dissenters as Jonathan Edwards or the reformist Quaker John Woolman (Shi 8-49), Thoreau's experiment at Walden Pond challenges the Calvinistic socioeconomic ideal and many of the accepted ideas of classical economy as expressed by such materialist thinkers as Benjamin Franklin. Thoreau, contrary to the ideology of his time, dreams of "a self-sufficient economy" in which "simplification leads to growth" (Birch and Metting 600). Thoreau's frequent references to the simple lives of different Indian tribes illustrates this attempt, especially in those chapters pertaining to his own theory of economics and his concept of the "half-cultivated field" (448; "Economy" 344-46; 376-77; "The Bean-Field" 447). Although *Walden*'s textual form embodies the cyclical pattern of subsistence of the Native Americans, it remains an incomplete model in that Thoreau relies on the village for his food supplies when neither the woods nor the bean-field yield a sufficient crop. Consequently, *Walden* glosses over these questions during the toughest of seasons in economical terms, winter and spring, by turning to local history and rich plant and animal life.

Walden's emphasis on nature's cornucopia finds its expression also in mood and tone. Though exhortative, the text expresses above all an overwhelming sense of exhilaration and abundance, especially when describing Walden Pond and its natural surroundings. Thoreau's ecstatic song of the micro- and macrocosmos of Walden Pond derives from his intimate, sensual, and engaged relationship with nature. This engagement, Thoreau contends, is motivated by "that portion of our most primitive ancestor which still survive[s] in us" (345). It is a bond between human nature and the natural environment that has been buried beneath a growing refinement, but still exists. Sociologist Norbert Elias contends that mankind's growing detachment from nature is caused by civilization's increasing dominance over nature's forces. This, he argues, goes hand-in-hand with a growing control of the inner self of humankind, which in turn is connected to a stronger self-control of the individual; and an increasing control concerning life within society (Elias 17). Moving to Walden Pond allows Thoreau to put the necessary distance between himself and society's restraints and refinement in order to uncover (or recover) the wilderness within and without. Cultivating the "wild according to [one's] nature," rather than controlling it, is the dream Thoreau pursues, a quest that is as much an exploration of the "out there" as of his inner self (488).

As is fit for such a quest, Thoreau's stay at Walden Pond re-enacts the journey theme so typical of the American Dream. Yet, as with his striving for poverty, *Walden* has remained a controversial quest. On the one hand, Thoreau's hermitage at Walden Pond is an integral tale in American literary history. On the other hand, scholars like to draw attention to the fact that while Thoreau, the self-proclaimed hermit, bathed in Walden Pond and kindled the hearth in his self-made hut, he was sustained by hearty meals at his family home. The author himself makes no secret of his whereabouts, which is still within reach of his social circle:

> I was seated by the shore of a small pond, about a mile and a half south of the village of Concord and somewhat higher than it, in the midst of an extensive wood between that town and Lincoln, and about two miles south of that our only field known to fame, Concord Battle Ground; .... (390-391)

Thoreau's wooden cabin at Walden Pond is not situated in a remote wilderness. The results of Robert A. Gross's research show us that the social climate of Transcendental Concord contrasts starkly with our understanding of individualism today. After all, it is "the great age of the patriarchal, Victorian family": one does not simply leave behind the familial household (Gross 508). Thoreau does not shut himself off from civilization by moving to Walden Pond. In "Visitors," he affirms that he probably "love[s] society as much as most" and that he "natu-rally [is] no hermit" (434). Throughout *Walden*, he discourses with a multitude of philosophical, historical, religious, and literary voices. Hence the paradox and controversy of a quest into the wilderness in which the explorer himself stays connected to family and society. The question remains: is Thoreau's a voice in the wilderness? Or is he merely an armchair-traveller, or worse, a hypocrite? Is *Walden* a dream fulfilled or failed?

If read strictly as social criticism, or as an example of radical individualism, *Walden* can be easily misread as a failed utopian dream of return, a retreat to nature. But, from its beginning, *Walden* is never meant as such. Rather, it is the experiment of a new beginning, a new approach to life. Ideally, it is to become an integral part of daily life, a perspective one cultivates anew every day, regardless of one's whereabouts. As Maxine Greene points out, "the American Dream has been a dream about beginnings, continually new beginnings" (179). To discover the universe anew for one's self requires a particular point of view, a view devoid of the prescribed cultural, intellectual, and aesthetic heritage of the world one inhabits.

Thoreau's cabin provided this unique point of view, being situated "by the *shore* of a small pond" (390) and "so low in the woods that the opposite *shore*" is his "most distant horizon" (391; emphasis added). The shore plays a crucial role in Thoreau's explorations of his inner self as well as nature. In *Cape Cod*, Thoreau calls the sea-shore "a sort of neutral ground, a most advantageous point from which to contemplate this world" (979). At the same time, he describes the shore as "a wild, rank place" (979). The rhetoric of positive yet neutral, vigorous yet disgusting, similar to the contradictions Emerson complained about when editing Thoreau's early work "A Winter Walk," is deliberate and intentional. For Thoreau the shore symbolizes the confrontation and merging of opposites. Here, the natural elements meet and intermingle; here, mankind encounters nature in its most crude and primary essence; here, mankind touches upon its own transience and must deal with the most essential questions of human life. In fact, the shore is the ideal space for Thoreau to "live deep and suck out all the marrow of life," to "drive life into a corner, and reduce it to its lowest terms"; here life's "whole and genuine meanness" intersects with its beauty (394). To set up house at Walden Pond means to occupy a sphere in between the wild and the rank, the mean and the sublime, where constant flux and eternal repose unite and overlap. His experiment at Walden Pond allows Thoreau a life at the frontier between wilderness and civilization. Like the sea-shore it is neutral because it distances him from village life; but it is advantageous in that it affords him the perfect starting point for a new daily beginning. Here he can "affect the quality of the day [which] is the highest of arts" while at the same time "front only the essential facts of life" (394).

In Thoreau's mind, Walden Pond is a shore in a much wider sense. It epitomizes wilderness for him, because it represents nature in all its diversity, being shore (390-391; 425), sea (463), mountain (391), and swamp (422) altogether. In many cultures, such places abound with meaning, both mythological and sacred. According to Mircea Eliade, mountains, as well as watery places, constitute holy sites or mythological sanctuaries. Every mountain functions as universal pillar (*axis mundi*) connecting heaven and earth. Waters represent openings, likewise allowing the "passage from one cosmic region to another" (37), here to the chaos of "*cosmic matter*, and . . . all that precedes and follows life" (41). Sacred mountains and waters not only link heaven, earth, and the underworld, but they become the centre of the world one inhabits and turn it into an image of the universe on a smaller scale. Looking back on his daily ritual morning bath, Thoreau writes: "I have been as sincere a worshipper of Aurora as the Greeks. I got up early and bathed in the pond; that was a religious exercise, and one of the best things which I did" (393). He elevates Walden Pond as the sacred and mythological centre of his universe, a centre that allows communication with the heavens, as well as with the chaotic and creative forces of the underworld.

The sandbank passages in the "Spring" chapter are probably the most famous ones in that regard, because they "illustrat[e] the principle of all the operations of Nature" (568). As Thoreau explains: "The whole cut impressed me as if it were a cave with its stalactites laid open to the light" (566). The focus on the thawing sand and its interior is intriguing in several respects. It is here we find a relationship with earth and nature in which plant, animal, and human life can no longer be separated. The sand, the human hand, the palm leaf, and the insides of Nature and human life interconnect organically, almost genetically, not unlike the "unique genetic relationship" (Wiget 225) of Native American emergence stories. Thoreau's relationship with the earth, though "somewhat excrementitious in its character" (568), is relatively free of the religious implications of cultivating the earth and human sin. At the same time, it goes hand-in-hand with a perspective and aesthetic point of view that is characteristic of most of his writings. He is intent on looking in an almost microscopic manner at the details of the natural universe and its interior rather than gaining views of the sublime or the beautiful. Often close-ups of the environment emphasize nature's earthy qualities, which are more often mean and rank than sublime. Indeed Thoreau's wilderness aesthetics move outside of the traditional conventions of the sublime and the beautiful.

To him beauty means fertility and flux, which necessarily includes Nature's "bowels" (568), as well as the pains and fluids connected to birth and creation.

The movement that results from Thoreau's close-up perspectives is thus a downward one, implying immersion rather than a horizontal panorama. Now and again the downward motion is counterbalanced by an upwards one, for example, in his observations on the trees surrounding Walden Pond, in his heavenward views or transcendental thoughts. Viewed as a whole, the depicted movement equals a continuous sequence of ups and downs as embodied in the metaphor of living "like a dolphin" (484). Thoreau's dynamics of immersion and resurfacing reject not only the European aesthetics of the beautiful and the sublime, but also the expansionist images of the frontier ideology.

All of the above aspects of an immersion in nature emphasize physical and sensual contact with the natural environment, whereby the senses are an integral aspect of cultivating the inner wild. It is through the bodily senses that humankind connects to nature.

Exploring Walden Pond and its surroundings becomes for Thoreau a universal quest in spiritual, mythological, cosmological, and physical terms that does not necessitate an actual stay in the remote wilderness. Situated at the edge of nature and culture, the pond challenges him to reconsider his relationship with wilderness and society. Living at Walden Pond reflects an approach to life that keeps body, mind, and consciousness alert and awake. This sustains Thoreau in his quest for an inner and outer wilderness, teaching him how to *be*, to "spend one day as deliberately as Nature" (95), in the here and now, regardless of the exact geographical position of his home. It is the inner freedom which enables us to discover wilderness wherever we live. He concludes: "I left the woods for as good a reason as I went there" (579), having by then found a means to fortify freedom and wilderness within.

While another essential quality of the American Dream, namely its equal accessibility for everybody, might have mostly been taken for granted by Thoreau himself, this assumption has come under attack during recent decades (Buell, "American Pastoral" 3-4). *Walden* does not avoid pointing out some of the inequalities in nineteenth-century American democracy—including slavery (350), the poverty of farmers (348-350) and laborers (346-349; 356-357), alcoholism ("Former Inhabitants" 528-532), and the confinements of domesticity as opposed to the freedom of the woods for females (329; 444). Thoreau's dissent has increasingly been reinterpreted as belonging to the hegemonic, exclusory, pastoral tradition. As Ann LaBastille puts it bluntly: "As a woman, I am not at all touched by *Walden*. It reads as if Thoreau disregarded half of the world's population" (67). Once again the question of *Walden* as a dream fulfilled or a disappointing fantasy surfaces.

Thoreau's writing is surely not exempt from the ideological coloring of his times. To claim that would be to ignore the facts and to place his texts within an intellectual vacuum. Yet, as Buell and Michael R. Fischer demonstrate, it is one thing to establish valid categories for decoding texts and their reinterpretation. It is quite another, however, to fill these classifications with one sweeping gesture and without due consideration of the context from which the respective literary works spring ("American Pastoral" 9-19; 111). In the case of *Walden*, and also of *The Maine Woods* and *Cape Cod*, "the *I*, or first person . . . is retained" (325) at the same time that it engages in a discourse with and mixes with a rather diverse stream of voices. Thoreau knows that in order to allow this dialogue to take place with the least interference from his own cultural baggage, it is necessary to relocate himself at Walden Pond to look for "the only true America":

> that country where you are at liberty to pursue such a mode of life as may enable you to do without [the dispensable comforts of life], and where the state does not endeavor to compel you to sustain the slavery and war and other superfluous expenses which directly or indirectly result from the use of such things. (486)

Clearly, the attraction of Thoreau's quest lies in the fact that his goal is a "mode of life" (486), which each individual has to seek for himself or herself, and whose achievement is not a matter of gender, race, politics, age, or creed. In fact, the wilderness appeal of Thoreau's writings has been and still is a strong one, especially for women writers such as Labastille and Annie Dillard. It illustrates that to fit *Walden* into an exclusivist and conservative literary category is problematic as well as myopic. As Buell summarizes: "Which dimension gets stressed depends partly on who is reading, partly . . . on the different locations of the individual texts along the ideological spectrum from radical to recessive" ("American Pastoral" 23).

Indeed, Buell's conclusion sums up *Walden*'s ambivalence concerning the various aspects of the American Dream, be it the achievement of riches, or an authentic striving for a better world that exists equally for any individual. Here lie both the timelessness and timeliness of *Walden*, revealing that the American Dream always involves teetering on the thin edge between success and failure. Rather than representing a triumphant journey, *Walden* carries within itself the failures and pitfalls connected to any quest. At the same time, it emphatically challenges some of the central assumptions of the American Dream, particularly those regarding the gain of material riches. To "advanc[e] confidently in the direction of [our] dreams, and endeavo[r] to live the life which [we have] imagined" (580), and to do so always according to the beat and the rhythm of the drummer that each of us hears (581), can by no means guarantee the successful realization of one's dream. But "[h]owever mean your life is," Thoreau encourages us, at least you "meet it and live it" (583) without sacrificing the dream itself.

WORKS CITED

Adams, James Truslow. *The Epic of America*. Boston: Little Brown and
    Company, 1931.
Birch, Thomas D. and Metting, Fred. "The Economic Design of Walden,"
    The New England Quarterly 66.4 (1992): 587–662.
Buell, Lawrence. "American Pastoral Reappraised," *American Literary History*
    1.1 (1989): 1-29.
———. "Henry Thoreau Enters the American Canon," *New Essays on Walden*.
    Ed. Robert F. Sayre. Cambridge: Cambridge University Press, 1992:
    23–52.
Cheng, Aimin. "A Comparative Study of Thoreau's and Taoist Concepts
    of Nature," *Thoreau's Sense of Place. Essays in American Environmental
    Writing*. Ed. Richard J. Schneider. Iowa City: University of Iowa Press,
    2000: 207–220.

Cronon, William. *Changes in the Land. Indians, Colonists, and the Ecology of New England*. New York: Hill and Wang, 1983.

Eliade, Mircea. *The Sacred & The Profane. The Nature of Religion*. New York and London: Harcourt, Brace & World, Inc., 1959.

Elias, Norbert. *Engagement und Distanzierung. Arbeiten zur Wissenssoziologie I*, 2nd ed. Frankfurt am Main: Suhrkamp, 1990.

Emerson, Ralph Waldo. *The Journals of Ralph Waldo Emerson*, Eds. Edward Waldo Emerson and Waldo Emerson Forbes. Boston and New York: Houghton Mifflin Company, 1911.

Fischer, Michael R. "*Walden* and the Politics of Contemporary Theory," *New Essays on Walden*. 95–113.

Greene, Maxine. "Observation. On the American Dream: Equality, Ambiguity, and the Persistence of Rage," *Curriculum Inquiry* 13.2 (1983): 179–193.

Gross, Robert A. "The Machine-Readable Transcendentalism: Cultural History on the Computer," *American Quarterly* 41.3 (1989): 501–521.

Harding, Walter. "Thoreau's Reputation," *The Cambridge Companion to Henry David Thoreau*. Ed. Joel Myerson. New York and Cambridge: Cambridge University Press, 1995. 1-11.

LaBastille, Anne. "'Fishing in the Sky,'" *New Essays on Walden*. 53–72.

Maiden, Emory V., Jr. *Cape Cod: Thoreau's Handling of the Sublime and the Picturesque*. Richmond: University of Virginia, 1972.

McGrath, James. "Ten Ways of Seeing Landscape in *Walden* and Beyond," *Thoreau's Sense of Place. Essays in American Environmental Writing*. 149–164.

Milder, Robert. *Reimagining Thoreau*. Cambridge: Cambridge University Press, 1995.

Shi, David E. *The Simple Life. Plain Living and High Thinking in American Culture*. Athens & London: The University of Georgia Press, 1985.

The Holy Bible. New International Version. London: Hodder & Stoughton, 1984.

Thoreau, Henry David. *Henry David Thoreau. A Week on the Concord and Merrimack Rivers. Walden; or, Life in the Woods. The Maine Woods. Cape Cod*. New York: The Library of America, 1985.

———. "Walking," *Walden and other Writings of Henry David Thoreau*. Ed. Brooks Atkinson. New York: Random House Inc., 1992.

———. *Walden*. Ed. Jeffery S. Cramer. New Haven and London: Yale University Press, 2004.

——. *The Writings of Henry David Thoreau: Journal.* Ed. John Broderick. Princeton: Princeton University Press, 1981– .

Tobin, Frank. *Meister Eckhart: Thought and Language.* Philadelphia: University of Pennsylvania Press, 1986.

Wiget, Andrew. "Reading against the Grain: Origin Stories and American Literary History," *American Literary History* 3.2 (1991): 209–231.

✑ *Acknowledgments* ✑

Brown, Lloyd W. "The American Dream and the Legacy of Revolution in the Poetry of Langston Hughes." *Studies in Black Literature* (Spring 1976): 16–18. Copyright Raman K. Singh. Reprinted by permission.

Canaday, Nicholas Jr. "Albee's 'The American Dream' and the Existential Vacuum." South Central Bulletin Vol. 26, No. 4 (Winter 1966): 28–34. Copyright The South Central Modern Language Association. Reprinted by permission.

Hawthorne, Julian. "Emerson as an American." *The Genius and Character of Emerson.* F.B. Sanborn, ed. Boston: James R. Osgood and Company, 1885.

Lemay, J.A. Leo. "Franklin's Autobiography and the American Dream." *The Renaissance Man in the Eighteenth Century.* Los Angeles: William Andrews Clark Memorial Library, 1978. Copyright The William Andrews Clark Memorial Library. Reprinted by permission.

Lisca, Peter. "*Of Mice and Men.*" *The Wide World of John Steinbeck.* New Brunswick, NJ: Rutgers UP, 1958: 130–43. Copyright by Rutgers, The State University. Reprinted by permission.

Miller, James E., Jr. "*My Ántonia* and the American Dream." *Prairie Schooner* 48, no. 2 (Summer 1974): 112–23. Copyright 1979 University of Nebraska Press. Copyright renewed 2002 by the University of Nebraska Press. Reprinted by permission.

Pinsker, Sanford. "*Huckleberry Finn* and the Problem of Freedom." The *Virginia Quarterly Review* Vol. 77, No. 4 (Fall 2001): 642–49. Copyright Sanford Pinsker. Reprinted by permission.

Stowe, Harriet Beecher. "Frederick Douglass." *The Lives and Deeds of Our Self-Made Men.* Chicago, IL.: M.A. Parker & Co.,1872.

Valdes, Maria Elena de. "In Search of Identity in Cisneros' *The House on Mango Street.*" *The Canadian Review of American Studies*, Vol. 23, No. 1 (Fall 1992): 55–72. Copyright University of Toronto Press.

Reprinted by permission of Canadian Association for American Studies (www.utpjournals.com).

Whitman, Walt. "Preface to *Leaves of Grass* (1855)." *Walt Whitman: Complete Poetry and Collected Prose*. New York: Literary Classics of the United States, 1982.

Yoder, Jon A. *Upton Sinclair*. New York: Ungar, 1975. Copyright Frederick Ungar Publishing Co., Inc.

Index

Characters in literary works are indexed by first name (if any), followed by the name of the work in parentheses

A

Abramson, Ben, 134

Adams, James Truslow, 59

    Epic of America, 67, 162, 213

Adams, John, 24

Adventures of Huckleberry Finn, The (Twain)

    Huck Finn in, xvi, 1–8

    Jim in, 1–2, 6–8

    Mary in, 5

    Aunt Polly in, 5

    problem of freedom in, 1–9

    racism in, 8–9

    romanticism in, 5

    satire and humor in, 4, 8

    Colonel Sherburn in, 4

    slavery in, 5, 8

    Tom Sawyer in, 2, 4–6, 8

African American

    disadvantages of, 37–40, 42–43, 203

    dreams, 174–175, 183, 203–212

    education, 180–181, 183–184, 206

    history, 171

    literature, 41, 44–45, 172, 203–205, 210

    racism, 173–174, 177–180, 183

    workers, 171, 179, 181–183

Albee, Edward

    The American Dream, 11–20

Alexander's Bridge (Cather), 142

Alger, Horatio, Jr., 23, 52–53

Ambassadors (James), 22

American

    Constitution, 39–40, 203–204

    democracy, 58, 109, 120–122

    dream, xv–xvi, 1, 8, 11–12, 16, 21–55, 58–65, 67, 69–71, 73–77, 79, 82, 97–98, 100, 105, 109, 120, 123–139, 141–152, 161–169, 171, 174–175, 178, 203–205, 210, 213, 216–217, 219, 221

    freedom, xv, 1–2, 6–9, 42, 82, 92, 147

    history, 40–41, 59, 64, 110, 188, 203, 216

    literature, 12, 22–23, 25–28, 109–110, 118, 187, 216

    mythology, 40, 67

    nightmare, xv

    pastoralism, 176

    poets, 109–111, 113–120

    social myths, xv

227